ENER**PH**IT

A STEP-BY-STEP
GUIDE TO
LOW-ENERGY
RETROFIT

James Traynor

© RIBA Publishing, 2019

Published by RIBA Publishing, 66 Portland Place, London, W1B 1NT

ISBN 978-1-85946-819-7

The right of James Traynor to be identified as the Author of this Work has been asserted in accordance with the Copyright, Designs and Patents Act 1988 sections 77 and 78.

All rights reserved. No part of this publication may be reproduced, stored in a retrieval system, or transmitted, in any form or by any means, electronic, mechanical, photocopying, recording or otherwise, without prior permission of the copyright owner.

British Library Cataloguing-in-Publication Data
A catalogue record for this book is available from the British Library.

Commissioning Editor: Alexander White
Production: Jane Rogers
Designed and typeset by Ashley Western
Printed and bound by Page Bros, Norwich
Cover image: Main entrance Rochestown: Donal Murphy Photography
Cover design: Kneath Associates

While every effort has been made to check the accuracy and quality of the information given in this publication, neither the Author nor the Publisher accept any responsibility for the subsequent use of this information, for any errors or omissions that it may contain, or for any misunderstandings arising from it.

www.ribapublishing.com

FSC
www.fsc.org
MIX
Paper from responsible sources
FSC® C023114

ENERPHIT

A STEP-BY-STEP
GUIDE TO
LOW-ENERGY
RETROFIT

James Traynor

RIBA Publishing

CONTENTS

Acknowledgements VI
ECD Architects VII
Preface: Prof. Wolfgang Feist (Universtity of Innsbruck) IX

1.0: Introduction

1.1: Purpose 002
1.2: Background 003
1.3: Attempts to retrofit 004
1.4: Newbuild standards 005
1.5: Retrofit standards 005
1.6: Drivers to retrofit 006
1.7: Barriers to retrofit 008
1.8: Finding a way forward 009
1.9: The importance of human comfort 010
1.10: EnerPHit for all? 011

2.0: What is EnerPHit?

2.1: Background to Passivhaus 016
2.2: Passivhaus in the UK 016
2.3: Passivhaus and thermal comfort 016
2.4: Passive House Planning Package (PHPP) 017
2.5: An introduction to EnerPHit 018
2.6: Certification options 018
2.7: Certification option 1 019
2.8: Certification option 2 019
2.9: Other ultra-low-energy standards 020
2.10: Other sustainable building refurbishment standards 022
2.11: Innovative solutions in retrofit: Energiesprong 023
2.12: Statutory compliance in the UK 023
2.13: The importance of quality control 025
2.14: The role of renewable energy 025
2.15: Step-by-step retrofit 026
2.16: Summary 026

3.0: The challenges of EnerPHit

3.1: Introduction 030
3.2: Achieving a successful retrofit 030
3.3: Understanding the barriers to retrofit 032
3.4: The specific challenges of heritage buildings 034
3.5: Overcoming the practical challenges of EnerPHit 036
3.6: Optimising the thermal envelope: external walls 037
3.7: Optimising the thermal envelope: ground floor 040
3.8: Optimising the thermal envelope: roof 040
3.9: Optimising the thermal envelope: windows and doors 041
3.10: Optimising the thermal envelope: solar gain/shade 041
3.11: Optimising airtightness 042
3.12: Optimising ventilation systems 042
3.13: Optimising the building form 043
3.14: Summary 043

4.0: Step-by-step to EnerPHit

4.1: A background to planned maintenance 046
4.2: Funding retrofit: the danger of political change 046
4.3: Funding retrofit: the danger of modest gains 048
4.4: The EuroPHit project: aims and outcomes 049
4.5: The EnerPHit retrofit plan and incremental improvement 049
4.6: Pre-certification for step-by-step retrofit 051
4.7: Aligning planned maintenance and step-by-step retrofit to EnerPHit 051
4.8: The economics of step-by-step retrofit 052
4.9: A case study in step-by-step EnerPHit: Stella Maris House 053
4.10: Implications for building management 059
4.11: BIM as a tool for step-by-step retrofit 060
4.12: Summary 061

CONTENTS

5.0: Targeting EnerPHit

5.1: Does retrofit matter? 064
5.2: EnerPHit as a retrofit target 064
5.3: District heating systems and EnerPHit 066
5.4: The capital cost of EnerPHit 068
5.5: EnerPHit comfort standard 070
5.6: EnerPHit Quality Standard 073
5.7: Eight reasons to target EnerPHit 073
5.8: Does EnerPHit certification matter? 074
5.9: Financing EnerPHit 074
5.10: Implementing EnerPHit for all 075
5.11: Summary 076

6.0: Residential case studies

6.1: Achieving EnerPHit in the residential sector 080
6.2: Wilmcote House, Portsmouth, UK: affordable housing 086
6.3: Rochestown, Phase 2, Dún Laoghaire, Ireland: sheltered housing 094
6.4: Ērgli Vocational School, Latvia: student housing 100
6.5: 105 Willow Street, Brooklyn, New York, USA: private owner-occupied 104
6.6: 2 Gloucester Place Mews, London, UK: Private rent, listed building 114

7.0: Commercial case studies

7.1: Achieving EnerPHit in the commercial sector 122
7.2: Evangelical Church, Heinsberg, Nordrhein Westfalen, Germany: public/community 128
7.3: University of Innsbruck, Tirol, Austria: higher education 136
7.4: Sparkasse Bank, Gross Umstadt, Hesse, Germany: offices 144

8.0: Delivering EnerPHit

8.1: How to approach EnerPHit 154
8.2: The practical challenges of EnerPHit 155
8.3: How to deliver EnerPHit 163
8.4: Summary 167

Postscript: Prof. Anne Power (London School of Economics) 168
Image Credits 170
Bibliography 171
References 175
Index 180

ACKNOWLEDGEMENTS

Dedication
This book is dedicated to the memory of Andrew Kimberley, Clerk of Works at Wilmcote House.

For the case studies, I would like to thank the following for their help and expertise: Stefan Oehler – Architect/Engineer (Sparkasse Bank, Gross Umstadt, Germany), Sebastian Walde – Pastor (Evangelical Church, Heinsberg, Germany), Prof. Ludwig Rongen – Architect (Evangelical Church, Heinsberg, Germany), Andree Dargan – Architect, DLR Council (Rochestown, Dún Laoghaire, Ireland), Sarah Clifford – Architect, DLR Council (Rochestown, Dún Laoghaire, Ireland), Erin Davidson – Architect, Feilden+Mawson (2 Gloucester Place, London, UK), Ulf Allers – Architect, Feilden+Mawson (2 Gloucester Place, London, UK), Steve Groves – Head of Building Maintenance, Portsmouth City Council (Wilmcote House, UK), Loreana Padron – Architect, ECD Architects (Wilmcote House, UK), Jake Stephen – Researcher, University of Southampton (Wilmcote House, UK), Mike Ingui – Architect, Baxt Ingui (20 Vesey Street, Brooklyn, New York, USA), Will Conner – Architect, Baxt Ingui (20 Vesey Street, Brooklyn, New York, USA), Laszlo Lepp – Senior Scientist, Passivhaus Institute (University of Innsbruck, Austria), Paul Ohnmacht – Associate Partner, ATP Architects, Innsbruck, Maximilian Frey – PR Assistant (DBA Communications, Innsbruck), Mare Mitrevica – Energy Consultant (Ērgli Secondary School, Ērgli, Latvia), Ervin Krauklis – Architect (Ērgli Secondary School, Ērgli, Latvia), Mariana Moreira – Energy Consultant (Stella Maris House, Wicklow, Ireland).

I would also like to thank Prof. Dr Wolfgang Feist (Passivhaus Institute), Prof. Anne Power (LSE), Jan Steiger (Passivhaus Institute), Giorgia Tzar (Passivhaus Institute), Sofie Pelsmakers (University of Aarhus), Nick Newman (Studio Bark), Thomas Bierbach (translation from German), Georgia Laganakou (illustrations), Gabriella Seminara (illustrations) and all my colleagues at ECD Architects and Keegans.

For their editorial work: Sarah Lewis, Mark Stephens, Elrond Burrell and Alex White.

My wife Kate for her encouragement and support looking after our children Josh and Adam, and my parents Jim and Barbara for providing a quiet refuge when writing this book.

To everybody: be the change you want to see in the world.

PROFILE

James Traynor is an architect, Passivhaus designer and Managing Director at ECD Architects, an award-winning architectural practice founded on the principles of sustainability and energy efficiency. These principles have guided the design approach to all energy-conscious design (ECD) projects since its inception in 1980, with the result that the practice is now renowned for its expertise in creating innovative ECD solutions which continue to improve the built environment.

ECD's first commission was Futurehome 2000, designed and built in 12 weeks in 1981, and shown on the BBC's *The Money Programme* as an exemplar of design for energy and cost efficiency. A series of low-energy housing schemes followed. Designed on passive solar principles with high insulation standards, these projects achieved significant reductions in space heating costs. Having cut its teeth on newbuild housing, the practice diversified to include education, community and commercial projects, and applied its sustainability principles to upgrading the energy efficiency of existing buildings – from individual homes such as the pilot Retrofit and Replicate project for Hyde Housing Association, and 13 of the TSB (now Innovate UK) Retrofit and Replicate projects, to high-rise developments such as the refurbishment of the residential towers on the Edward Woods Estate – a flagship renewable energy project for the London Borough of Hammersmith and Fulham.

Today, the company is one of the few architectural practices to be BRE BIM certified. It has offices in London and Glasgow and is a member of the N-Able Group, enabling it to add value and broaden the range of services it provides to clients. Its designs provide a contemporary response to people and place which is progressive and transformative. The practice's work engages with the culture of our age, focusing on narrative architecture that is meaningful, functional and accessible.

ECD was a founder member of the UK Passivhaus Trust, and is a strong advocate of Passivhaus design. Winning the refurbishment of Wilmcote House in 2013 enabled the company to hone these skills with regard to retrofit. Designed to the EnerPHit standard, Wilmcote House was selected by the European Commission and the International Passivhaus Institute as the only UK case study in the innovative EuroPHit programme (step-by-step retrofit). Completed in 2018, ECD's retrofit of Wilmcote House has become a national and international reference for high-quality large-scale refurbishment reports. The impact on existing residents has been evaluated by the London School of Economics (LSE) in its *Retrofit to the Rescue* report published in 2019.

PREFACE

The availability of fossil fuel has led to ever-increasing energy consumption across the globe, due to it being cheap, efficient and easy to source.

Now, fossil energy is approaching a necessary end. The findings of climate change researchers are undeniable, and the damage to our planet is already taking effect. Fossil fuels must be replaced by a sustainable supply.

The heating of buildings is the single highest source of energy consumption, accounting for approximately one-third of usage in Europe. The majority of buildings that will require heating in 2060 already exist today. Moving to a sustainable energy system is about redeveloping these buildings to be fit for renewable energy.

The solution lies in improving energy efficiency. In the case of buildings, it is primarily a matter of reducing the high heat losses through old exterior components. These are typically poorly insulated, and/or prone to leaking. The subsequent improvement is possible almost everywhere with reasonable effort – and this not only saves energy, but also improves indoor comfort.

The refurbishment of old buildings with energy-efficient components has created a large field of activity at all levels of qualification: from the planner to the plasterer, and the engineer to the installer. These activities create added value and increased quality of life. The knowledge required for conversion can be easily learned and implemented.

It only took a few decades to build the structures that drive today's consumption of carbon-based fuels, so it should be possible to sustainably refurbish these within a few decades.

The book gives a positive message: transformation is possible, and it is affordable. This is evidenced by a large number of completed refurbishments.

James Traynor has done a very good job of providing the tools architects, engineers and craftspeople need to be able to successfully carry out this necessary transformation and retrofit for energy-efficient housing.

Prof. Dr Wolfgang Feist,
University of Innsbruck

1.0: Introduction

1.1: PURPOSE

This book considers the importance of building refurbishment and the Passivhaus EnerPHit standard as a means of achieving improved thermal comfort for building users and reduced carbon emissions in the building sector. Both are vital in order to meet the international targets set out in the United Nations Framework Convention on Climate Change (UNFCCC) and the Paris Climate Agreement of December 2015.

Much has been written on the importance of Passivhaus. Developed in the early 1990s by academics Bo Adamson (Lund University, Sweden) and Wolfgang Feist (Institute for Housing and Environment, Darmstadt, Germany), the first Passivhaus building was created in 1991 in Kranichstein, Darmstadt. With tens of thousands of completed projects around the world and clear evidence from these that performance in use closely matches the design model, it has since become recognised as the gold standard in building performance. Passivhaus was originally developed as a voluntary standard, but has now been adopted by many local authorities as a means of both reducing carbon emissions and ensuring buildings perform as designed.

However, much less has been written on the application of Passivhaus to existing buildings. The first existing building to be refurbished to the Passivhaus standard was the Ebok office building in Tubingen, Germany, completed in 2003. Following these early refurbishment projects by the Passivhaus Institute (PHI) in Darmstadt, Germany developed the EnerPHit standard in 2010. It employed the same energy performance methodology but, in recognising the difficulty of refurbishment, would accept a marginally lower standard. For example, in an existing building it may not be possible to insulate the ground floor or basement level, and it can be extremely difficult to change the orientation of the building or significantly alter the building form. Therefore, alternative methods need to be employed to improve the building fabric and reduce heat losses. Nevertheless, the performance standard for refurbished buildings is still significantly better than typical newbuild standards in most countries.

This book recognises the benefits and challenges of EnerPHit as a means of achieving improved building performance, and shows how this has been applied to a series of building typologies around the world. Passivhaus – and more recently EnerPHit – has been most widely applied in the domestic housing sector, with many examples in the UK alone; however, there are relatively few examples of EnerPHit applied in non-domestic sectors. A range of building typologies and projects from around the world have been selected as case studies to represent both the challenges and opportunities for deep retrofit to the EnerPHit standard. These case studies include a church, university, commercial bank, affordable housing, sheltered housing, student housing, private owner-occupied housing and private rented housing in a listed 'heritage' building. In each case, the standard EnerPHit methodology was used to inform the performance target, with individual challenges that required a specific response in design, delivery and execution. Where available, pre- and post-retrofit studies that were undertaken by the project team or third parties to demonstrate actual performance against targets have been referenced.

While this book is primarily addressed to architects, engineers, surveyors and contractors, it is also written to inform both building owners and policymakers of the benefits of EnerPHit to improve performance and reduce carbon emissions. Building owners with a long-term interest in their assets need to understand the impact of this methodology in terms of improved comfort and reduced running and maintenance costs, alongside the impact of the physical works and capital cost. Policymakers seeking to implement carbon reduction targets for 2050 must also understand the importance of this rigorous methodology and the need for consistent support, advice and legislation to enable building owners to achieve these targets.

While only two of the eight case studies presented are in the UK, the background issues and implications of EnerPHit are primarily applied to the UK context and important lessons are drawn from other countries, most notably Germany, which has the highest uptake of EnerPHit projects. Alternative local or national methodologies are also referenced for measuring energy performance and contrasted against the Passivhaus methodology to understand relative benchmarking both in design and in use.

Significantly, there is feedback from the building users – perhaps the most important aspect of a successful retrofit. Many questions are considered in each case, and feedback gathered to inform future retrofit projects. Were the building users involved in the design development of the project? Did the building users remain in occupation during the works, and was this successfully managed? Are they satisfied with the outcomes of the retrofit? Does the building perform as designed?

Unlike newbuild projects, retrofit schemes benchmark against both existing energy performance and existing thermal comfort. In EnerPHit schemes this means significant improvement in both measures, but a fair comparison would assume that the existing building was heated, cooled or ventilated to adequate levels, e.g. World Health Organization thresholds. If that were the case, the percentage reduction in carbon emissions or energy bills would match modelled expectations. However, in many cases, this is not the reality. The very reason for the retrofit may be due to the poor thermal comfort, perhaps caused by fuel poverty and the inability of building users to adequately heat the building. As a result, the building users are able to adequately and affordably heat, cool and ventilate their building but it can cause a 'rebound effect' (also known as the 'Jevons paradox') which reduces the theoretical carbon savings and environmental benefits.

This rebound effect can apply to a diverse range of building types, as described in the case studies for Wilmcote House and Sparkasse Bank. While this rebound may include legitimate improvement and does not necessarily affect performance against the EnerPHit standard, it should nevertheless be considered when estimating the potential benefits of wider application and carbon reduction targets. Pre-retrofit evidence[1] from Wilmcote House clearly demonstrates the need to understand actual energy consumption rather than estimated consumption.

Finally, the conclusion considers the evidence from the case studies and other relevant data compared against the global and national targets for carbon reduction by 2050, considering the practical challenges and the means of overcoming these in a 'step-by-step' retrofit plan over the next 30 years. It also reflects on the benefits of a widespread retrofit programme to the EnerPHit standard, and how this compares to current targets (or lack of) for the improvement of existing buildings, other refurbishment initiatives and the wider social and health benefits to building users.

1.2: BACKGROUND:

There are around 27.1 million dwellings in UK, 80% of which will still exist in 2050.[2] At present these dwellings represent approximately 27% of UK CO_2 emissions.[3] Almost 40% of housing in England pre-dates 1945,[4] and about 15% of the UK's CO_2 emissions can be attributed to the burning of fossil fuels to provide space heating in housing.[5] As current rebuilding rates are delivering only approximately 120,000 new homes per year, we clearly cannot rely on newbuild to deliver the seismic shift needed to achieve the targets set by the Climate Change Act 2008. Neither can we rely on demolition of the worst-performing stock. The acute housing shortage in the southeast of England[6] and the partial failure of the Pathfinder scheme[7] in the northwest of England show in different ways that we cannot demolish and rebuild our way out of this problem.

Retrofit is distinctly different to refurbishment or repair, which have traditionally been the methods used to treat existing buildings. This has generally been either for essential maintenance purposes or for cosmetic reasons, to update or modernise the appearance of the building. Instead retrofit aims to upgrade an existing building to meet wider objectives: reducing energy consumption and improving thermal comfort. Retrofit also typically includes other works, including essential maintenance and improvements to the aesthetic appearance of the building, which are carried out at the same time.

Retrofit is typically cheaper than demolition and rebuild. While there may be other reasons to consider redevelopment, such as increased density, it is usually more cost-effective to refurbish. The questions then become how to retrofit, to what standard, and how can this be done with building users in situ? If we consider the targets set out in the Climate Change Act and subsequent international agreements such as the Paris Climate Agreement (2015), existing buildings need to be 'zero carbon' by 2050. But if af all existing buildings *were* upgraded to be zero carbon, this would mean that over 2,000 buildings per day, every day, until 2050 would need to be upgraded to meet this target.

1.3: ATTEMPTS TO RETROFIT

There is much to be done over the next 30 years. If we are to have any chance of achieving these targets, the work needs to start now.

In recent years, the UK government has attempted to leverage change and encourage retrofit through initiatives such as the high-profile, but ultimately unsuccessful, Green Deal scheme. The failings of this scheme are well documented both in the uptake, cost-effectiveness[8] and the quality of installations carried out. Indeed, this author was involved in the largest Green Deal scheme and saw at first hand the impact of piecemeal measures and poor-quality installations. Following the closure of the Green Deal scheme, the UK government commissioned Dr Peter Bonfield to lead a review[9] into the failings of previous retrofit schemes and provide recommendations for the future. The recommendations in the 'Every Home Counts' report included 'cross-cutting' themes including the following:

- Consumer protection
- Advice and guidance
- Quality and standards
- Skills and training
- Compliance and enforcement

It also included sector-specific themes:

- Insulation and fabric
- Smart meters
- Home energy technologies
- Application to social housing

Under 'quality and standards', the review recommended the development of an overarching standards framework for end-to-end delivery of retrofit measures. The existing code of practice and specification for installers of energy-efficiency measures (PAS 2030) was particularly criticised as not fit for purpose, and this document has subsequently been rewritten by industry experts. An updated version was released in 2017, which requires three fundamental principles to be followed as described below:[10]

- Designers are to provide an adequate and site-specific design for each installation, and no installation may proceed without a design. Installers are to check the design is satisfactory before installation, referring back to the designer where amendments are required.

- Designs and installations must have a 'whole-building focus', with understanding of the interaction between different building elements, both physical junctions (such as wall to roof details) and technical relationships (such as airtightness and ventilation strategy). This strategy should include measures that may already be installed, those that are being considered as part of the works, and those that may be undertaken at a future date.

- When upgrading insulation, the impact on ventilation must be considered. Background ventilation must be provided via trickle vents to all rooms, and extract ventilation provided to 'wet rooms', i.e. kitchens and bathrooms. Where multiple measures are installed and deep retrofit achieves airtightness levels lower than 5 $m^3/m^2/hr$ at 50 Pa, all rooms must have ventilation via air inlets with extraction from wet rooms.

These seemingly obvious requirements were not stipulated under previous retrofit schemes. In conjunction with the development of a new 'EHC (Every Home Counts) Quality Mark' equivalent to the Microgeneration Certification Scheme (MCS) for renewable energy installations, it is hoped that these recommendations and the forthcoming PAS 2035:2018 (specification for the energy retrofit of domestic buildings) will result in a more comprehensive, holistic approach to future retrofit.

1.4: NEWBUILD STANDARDS

It is well known that buildings are typically designed to meet, rather than exceed, statutory performance requirements. While some clients choose to target higher standards, it is not the norm. Building regulations in all countries tend to increase requirements over time, which means that older buildings typically perform to a lower standard. As a result of the 2002 EU EPBD (Energy Performance of Buildings Directive), standards for energy performance in buildings have been increasing over time, particularly over the last 20 years as EU governments have sought to reduce carbon emissions. Under current building regulations in the UK (Part L 2016 amendment) carbon emissions have reduced by approximately 55% against 2002 regulations.

The nZEB (near-zero energy in buildings) standard is the culmination of this incremental improvement in the thermal performance of new buildings. Approved in 2010 and effective across the EU from 2020 and all public buildings from the end of 2018, it requires all new buildings to achieve a near-zero energy balance between consumption and production. All EU countries are required to demonstrate how they achieve this standard. While it is noted that there are numerous ways of achieving this to suit both the location and building typology, it is acknowledged that in northern climates the envelope or fabric of the building is extremely important, and Passivhaus offers a means of achieving a very low energy consumption.[11] The zero-energy target to 15kWh will reduce the heating and cooling energy needs at 10 kWh/m^2/a or better in most cases (Passivhaus level) by:

- enhanced performance of the envelope thanks to improvements

- cost reduction in technologies and an extension of their use and integration (e.g. low-emissivity plastic films to reduce weight and costs of triple-glazing, vacuum insulation, aerogel and other super-insulation technologies to obtain higher insulation levels for the same thickness, especially useful in retrofits)

- windows and openings designed for easier use and control for night ventilation, demand-controlled ventilation (occupancy, CO$_2$ driven).

It should be noted that while Passivhaus or EnerPHit may achieve nZEB, it is not a statutory compliance tool. In fact, the performance of the building fabric in an nZEB-compliant building may be significantly worse than Passivhaus if the energy demand can be matched to low carbon sources. Chapter 2 considers alternative methodologies that might be followed to achieve this standard.

In 2008, the UK proposed to implement zero carbon in all new buildings by 2016, but this was scrapped with the Code for Sustainable Homes in 2014. At the time of writing it is unclear whether nZEB will be implemented in the UK; however, the long-term targets for carbon emissions remain and international obligations suggest that the UK will need to implement nZEB, or something very similar, very soon.

1.5: RETROFIT STANDARDS

Until very recently the retrofit of buildings to improve energy performance has not been mandated, and even where threshold standards exist the performance requirements are relatively low (see UK building regulations Part L1B or L2B). Both EU and UK policies have proved limited and/or relatively ineffective in tackling carbon emissions from the existing building stock.

While the 2002 European Performance of Buildings Directive (EPBD) encouraged EU countries to introduce certification schemes for their existing stock, which led in the UK to the introduction of Energy Performance Certificates (EPCs) and other initiatives, the translation of this to improved building performance has had limited effect. The EPC output is typically ignored, and the methodology for preparing them – Reduced Data Standard Assessment Procedure (RdSAP) – is very limited. The performance of existing buildings has therefore lagged, with no requirement until recently for building refurbishment. While the UK government has introduced a 'consequential improvements' clause requiring energy-efficiency improvements when major works are proposed, this is not enforced for domestic dwellings, which represent over 40% of total energy consumption.

The existing refurbishment performance targets in the UK (Part L2B) are relatively low and need to be significantly increased to meet government carbon reduction commitments for 2050. The recent introduction of the Minimum Energy Efficiency Standard (MEES) in March 2018 is the first step in enforcing thermal improvements in the worst-performing parts of the building sector (Band F and G properties) and will require building owners, both public and private, to achieve a minimum Band E performance. However, these modest improvements to achieve limited standards may compromise the future ability of the building owner to meet more stringent targets.

The challenge in setting refurbishment standards is how to achieve realistic improvements which are both affordable and sensible, without preventing the improvements necessary to achieve the zero-carbon standard. If we accept that existing buildings will ultimately need to achieve the same nZEB performance currently proposed for new buildings by 2020, we might consider the EnerPHit standard for the refurbishment of buildings.

Implementing this across all building types in a single project will almost certainly be cost-prohibitive for most building owners. However, if the necessary measures could be planned over a 30-year investment programme and built into regular maintenance programmes, it becomes an appropriate solution. In Chapter 4, the outcomes from recent EuroPHit programme are assessed. These implemented planned measures as part of a retrofit plan allow for future upgrades to achieve zero carbon as funds allow.

If EnerPHit is the right methodology for building retrofit and is flexible enough to be affordable and achieve long-term targets: how can we ensure this target has been achieved? Several studies have shown that the 'performance gap' between energy consumption as predicted against actual[12] can be as much as five times, and there is increasing awareness of the effects of poor quality control in both newbuild[13] and building refurbishment.[14] There is therefore an urgent need to tackle this issue. In conjunction with Building Information Modelling (BIM), it is hoped that the requirement for all UK government-funded projects from April 2016 to follow the Government Soft Landings (GSL) methodology[15] will improve the handover and commissioning of buildings and reduce the gap between predicted and actual performance.

Fortunately, post-occupancy studies undertaken over the last 25 years have consistently shown that Passivhaus buildings perform in line with design predictions. While energy consumption is strongly affected by building user choice, the differences are much less pronounced in Passivhaus and EnerPHit buildings.

1.6: DRIVERS TO RETROFIT

The retrofit of our building stock, especially in the residential sector, is of key importance in reducing our carbon emissions. UK buildings currently produce approximately 88 $MtCO_2e$ per annum (2015) from the burning of fossil fuels to provide space heating and hot water, which represents 17% of total UK carbon emissions. Of this total 64 $MtCO_2e$ (13% of total carbon emissions) is produced in the residential sector with the remaining emissions produced by the commercial sector (13 $MtCO_2$) and public sector (9 $MtCO_2$).[16]

By 2050, the UK government is seeking to reduce carbon emissions by 80% from 1990 levels. Since 2009, the government has set a series of four-yearly Carbon Budgets demonstrating how it intends to reduce carbon across all sectors. Given the difficulty in achieving this cross-industry, the building sector has been identified as a key target to fully decarbonise by 2050. The latest release of the 5th

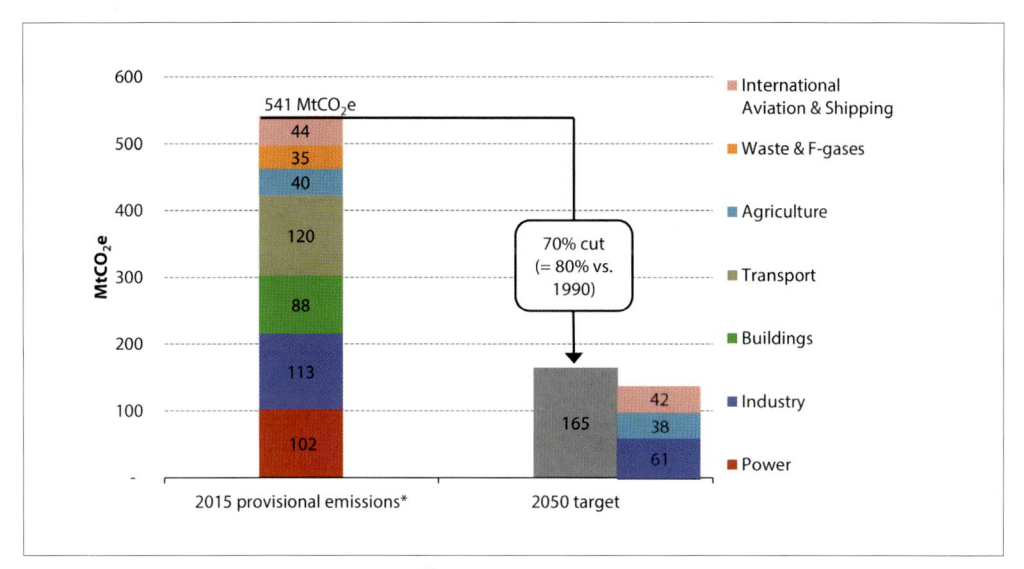

Fig 1.1: Hard-to-reduce sectors and the 2050 target[17]

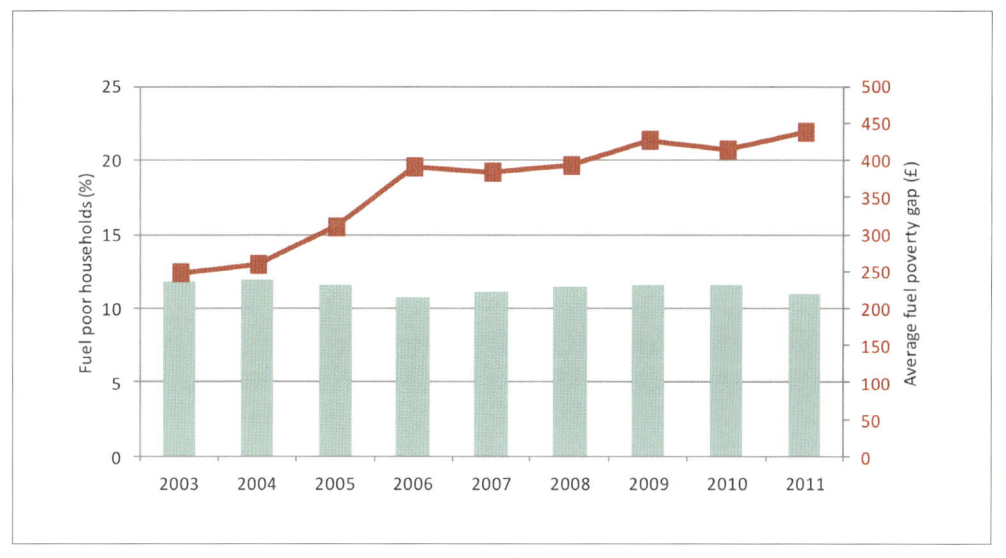

Fig 1.2: Fuel poverty in England (%) and the fuel poverty gap (£)[18]

Carbon Budget for 2028–32 shows (see Fig 1.1) that the majority of the 165 MTCO$_2$e target is already accounted for, before buildings, transport, waste and power are even considered. The UK housing stock is also one of the oldest and worst insulated in Europe.[19] With only 15% of homes built since 1990, most are expected to remain in situ by 2050 so there are more than enough buildings to retrofit.

Deep retrofit
Deep retrofit is an effective solution in tackling demand at its source and futureproofing buildings.

The outcomes of good-quality deep retrofit schemes are improved thermal comfort and dramatically reduced fuel bills. This is particularly important for those on low incomes, where fuel poverty can seriously damage the health and wellbeing of residents who must choose to eat food rather than heat their homes. Fig 1.2 shows that the financial impact on those households has dramatically increased with the widening of the financial gap.

Introduction 7

1.7: BARRIERS TO RETROFIT

Targets cannot be set in isolation. It is necessary for regulators to understand the practical challenges of meeting these targets before enforcement becomes mandatory. For new buildings, the challenges are less demanding, as the design can be optimised to suit the requirements. Design factors that can be optimised include orientation, building footprint, window sizes, distribution of services and material selection. However, for existing buildings it may be impossible to change the orientation or building footprint, which means improvement may require an extensive upgrade to the building fabric or higher performance components. Existing buildings bring additional challenges, such as unknown or unexpected materials resulting from incomplete building records. Many existing buildings (especially residential) may remain in occupation during refurbishment with access restrictions causing delays and/or additional cost. Financial constraints are a limitation on any project, and refurbishment budgets are often limited to little more than an annual maintenance budget for urgent repairs. This allowance does not typically include enhanced thermal performance, and such measures are usually driven by the availability of funding.

In this context of increasing standards with limited funding, it is important for building owners to understand the future destination of regulations and how building improvements can be phased over time without compromising future works. Unfortunately, many energy-efficiency refurbishment projects in UK over the last 10 years have been driven by the availability of external funding for piecemeal measures. Many of these projects have not considered the building as a whole, or improvements as part of a long-term refurbishment plan. In many cases the detailing has been poor, with little consideration of the interaction between elements, resulting in unintended consequences that can lower performance and cause the building to deteriorate. In some cases, this has resulted in reduced thermal comfort and increased health issues for building occupants. Improvements should be considered as part of a plan phased to suit client budgets, with a clear understanding of the impact of the measure proposed. For example, improving windows without allowing for adequate ventilation (either passive or active) will result in increased risk of condensation.

For building owners with a long-term interest in the condition of their assets, the need for careful stewardship of their building is self-evident. However, many buildings, both commercial and residential, may be short-term investments and refurbishment will either be essential maintenance or driven by other market factors. For these buildings, improvements to the thermal performance of the building are likely to be of secondary importance and driven by the need for consequential improvements (as per UK building regulations Part L2B) arising from other works. Unfortunately, these lower standards may 'lock in' lower performance over the long term, and prevent future upgrades. In addition to commercial barriers there are often legal barriers preventing enhanced performance. For example, leasehold contracts typically exclude any possibility of the recovery of monies arising from 'betterment'. This means that the freeholder or managing agent is unable to recover any money for works carried out which exceed building regulations. For the vast majority of properties, even the limited standards required by building regulations (Part L2B) are not enforced unless the extent of works triggers 'consequential improvements'.

The UK building stock is incredibly diverse, with occupied buildings, both commercial and residential, dating back over 1000 years. Many of these buildings are of architectural importance and as such are listed or are else in conservation areas, meaning that any change to the visual appearance of the building may not be possible or desirable. While improvements to the energy efficiency of the building fabric can be achieved without changing the external appearance of a building, this often raises other issues. For example, solid-wall properties are typically classed as 'hard to treat' with no internal cavity to insulate. They also often pre-date 1945, meaning they are more likely to be in conservation areas. Therefore, the only opportunity to insulate the external walls is along the internal face of the wall, which causes disruption for occupants and some loss of valuable floor area.

Internal wall insulation also needs to be carefully considered, as it can increase condensation risk if not properly detailed. Older properties may also have latent defects which need to be addressed prior to any energy-efficiency works. This may include structural defects such as subsidence, incomplete damp-proofing at ground or flashings at roof level, causing moisture ingress to the wall. Even when external wall insulation is possible, it will usually be necessary to relocate existing wall-mounted services and extend window sills to suit.

1.8: FINDING A WAY FORWARD

If we accept that buildings have a crucial role to play in achieving carbon reduction targets, and we accept that in most developed countries the majority of buildings that currently exist will still remain in 2050, the need to properly address building refurbishment is imperative and urgent. Despite the technical challenges identified above and discussed in more detail in Chapter 3, for many properties these can be overcome with careful planning and attention

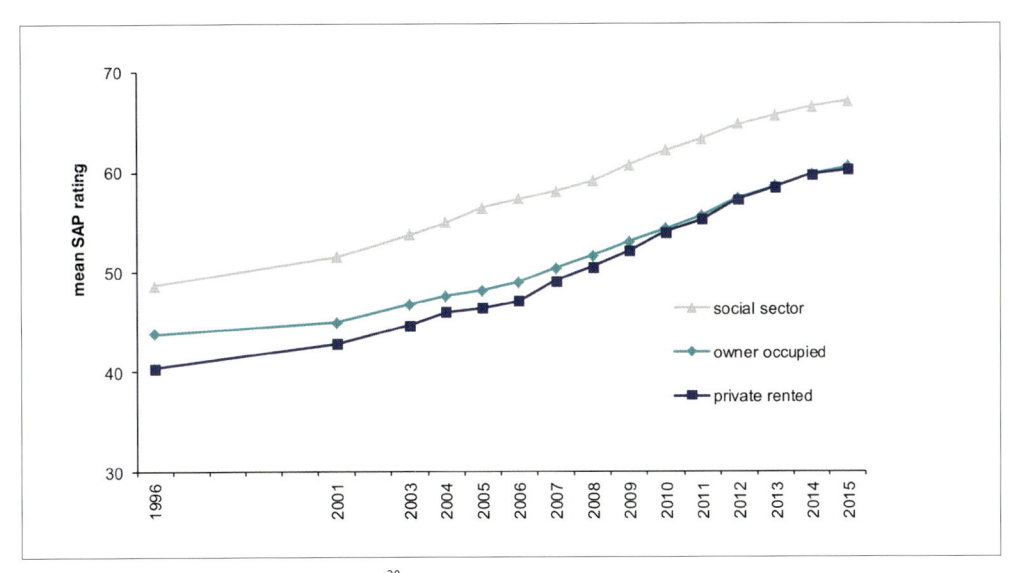

Fig 1.3: Mean SAP rating by tenure, 1996–2015[20]

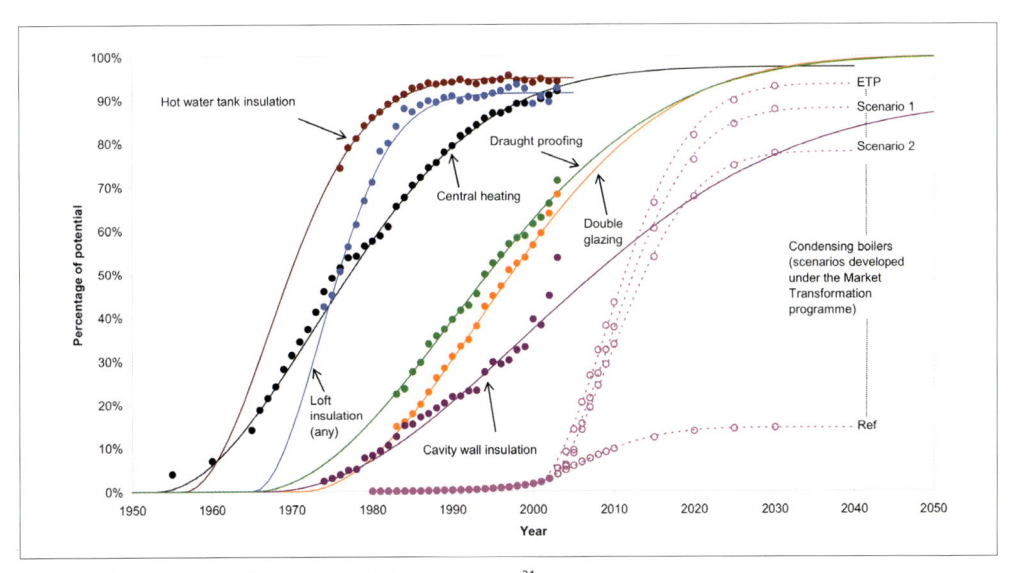

Fig 1.4: Market penetration of home energy-efficiency measures[21]

to detail. However, studies[22] have shown that the technical challenges are often not the biggest obstacle to deep retrofit. Rather obstacles can include more human issues, such as inertia caused by disruption, anticipated or actual; lack of interest due to other priorities; and financial constraints due to the relatively low (although increasing) price of energy against the increasing cost of refurbishment. In addition, legal barriers[23] can prevent energy-efficiency measures where the freeholder of the building is unable to re-charge improvements to leaseholders. While essential maintenance can include energy-efficiency measures, there is no possibility of recovering monies where the works exceed current building regulations. As noted above, these short-term energy-efficiency measures can often lock in moderate improvements, making future improvements more difficult. For building owners with a long-term interest in the performance of their building this is clearly not desirable, and some have chosen to exceed current building regulations in order to avoid future upgrades and reduce both ongoing running costs and maintenance. However, these exemplar projects are not the norm and, where refurbishment does occur, energy efficiency is often not the first priority.

Nevertheless, energy efficiency of buildings has gradually improved over the last 30 years. For example, in the UK the average SAP rating of residential properties has increased approximately 38% from 45 in 1996 to 62 in 2015.[24] Some of this is due to demolition and newbuild; however, with relatively low levels of replacement (approximately 2%), refurbishment of properties has made an impact on energy efficiency and carbon emissions, especially in the affordable housing sector (see Fig 1.3). For many people in the UK energy efficiency is synonymous with loft insulation and double-glazing – which have, like central heating, become the norm in most properties (see Fig 1.4). These measures have proved popular in both the private and public sector, and have undoubtedly resulted in substantial reductions in energy consumption. While loft insulation has been installed in many thousands of properties over the last 30 years the typical depth of insulation installed is relatively modest and can easily be improved. Similarly, double-glazing has reduced draughts and overall heat loss; however,

the quality of both products and installation have varied enormously. While products have improved through legislation, i.e. U-values and thermal breaks within window frames, the continuing poor quality of installation can result in increased and unnecessary heat losses at the junction with the wall.

Setting aside for a moment the variable quality of installations, we might consider the success of these retrofit measures in their widespread application and the extensive supply chain that has developed over the last 30 years. In the private sector these improvements were typically driven by consumer demand from increased sale values (perceived or actual) and thermal comfort (reduced draughts and noise), and in the public sector by regulation and reduced maintenance (perceived or actual). If the marketing success of this sector could therefore be harnessed to increased performance standards, and quality control is built into the process through a reliable completion test, we might achieve actual improvement on a large scale. Indeed, the recommendations of the Bonfield review[25] suggest how this might be achieved. However, while improvements to both products and installations are important, they must be considered in the context of the whole-building performance and thermal comfort.

1.9: THE IMPORTANCE OF HUMAN COMFORT

While carbon reduction is an imperative, and energy consumption is often (although not always) directly linked to this target, we should not forget that buildings are primarily designed to serve human needs and comfort. Given that many existing buildings fail to provide good levels of thermal comfort, this should be a key driver when tackling our ageing building stock. Other triggers for refurbishment may include the rising cost of energy and the disproportionate cost of heating an inefficient building, which in the housing sector may result in fuel poverty. In 2014, 17% of English households were defined as being in fuel poverty, with around one in five people finding it difficult to afford the cost of heating their home. Living in a cold home can result in a series of avoidable health-related problems, both physical and mental, and has been linked to increasing rates of death.[26]

While thermal comfort is subjective, studies have shown[27] that most humans are comfortable at temperatures of 20°C to 22°C, although this may be altered by levels of activity, clothing or humidity. Given seasonal variance in most climatic zones, we rely on our buildings to moderate external conditions to suit our needs. In practice this can mean heating them in winter and cooling them in summer, depending on the climatic zone. The degree to which the building is able to moderate seasonal temperature changes is usually determined by the efficiency of the heating or cooling system, and the building user's ability to pay the running costs. Users of poorly insulated buildings often experience a high degree of discomfort caused by radiant asymmetry. A room thermostat located midpoint on a wall may suggest that the room is at a comfortable temperature, but the building user could still experience a cold, draughty floor while at the same time suffering from uncomfortably high temperatures at head level caused by stratification. Similarly, a poor-quality, badly fitted window will increase temperature difference across the room and cause increased air movement and draughts. Indeed, in the UK this phenomenon has traditionally been actively encouraged by locating radiators under windows, which has also contributed to increased heat loss through poor-quality windows.

Where rooms are not sufficiently heated and surface temperatures drop below 12°C, even moderate levels of humidity combined with poor ventilation can cause mould growth. The worst-affected locations are typically in high-moisture zones such as bathrooms and kitchens, and where these coincide with thermal bridges or lower levels that may be less well ventilated. Mould growth obviously causes further deterioration to the building fabric and further reduces air quality, with a proven link to increased rates of asthma.[28] Air quality is an increasingly important issue in cities, with high levels of air pollution an increasing concern for the impact on human health. Indoor air quality is therefore linked to the local air quality, as ventilation has traditionally meant opening windows. Where insufficient ventilation is provided, levels of CO_2 can increase, causing uncomfortable 'stuffy' conditions which can also lead to increased headaches, inability to concentrate and sleepiness.

Numerous studies of completed Passivhaus/ EnerPHit buildings have shown that significant improvement in the building fabric and resulting reduction in both heat losses and overheating risk can dramatically reduce energy costs and improve thermal comfort. With a highly insulated building envelope and mechanical ventilation with heat recovery (MVHR) there is no radiant asymmetry, as all internal surfaces are the same ambient temperature and correspond to the room thermostat. Therefore, there are no draughts and thermal comfort is significantly improved. There is also no risk of mould growth, as the modest heating demand ensures internal surface temperatures remain well above 12°C, while constant ventilation provided by MVHR ensures all areas are adequately ventilated with fresh pre-warmed air. Incoming air is filtered, improving quality and removing many of the toxins present in our polluted cities. With improved ventilation and warm, stable temperatures humidity levels are also typically lower, leading to more comfortable living conditions.

1.10: ENERPHIT FOR ALL?

There are a number of benchmarking options when considering building retrofit, and the designer and client should understand what these offer before selecting a preferred route. While Passivhaus and EnerPHit provide a rigorous methodology for measuring building performance, they are solely focused on the building and its occupants, and unlike BREEAM and LEED they do not measure wider sustainability factors such as embodied energy, sustainable procurement, transport or pollution controls, which may be important to the client. Nevertheless, EnerPHit does offer a proven methodology to both improve performance and raise quality in construction, and over the following chapters I will set out the reasons why I believe the EnerPHit methodology can be applied to virtually all building types.

CHAPTER 2 explains the background to the EnerPHit standard and summarises the key aspects of the standard and its relationship to Passivhaus. It includes key assumptions about building design and services, as well as their implications. It also looks at recent changes to the standard and its future development.

CHAPTER 3 considers the technical challenges of implementing refurbishment schemes to the EnerPHit standard and the key factors faced by the building owner, consultant and contractor, such as heritage, cost and skills. It also discusses practical solutions adopted by others that offer lower, but acceptable, standards of performance

CHAPTER 4 assesses the funding challenges of deep retrofit, referencing the recent EuroPHit project and other good examples of incremental retrofit. It considers the wider implications of limited measures, i.e. insufficient insulation to fabric, to lock in modest gains that prevent future improvements. It also looks at what measures to take, what these might cost, and when and how to avoid pitfalls in the sequencing of projects.

CHAPTER 5 discusses the case for EnerPHit and the role of benchmarking in driving standards, ensuring quality in delivery and evidence of performance in future decision making, as well as other reasons for doing deep retrofit – including health, security and aesthetics.

CHAPTER 6 outlines the nature of the residential sector and describes five key retrofit case study projects across a broad range of building types and locations which have been designed to achieve EnerPHit. In each case, the key challenges are considered, as well as how these were successfully addressed. It also looks at the impact on the building users and owners, and whether this is a methodology they endorse and a process they would repeat.

CHAPTER 7 outlines the nature of the commercial sector and describes three key retrofit case study projects across a broad range of building types and locations which have been designed to achieve EnerPHit.

CHAPTER 8 considers how to approach EnerPHit, the necessary practical measures to achieve EnerPHit on a typical retrofit project, and how this can be delivered.

2.0: What is EnerPHit?

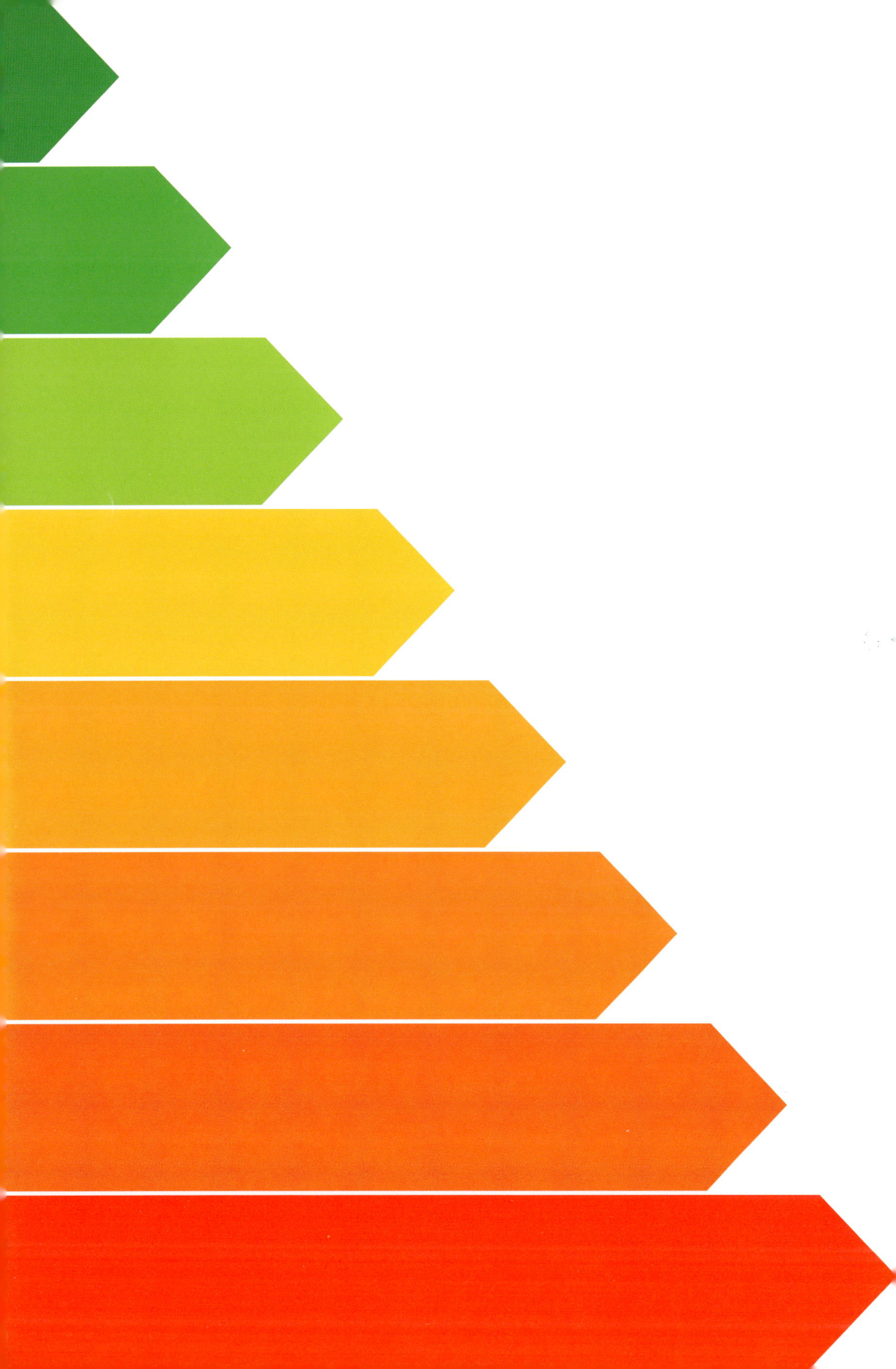

2.1: BACKGROUND TO PASSIVHAUS

The Passivhaus methodology was originally developed in the early 1990s by academics at Lund University (Sweden) and the Institute for Housing and Environment (Darmstadt, Germany). The methodology incorporates all aspects of the physical performance of a building in its local context, using local weather files suited to each location. The Passivhaus standard requires a highly insulated airtight building envelope with a mechanical ventilation system to provide heat recovery. This standard provides a performance threshold level at which an occupied building can provide thermal comfort to its users without a secondary heating system. With over 30,000 completed schemes and increasing evidence of performance in use, this standard has become increasingly important as building owners and designers seek to reduce energy consumption and carbon emissions.

2.2: PASSIVHAUS IN THE UK

Since the first Passivhaus project in the UK was completed in 2009 at Denby Dale, the Passivhaus standard has grown considerably, with over 250 schemes completed by end of 2013. There are currently over 450 certified Passivhaus designers/consultants and seven certifiers in the UK. There are also an increasing number of PH-certified tradespeople and an increasing number of UK manufacturers producing PH-certified products. The Passivhaus Trust was launched in 2009 to support the growth of Passivhaus projects in the UK, and since then several public and private sector clients have delivered Passivhaus projects. Nevertheless, it remains a niche pursuit for informed clients and consultants who believe that UK building regulations are not rigorous enough and wish to target ultra-low-energy performance.

While the standard is not currently supported under UK legislation, there are reasons to believe this may change in the near future.[1] Increasing energy performance legislation in UK regions, most notably in London and Scotland, and active support from local authorities, most notably in Exeter and Norwich, suggest that it is now being seen as an effective methodology for exceeding current standards.

2.3: PASSIVHAUS AND THERMAL COMFORT

The Passivhaus standard is primarily focused on energy, both in terms of space heating and primary energy. It sets fixed performance targets to ensure the building is optimised, and to minimise risk for both energy consumption and overheating. However, it is also a standard which provides improved thermal comfort. The functional definition of a Passivhaus is 'a building, for which thermal comfort … can be achieved solely by post-heating or post-cooling of the fresh air mass, which is required to fulfil sufficient indoor air quality conditions … without a need for additional recirculated air'.

Thermal comfort is defined in BS EN ISO 7730:2005 (10) as 'that condition of mind which expresses satisfaction with the thermal environment'; however, it is influenced by several subjective human perceptions, and a direct cause and effect of thermal comfort can be elusive. Nevertheless, there are two key influencing factors:

- **Occupant parameters: physical activity and clothing**

- **Environmental parameters: air temperature, mean radiant temperature, air speed and relative air humidity**

Thermal comfort is achieved primarily through implementation of 'passive' measures. In practice, this involves a highly insulated thermal envelope and high-performance components such as windows and doors, which reduce heat losses to a minimum. Supplementary 'active' measures include MVHR, which provides sufficient background ventilation that can be boosted to suit occupancy levels and activity.

Thermal comfort is also subjective, and numerous studies have shown that it is impossible to achieve 100% satisfaction levels as the occupant parameters will always vary and personal preference will influence building user feedback. However, incorporating opportunities for building users to modify their environment has been proven in recent years to increase thermal comfort. This might mean ensuring building users are able to control ventilation (by opening windows) or control lighting (by switching on lights). When given such measures, studies have shown that building users are willing to accept a broad range of 'comfortable' temperatures typically linked to local external ambient temperatures. People in colder climates are usually willing to accept cooler internal conditions than people in warmer climates.

It also supports building users who wish to adapt their thermal comfort by opening windows. MVHR provides ventilation rather than cooling and, although the cooling effect of MVHR can be effective in temperate conditions, it is less effective in periods of prolonged heat. While the high-performance building envelope of a Passivhaus prevents excessive heat gain, it also reduces heat loss. Therefore, over an extended cold or hot period the internal environment provides considerable inertia. This means the internal environment can take longer to cool down, which is a benefit in winter but a potential problem in summer. In these conditions building users are advised to open their windows, preferably at night to benefit from night cooling and/or natural cross-ventilation as they would in a conventional building. See case study 7.3 (University of Innsbruck).

2.4: PASSIVE HOUSE PLANNING PACKAGE (PHPP)

Passivhaus buildings are modelled in a very detailed Excel spreadsheet or Passive House Planning Package (PHPP), which has been developed and refined over the last 20 years (currently at version 9) based on results from monitored buildings.[2] It is one of the most accurate energy-efficiency and calculation design tools available. PHPP is used as one of the primary compliance tools for Passivhaus or EnerPHit certification and, critically, unlike other certification tools it incorporates measured data from the project, which ensures quality in construction. While Passivhaus buildings also experience a range of performance levels depending on user interaction average, energy consumption is significantly lower than other 'low-energy' buildings.

PHPP provides a verification tab which is used throughout the development of the design to confirm whether the proposals achieve the relevant standard.[3] The model incorporates 38 active worksheets requiring the designer to insert detailed information on the building size, shape, thermal envelope (i.e. U- and psi values) and components. It also includes information on building occupancy, lighting, heating/cooling/shading and hot water strategy, unregulated energy demand[4] and energy sources (including renewable energy sources) which, combined with local weather files, calculate estimated energy demand. While PHPP is a very detailed design tool, it should not be confused with statutory tools such as SAP or SBEM (UK energy compliance tools). It should also be noted that this tool is not designed to calculate carbon emissions, although the data output can be compared against energy sources to calculate carbon emissions.

The PHPP is a 'steady-state' model which calculates a series of monthly energy balance calculations performed broadly in accordance with EN ISO 13790:2008 for determining the heating demand according to annual and monthly methods. In addition, PHPP also contains algorithms to calculate peak heating and cooling loads and assess overheating risks based on a single-zone thermal model. It is primarily a tool to help the designer refine and optimise the building design. As a steady-state single-zone model, it requires all boundary conditions to be accurately shown, which may not at project inception requiring appropriate assumptions be possible.

Despite its apparent complexity, it can also be used from the earliest stages of design development. With experience and using typical default values, the designer can quickly gauge the relative performance of several high-level design options such as orientation and proportion of windows. In recent years a modelling tool (designPH) has been developed as a plug-in to SketchUp[5] to assist architects in the translation of their designs into PHPP, and other tools are being developed as plug-ins to Revit[6] (i.e. Passivlink) as well as other 3D modelling software.

The most recent version, PHPP 9 (2015) introduced a number of new features including a 'Variants and Comparison' function, which enables the designer to compare the performance of a number of different design options, and a 'PHeco' tool which allows the user to understand the cost benefit of each. This is particularly useful on existing building retrofits where designers wish to compare performance against an existing building.

2.5: AN INTRODUCTION TO ENERPHIT

EnerPHit was launched by the Passive House Institute (PHI) in 2010 as the target standard for the refurbishment of buildings. It uses the same methodology as the Passivhaus standard, but with a slight relaxation to reflect the complexity of existing buildings. It uses the same five principles to ensure that design proposals address all the key aspects of building performance.

- **Building envelope:** This should be a continuous layer without gaps around a building, which minimises heat transfer relative to the function of each element, whether it is a window, wall, floor or roof. Threshold levels of performance are required for each element to ensure overall integrity. In the case of windows this includes performance losses arising from installation in the wall. The efficiency of the envelope relative to floor area (often known as the 'form factor') also plays an important part in reducing energy demand.

- **Airtightness:** The airtight layer plays a crucial role in reducing heat losses from draughts as well as protecting the building fabric from condensation. The measurement of airtightness should be done at key stages during construction to ensure that performance on completion meets threshold criteria.

- **Solar gain:** Windows are typically required in all building types, and seasonal variations need to be carefully modelled to provide sufficient heat in the winter while avoiding overheating in the summer. In practice this can mean a combination of physical shading and/or selection of appropriate glazing.

- **Thermal bridges:** A thermal bridge is a localised weak spot in the envelope of a building where heat losses are substantially greater than surrounding areas. This weakness is a result of insufficient insulation and could be a repeating element such a structural column, or a continuous element such as a lintel, or the junction of two primary elements such as the wall and floor. Careful detailing is required to ensure thermal bridges are avoided wherever possible, although this can be more challenging in existing buildings.

- **Ventilation:** This means providing optimal indoor air quality for the health and comfort of residents while avoiding uncomfortable draughts and associated heat losses caused by excessive uncontrolled ventilation. In practice this means using MVHR to extract from rooms with high humidity (e.g. bathrooms and kitchens) while supplying fresh preheated air to other areas (e.g. living rooms and bedrooms).

Applying these five measures means buildings are designed to achieve specific performance outputs for a range of measures such as space heating/cooling demand, space heating/cooling load, frequency of overheating, frequency of excessive high humidity, airtightness, non-renewable primary energy demand (PE) and primary energy renewable (PER).

2.6: CERTIFICATION OPTIONS

There are two routes for achieving EnerPHit certification. The first is the achievement of the specific heat demand and other criteria set out below, and the other is the use of Passivhaus-certified products on an elemental basis. The recent publication of the *Building Certification Guide*[7] provides clear guidance on the benefits, criteria, costs and methodology for achieving certification.

Certification is a voluntary process and is not currently enforced by local authorities. However, users of the Passivhaus methodology benefit from improved quality control because the contractor is required to demonstrate actual performance to achieve certification. Ensuring this is achieved therefore becomes a key component in the employer's requirements and a contract deliverable.

2.7: CERTIFICATION OPTION 1

Achieving the necessary performance outputs for the five key performance criteria is typically harder in existing buildings than in new buildings. Whereas a new building can often be optimised by adjusting the orientation, modifying window sizes, improving the form factor, avoiding thermal bridges and so on, these design tools may not be available in the case of existing buildings. Therefore, in developing the EnerPHit standard, PHI identified a series of lower targets that may be used for building refurbishment projects, which are summarised in Table 2.1.

Passivhaus buildings are required to deliver a space heating demand of less than 15 kWh/m²/a, whereas EnerPHit can achieve less than 25 kWh/m²/a. The airtightness of a Passivhaus building shall be not more than 0.6 n50 1/h, whereas an EnerPHit building can achieve a pass at 1.0 n50 1/h.

2.8: CERTIFICATION OPTION 2

PHI also recognises that even this reduced standard may be difficult to achieve for some building types. For example, in historically important buildings, it may not be possible to change the external appearance of the building. Therefore, an alternative route to compliance under EnerPHit using

	Passivhaus standard	EnerPHit standard (method 1)
Space heating		
Heating demand	<15 kWh/(m²/a)	<25 kWh/(m²/a)
Heating load	<10 W/M²	n/a
Space cooling		
Cooling demand	<15 kWh/(m²/a)	<25 kWh/(m²/a)
Cooling load	<10 W/m²	n/a
Frequency of overheating (>25°C) %	10%	10%
Frequency of excessively high humidity (>12 g/kg) %	20%	20%
Airtightness	<0.6 n50 1/h	<1.0 n50 1/h
Non-renewable primary energy (PE)	<120 kWh/m²/a	<120 kWh/m²/a
Primary energy renewable (PER) demand	<30, 45, 60 kWh/m²/a	<30, 45, 60 kWh/m²/a
PER generation relative to building footprint area	<0, 60, 120 kWh/m²/a*	<0, 60, 120 kWh/m²/a*

Table 2.1 Targets for building refurbishment projects
*Classic, Plus or Premium options.

Passivhaus-certified components is offered whereby improvements are made on an elemental basis. PHI-certified components include the following elements:

- Wall and construction systems
- Floor slab insulation systems
- Roof parapet and balcony connections
- Facade anchors
- Window frames
- Window connections
- Front doors and sliding doors
- Post-and-rail facades
- Roof windows and skylights
- Roller shutters and external blinds
- Glazing
- Mechanical ventilation systems
- Compact heat pump units
- Exhaust systems

To achieve EnerPHit by using certified components, it would typically be necessary to use a PH-certified MVHR system and triple-glazed windows. For complex or historically important buildings, it may not be possible to improve the thermal envelope with external insulation. On these buildings internal wall insulation to at least 25% of the external wall area can be provided, and is described as EnerPHit(i). An example of this approach is shown in case study 7.2 (Evangelical Church, Heinsberg).

2.9: OTHER ULTRA-LOW-ENERGY STANDARDS

The forthcoming nZEB standard will become effective across all new buildings in the EU in 2020 and public buildings in 2018. EPBD Article 7 requires all member states to enforce improvements to the energy efficiency of existing buildings when these undergo major refurbishment, 'in so far as this is technically, functionally and economically feasible'. While there is no single EU-wide methodology for nZEB, the onus is on member states to put forward measures to achieve this, and it is widely recognised that Passivhaus offers an acceptable methodology for achieving nZEB, especially when coordinated with renewable energy sources.

The PHI recognises that for some buildings and clients it may not be possible to achieve all aspects of the Passivhaus or EnerPHit standard – perhaps due to poor form factor, poor orientation, availability of components or a challenging location. In these situations, an alternative low-energy building standard is available. Here, the space heating demand for both newbuild and refurbishment projects is relaxed to 30 kWh/m^2/a and the airtightness threshold is set at 1.0 to match the EnerPHit standard.

Although the Passivhaus/EnerPHit/low-energy building standards have been widely adopted by many clients and some local authorities, they are typically not statutory, and are not the only ultra-low-energy standards for buildings in Europe. Minergie-P is the Swiss equivalent of the Passivhaus standard, providing similar thermal performance, and offering an even higher standard for primary energy consumption. Minergie-P+ achieves a further 25% reduction in total energy demand by incorporating more advanced services technologies. Other low-energy building standards include various 'Passive House' variants as developed by Norway (standard NS 3700:2010 – new buildings only); Sweden (Forum för Energieffektiva Byggnader); Denmark (Lavenergiklasse 1 from the Danish building code) and the French BBC Effinergie system. However, the Passivhaus standard is also widely used in these countries.

The UK Code for Sustainable Homes was withdrawn in 2014, and there is currently no equivalent UK standard for ultra-low-energy buildings. However, the Association for Environment Conscious Building (AECB) promotes the Passivhaus standard through its Carbonlite programme as the 'Gold' standard. It also offers an alternative 'AECB' standard (previously known as the 'Silver' standard), which can be used on both newbuild and refurbishment projects.** The AECB standard uses the Passivhaus methodology with a further relaxation in performance standards, as can be seen in Table 2.2.

	Passivhaus (PH) standard	EnerPHit standard	PH low-energy standard	AECB standard**	UK Part L1A 2013 (newbuild) approximately
Space heating/ cooling demand	15 kWh/m²/a	25 kWh/m²/a	30 kWh/m²/a	40 kWh/m²/a	54 kWh/m²/a
PE/PER demand*	120 kWh/m²/a *	120 kWh/m²/a *	120 kWh/m²/a *	120 kWh/m²/a *	190 kWh/m²/a
Airtightness (n50)	0.6 n50 1/h	1.0 n50 1/h	1.0 n50 1/h	1.5 n50 1/h	5.0 n50 1/h
Thermal bridges	0.01 W/MK***	As PH standard	As PH standard	As PH standard	0.05 or 0.15 W/MK
Overheating frequency (>25°C) %	10%****	10%****	10%****	10%****	Not measured

Table 2.2: Comparison of low-energy building standards

*Following the release of PHPP v9 the PE/PER demand varies to suit the region and inclusion of renewable energy sources. The figure shown above is the previous threshold level for non-renewable electricity consumption.

**The AECB recommends this standard for newbuild. While this target can be used for retrofit projects, designers are advised to pay attention to increased moisture risk.

***This figure (or lower) is considered 'thermal bridge free'. While higher figures may be used, these must be entered into PHPP to determine suitability.

****PHI recommends a maximum of 5% is used.

Typical

Passivhaus/EnerPHit

EPC (Energy Performance Certificate)

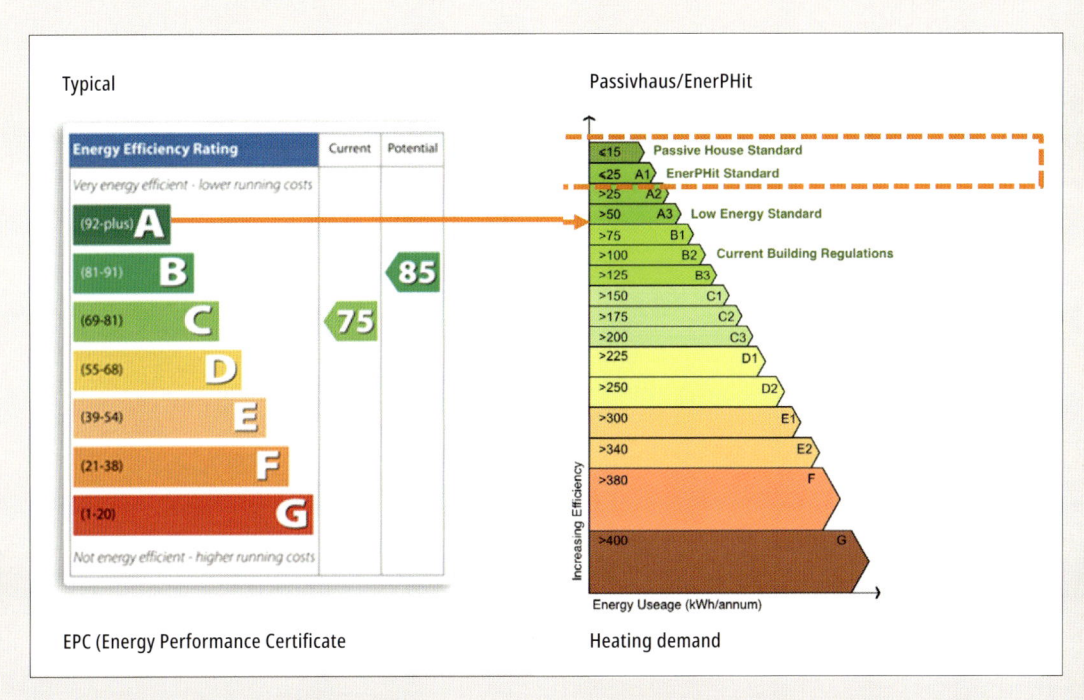

Heating demand

Fig 2.1: Comparison of energy performance (EPC)

What is EnerPHit? 21

2.10: OTHER SUSTAINABLE BUILDING REFURBISHMENT STANDARDS

There are other aspects of sustainability that building owners and clients may want to consider when refurbishing their buildings. Energy performance is usually measured and weighted as part of a range of improvements; however, the methodologies used to calculate energy performance are generally less sophisticated than PHPP and more prone to variance. Examples of these standards and methodologies are given below.

BREEAM

BREEAM UK Domestic Refurbishment (2014); BREEAM UK Non-Domestic Refurbishment & Fit-Out (2014) and BREEAM International Non-Domestic Refurbishment (2015).

These standards measure the following sustainability factors:

- Building management
- Health and wellbeing
- Energy performance
- Water
- Materials
- Waste
- Pollution
- Innovation

LEED

LEED (USA) for New Construction and Major Renovations (2005).

This standard measures the following sustainability factors:

- Sustainable cities
- Water efficiency
- Energy and atmosphere
- Materials and resources
- Indoor environmental quality
- Innovation and design process

ActiveHouse

ActiveHouse (EU) for All Building Types.

This standard measures the following sustainability factors, and can be applied to both new and existing buildings, although national energy calculation methodologies are used rather than a universal standard. The highest target for energy demand is currently only 40 kWh/m^2/a.

- Energy
Energy demand
Energy supply
Primary energy performance

- Comfort
Daylight
Thermal environment
Indoor air quality

- Environment
Environmental loads
 (LCA methodology)
Fresh water consumption
Sustainable construction

SKA

SKA (UK – RICS) for Non-Domestic Fit-Out.

This standard is limited to fit-out projects only, and does not include the performance of the whole building. The online tool encourages good practice and can be tailored to suit the scope of the project. It measures the following sustainability factors:

- Energy
- Materials
- Pollution
- Project delivery
- Transport
- Waste
- Water
- Wellbeing

2.11: INNOVATIVE SOLUTIONS IN RETROFIT: ENERGIESPRONG

Energiesprong is a retrofit methodology developed in the Netherlands which uses offsite manufacturing to significantly speed up the process of refurbishment. While energy performance targets (space heating: 30 kWH/m^2/a) are typically lower than Passivhaus or EnerPHit standards, they are better than UK Part L newbuild and a significant improvement on existing performance. Energiesprong projects typically incorporate renewable and low-carbon energy sources to provide heating and hot water. They also offer innovative financing solutions (see para 5.11), whereby the costs of the retrofit measures are recovered through energy bills. A number of housing providers in the UK are currently developing Energiesprong projects, most notably Nottingham City Homes – see Fig 2.2. Further information is available at: http://energiesprong.eu

2.12: STATUTORY COMPLIANCE IN THE UK

The design tool PHPP is not a statutory compliance tool, which means designers and their clients in the UK are still required to calculate energy consumption using SAP 2016 and residential buildings using the Building Research Establishment Domestic Energy Model (BREDEM). Non-residential buildings use simplified building energy model (SBEM) software to calculate predicted energy consumption. In existing residential buildings, an RdSAP is used to estimate likely energy consumption; however, this uses generic data for certain elements (e.g. thermal bridging) and must be treated with extreme caution where buildings have received a deep retrofit, because it is likely to significantly underestimate actual performance.

As noted, the EPBD was introduced in 2002 by the EU to promote and improve the energy performance

Fig 2.2: Energiesprong in Nottingham[8]

Band	SAP rating (1–120)	Estimated carbon emissions kg/CO_2/m²/year*	Estimated space heating demand (kWh/m²/year)
A	92+	<7.0	<32
B	81–91	7–14	33–65
C	69–80	14–22	66–100
D	55–68	22–29	101–135
E	39–54	29–37	136–170
F	21–38	37–43	171–200
G	1–20	>43	>200

Table 2.3: EPC bands
*Assuming gas heating. Emissions factor = 0.216 (SAP 2012)

of both new and existing buildings by requiring measurement of estimated performance. For every house sold or rented in the UK since 2008, an EPC has been generated. EPCs show eight bands from A to G. Each band is associated with annual energy consumption or RdSAP rating. While this data is based on somewhat generic information, it does provide an indication of current performance levels and trends. Between 1996 and 2012, the average SAP for existing properties increased from 45 to 59 (as shown in Fig 1.3). However, this compares to a current average SAP rating of newbuild properties of 81.

There are important differences between SAP[9] and PHPP,[10] which means that it is difficult to make a direct comparison. These differences include the following:

- Internal heat gains (PHPP assumes lower internal heat gains and therefore results in increased heat demand)

- Accuracy of weather files (SAP uses a single weather file for the whole of the UK, whereas PHPP uses 22 different weather files resulting in increased accuracy)

- Treatment and measurement of air permeability (PHPP assumes much higher performance)

- The efficiency of ventilation systems (SAP appendix Q only measures size and fan speed whereas PH-certified ventilation systems also measure efficiency)

- The efficiency of unregulated energy loads (i.e. domestic appliances) is not included within SAP, but it is included in PHPP – this can make a significant difference to energy consumption

- Floor and wall areas (different methodologies for calculating these with PHPP typically assume higher figures and therefore increased heat loss); PHPP uses treated floor area (TFA) whereas SAP uses gross internal area (GIA)

- Treatment of thermal bridges (PHPP requires all thermal bridges to be calculated on the basis of the external envelope; SAP typically uses generic psi values for thermal bridges based on the internal envelope, which underestimates heat loss; RdSAP does not include psi values at all)

One fundamental difference between SAP and PHPP is the purpose of the original tool and the resulting output. Whereas SAP reports carbon emissions and energy cost, PHPP reports energy consumption in terms of space heating and primary energy demand. While carbon emissions and cost are important measures, there is increasing concern in the UK[11] that SAP may not provide sufficiently accurate data on building performance, and a new replacement tool may be required.

2.13: THE IMPORTANCE OF QUALITY CONTROL

Unlike most methodologies and certification routes, Passivhaus/EnerPHit incorporates both measurement of as-built performance on site and third-party sign-off. This has protected the overall quality of the standard and enabled the client and consultants to enforce actual performance of the building. While there will always be some difference between modelled performance and actual performance due to the role of the building user, the performance gap is significantly lower in Passivhaus/EnerPHit buildings than typical newbuild or refurbished buildings, where the difference can be up to 500% more than expected.[12]

Post-occupancy studies in both Germany[13] and the UK[14] have shown that Passivhaus schemes deliver consistently reliable outputs and buildings typically perform as intended. The percentage difference between space heating prediction and performance in Passivhaus buildings is significantly less than other recent low-energy buildings. One of the key variables affected by human behaviour are the internal heat gains (IHG), which are largely determined by the occupancy levels. These can make a significant difference to overall space heating/cooling demand. While this factor is modelled in the IHG tab of PHPP, occupancy levels are fluid and the building should be able to accommodate a reasonable degree of flexibility.

2.14: THE ROLE OF RENEWABLE ENERGY

While Passivhaus projects typically reduce energy consumption to very low levels, this can be offset by users making inefficient use of their building or else increasing energy consumption from unregulated

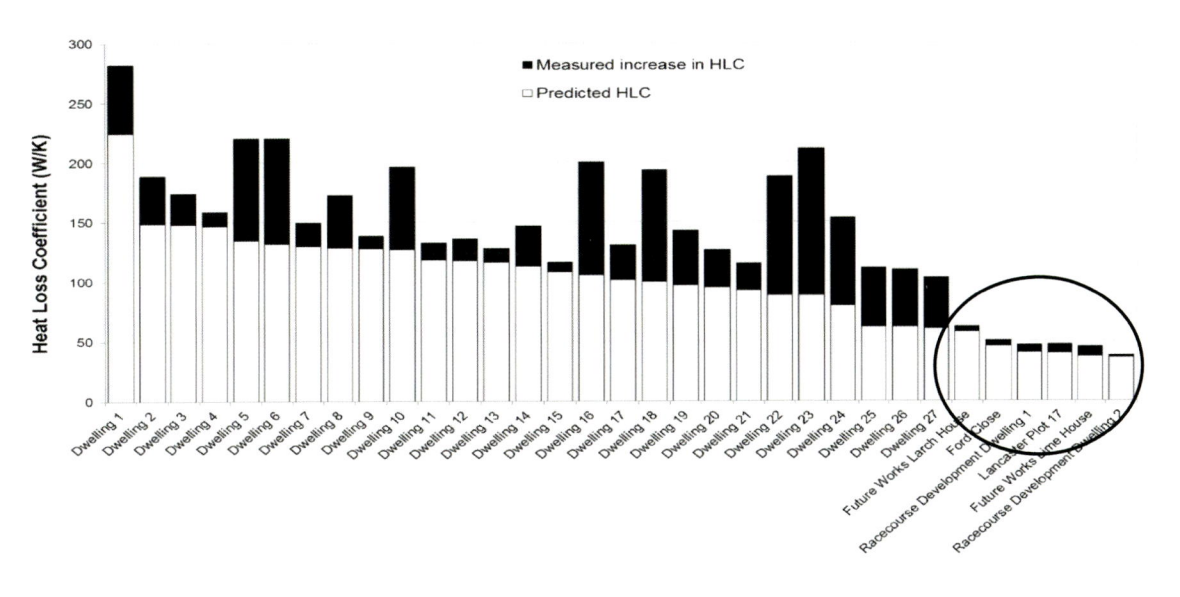

Fig 2.3: Performance in use of 33 new 'low-energy' dwellings under electric co-heating test by Leeds Beckett University (note: six highlighted projects are Passivhaus certified)[15]

loads such as home entertainment systems or inefficient white goods.

In response, PHI launched the PassREg[16] project in 2012, in partnership with the EU, to support Passivhaus schemes and renewable energy in achieving the nZEB standard. This project involved numerous local authorities across Europe in a variety of exemplar projects which integrated Passivhaus/EnerPHit solutions with local renewable energy to achieve a near-zero energy balance. Front runner regions including Hannover, Brussels and Tyrol provided several demonstration projects, with input from countries including the Netherlands, France, the UK, Latvia, Italy, Croatia and Bulgaria.

Following the successful completion of the PassREg project in 2015, the Passivhaus/EnerPHit standards were augmented by the Passivhaus/EnerPHit Plus and Passivhaus/EnerPHit Premium standards, which were introduced to enable designers to measure and coordinate renewable energy sources into a Passivhaus/EnerPHit building. While there are very few buildings that have achieved this standard, it recognises excellence and enables the incorporation of renewable energy sources, which will play an increasingly important part in future retrofit schemes as the grid is decarbonised[17] and electricity becomes a credible heating source for low-energy buildings.

2.15: STEP-BY-STEP RETROFIT

In 2016 the PHI launched a step-by-step accreditation process to EnerPHit. Based on the outcomes from the EuroPHit field trials (see Chapter 4), it offers a route to long-term certification over multiple phases. Recognising that many clients are unable to afford the full cost of a deep retrofit in a single project, PHI developed the EnerPHit retrofit plan (ERP) as part of PHPP 9, which allows the client and design team to develop a long-term strategy for the refurbishment of their building or indeed portfolio of buildings. This methodology also reduces the likelihood of short-term measures which could lock in modest gains and prevent future improvements that may be needed to satisfy legislation in 2030 and beyond.

It also recognises that the sequencing of works is critical to avoid potential detailing conflicts and unintended consequences. The ERP must therefore consider both the energy and cost impact of interim measures and the physical detailing of key building junctions to allow for phased implementation. For example, the installation of high-performance windows and improved airtightness in advance of a ventilation system could result in reduced air quality and increased risk of mould growth. Similarly, the coordination of windows and external wall insulation should be carefully considered to avoid the risk of thermal bridging.

Other reasons for considering a step-by-step approach may include the impact on existing building users. Whether the building is for commercial or residential use it may be necessary to limit the extent of works or omit measures that are impractical in occupied buildings. For example, an uninsulated ground floor is a significant heat loss area. However, it is usually impossible to insulate this with building users in occupation. Alternative measures need to be considered to reduce thermal bridging and the resulting heat losses. This could include the extension of wall insulation below adjacent ground levels, creating a thermal 'skirt' around the base of the building. If the works can be limited to a single facade at a time, it may be easier to provide separate access arrangements for contractors, reducing the size of the building site and limiting the impact on building users.

2.16: SUMMARY

Building retrofit is a complex and challenging task, especially where building users remain in occupation. Having determined that a building retrofit is necessary, the next question a client should ask is 'What standard is being targeted, and why?'

There are several building refurbishment and sustainability standards which might be considered; however, the EnerPHit standard is perhaps the most rigorous standard available. This is due to its holistic approach to energy demand, which considers the whole building as a system within a specific environment. It is also due to the incorporation of feedback from previous examples and independent certification of each project using measured data from the actual building, and – with the release of PHPP 9 – due to its flexibility in delivery.

3.0: The challenges of EnerPHit

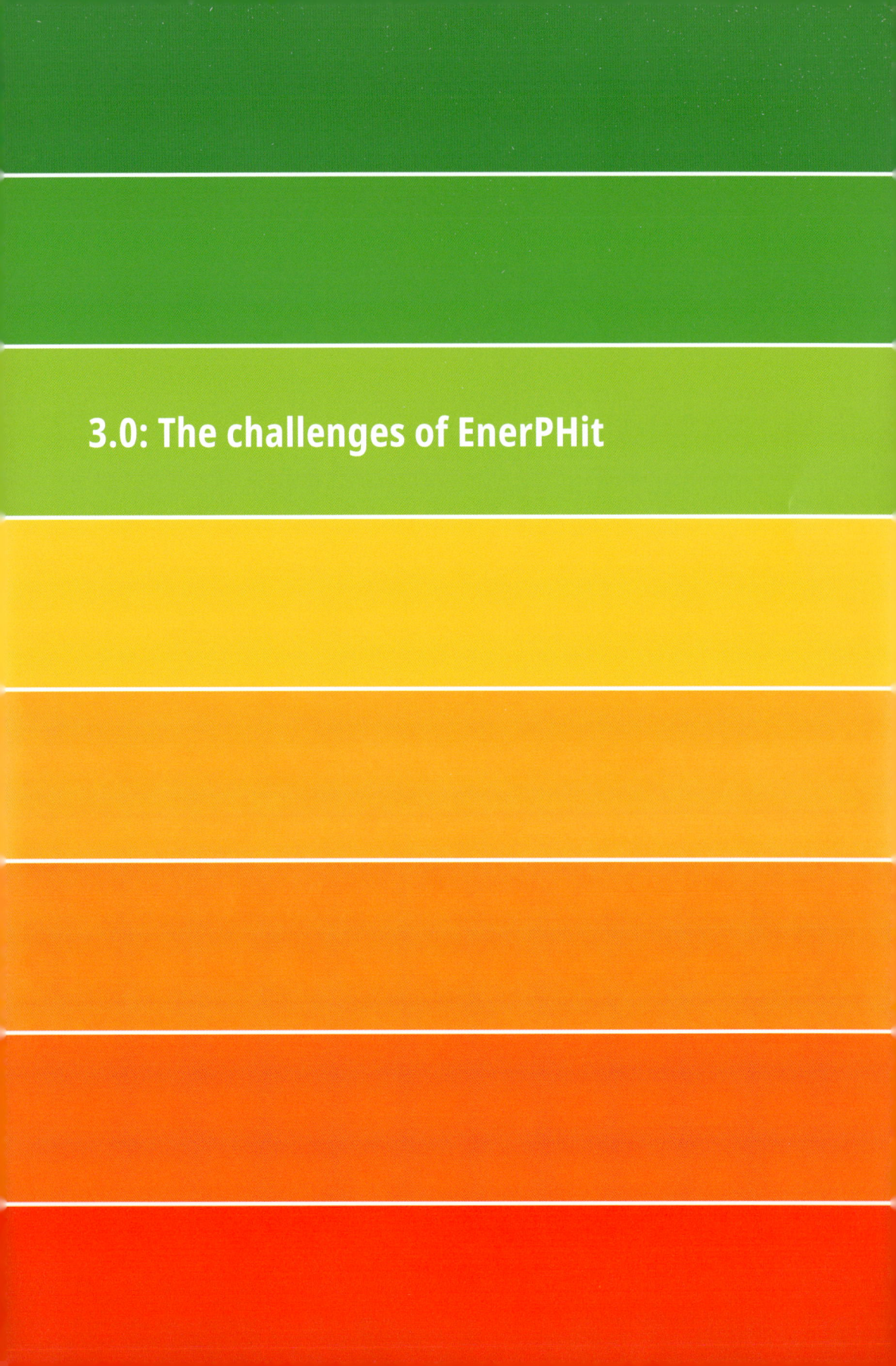

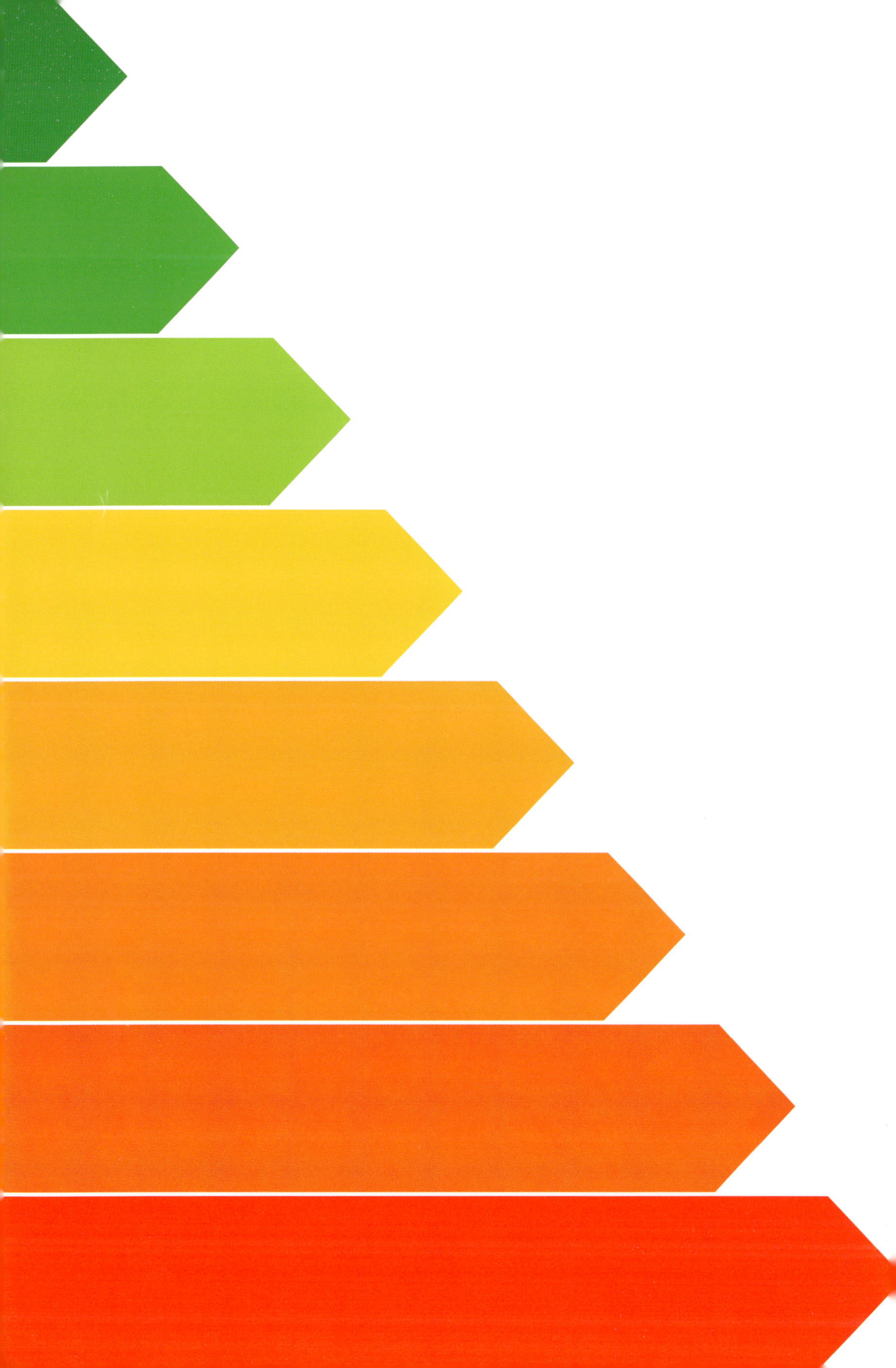

3.1: INTRODUCTION

To achieve the EnerPHit standard a building will typically require a deep retrofit involving a holistic whole-building upgrade to all building elements and components, including walls, floor, roofs, windows, doors and services. This can be very disruptive to the normal operation of the building and its users and occupants, especially where internal insulation is used. Therefore, the sequencing of the works needs to be carefully planned so that building users and especially residents can remain in situ throughout. Each member of the project team needs to understand the specific risks and rewards of targeting, designing and delivering to the EnerPHit standard. As with all construction projects, success is measured in terms of quality, programme and cost. Each member of the team therefore needs to understand the implications of these additional requirements.

The client should be aware of both the benefits and challenges in achieving EnerPHit on their specific building before undertaking the project. For example, in an occupied building it may be necessary or desirable to phase the works. Where the building is vacant, the challenges will be greatly reduced; however, there will still be important design factors to address, and the client should ensure that the design team have the necessary skills to deliver the appropriate solutions. Fortunately, there are now over 450 certified Passivhaus designers/consultants in the UK alone, with several certifying bodies and increasing awareness of Passivhaus delivery throughout consultant teams.

The consultant team should incorporate a Passivhaus designer/consultant, and all members of the team should be aware of the additional implications of achieving EnerPHit for the specific building. They should also understand both the typology and the condition of the existing building, and any constraints this imposes on the design solution. It is also necessary to know the procurement options available to ensure that EnerPHit is designed in to the employer's contract requirements, and a list of suitably qualified contractors should be invited to tender. In the UK, there are an increasing number of both small and large contractors who have delivered Passivhaus schemes, with at least two open frameworks available for the procurement of suitable contractors.[1]

During tender, the contracting team should be aware of the additional quality control procedures required on site to ensure contract compliance and a smooth handover on completion. This typically means ensuring that components are correctly assembled, the airtight layer is not damaged and that services are properly commissioned. This requires an ongoing quality control process, with regular checks to ensure compliance and avoid costly rework pre-handover. This in turn requires careful pre-construction planning of sequencing and management of trades on site, with the site manager or foreman typically responsible for coordination. This person may also be the airtightness champion who ensures, via toolbox talks and daily inspections, that all subcontractors understand the importance of maintaining the thermal airtight envelope. Any breaches should be picked up and dealt with in interim airtightness tests, to avoid problems at the end of the project and ensure compliance.

While EnerPHit might be described as the gold standard for retrofit, many of these challenges are common to all types of deep retrofit. Fortunately, there have been a number of successful deep retrofit pilot projects in recent years, and there are useful lessons to be learned. The number of successful retrofit projects achieved to date is well below UK government targets, which means it is important to understand the barriers to retrofit and how these might be overcome.

3.2: ACHIEVING A SUCCESSFUL RETROFIT

In the UK several retrofit pilot projects have been undertaken to assess the challenges and opportunities of building retrofit, most notably the Retrofit for the Future programme (2009–11) undertaken by Innovate UK (formerly the Technology Strategy Board). This project included approximately 90 existing residential properties owned and managed by Housing Associations and representing a variety of housing typologies. This author was responsible for four of these projects, and saw at first hand the challenges of achieving deep retrofit on a variety of existing building typologies. While these building research projects achieved substantial improvements, and some achieved EnerPHit, there were many important technical, financial and human lessons learned, which are described in the summary report[2] and a book on the subject by Marion Baeli.[3] The *Retrofit for the Future* report identified six interconnected themes for any successful retrofit:

- Retrofit planning
- Building fabric
- Indoor air quality
- Services
- Working on site
- Engaging residents

Retrofit planning is essential if the project is to succeed. This includes all aspects of the project, from the setting of initial performance requirements through to engagement of the relevant specialists for the detailed design and procurement of the works, to arrangements for monitoring during construction and after completion. Innovative retrofit requires multiple parties, but there should always be an effective lead consultant or retrofit coordinator ensuring that the right targets are set and delivered through design and construction.

The building fabric is undoubtedly the single biggest factor determining the ultimate performance of the retrofitted building. Heat loss can occur through all parts of the building envelope, and any areas that remain uninsulated are vulnerable. The building form is also an important factor in determining heat loss, and buildings with a complex footprint, in plan or section, will be prone to increased heat loss. The building should therefore be regarded as a whole system, and any retrofit measures should address all parts of the building envelope in a 'whole-building retrofit'. For solid-wall properties the insulation would ideally be placed on the outer face of the wall and create a continuous thermal envelope at the roof and ground. Similarly, where external wall insulation is not possible, any internal insulation should be continuous.

Air quality and ventilation should be considered alongside improvements to the building fabric in all retrofit projects. Whether the existing air quality is good or bad, any improvements to the fabric will have an impact on air quality, which must be considered to avoid unintended consequences.[4] Improved airtightness of less than three air changes per hour (avoiding the use of trickle-vent windows) will typically require some form of background ventilation, whether MVHR or passive stack. In both cases, this should be carefully coordinated with the airtight envelope to ensure there is no leakage, but that sufficient ventilation is provided in accordance with statutory requirements (in the UK this is dealt with in Part F of the building regulations).

Building services, whether existing or new, should be considered from the outset of any retrofit project. The location, coordination and integration of these services will be a critical part of the design and construction process. Where MVHR is used, this should ideally be located near an external wall with good access. Any penetrations through the airtight layer should be properly sealed with appropriate tapes or grommets to avoid air leakage. Where existing meters are located on an external wall and within the proposed insulation zone, the meters should be brought forward to ensure thermal continuity. However, the meter box can only be moved by the statutory provider, and therefore close coordination and planning are required from the outset to avoid delay. The effective functioning of all services, but especially ventilation, heating and hot water, will be a key part of the commissioning and handover process, and the building user should be given a simple guide in plain English on how to use their building most efficiently.

Site operations can have a significant impact on the effectiveness of any building retrofit. Quality control is essential if the performance requirements of the brief are to be achieved. This is particularly true where residents remain in situ during the works. The contractor typically takes ownership of the site during the works, and is responsible both for delivering the employer's requirements and maintaining the health and safety of all people who may be affected by the works under CDM regulations. A clear understanding of performance requirements, roles and responsibilities with clear communication is always required to avoid performance conflict, confusion and delay. Offsite manufacturing can often have an important part to play in improving quality control and speed of construction, as can be seen in the Energiesprong model.

Residents or building users are among the most important factors in determining the success of a building retrofit. If the building users are not involved in the process, they are unlikely to be engaged in optimising their use of their building post-completion. This can be seen in the wide variation in energy consumption for similar dwelling types. This is also true of Passivhaus/EnerPHit buildings, although this gap is significantly smaller than traditional buildings. The performance of the building is much more closely aligned to the design intent, and therefore the margin for user difference has less impact.

3.3: UNDERSTANDING THE BARRIERS TO RETROFIT

While there are strong drivers towards retrofit, the uptake of these schemes has been very limited, and much lower than required if we are to achieve UK and global targets for carbon reduction. There are valid obstacles to building retrofit, and understanding these barriers is of key importance if we are to achieve the dramatic carbon reduction that is needed. The *Breaking Barriers* report[5] identified eight key barriers to whole-house retrofit that must be addressed if we are to achieve successful retrofit on a wide scale:

- Economics
- **Education and skills**
- **Political**
- **Consumer**
- **Coordination and supply chain**
- **Practical installation issues**
- **Performance**
- **Pilots**
- **Legal***

*Added by this author

There are economic barriers to whole-building deep retrofit, and most deep retrofit schemes undertaken to date have been pilot projects where funding has been made available for a variety of other reasons. The examples included within the case studies in chapters 6 and 7 are typical examples of such non-domestic deep retrofit schemes. The retrofit drivers for these projects may have been fuel poverty (Wilmcote House), corporate sustainability objectives (Sparkasse Bank) or increasing maintenance problems (University of Innsbruck). However, the short-term economic barriers faced by most building owners have been avoided in these projects by a combination of long-term finance and public subsidy. Similarly, the Retrofit for the Future project showed how deep retrofit could be achieved in the residential sector when 100% funding is provided and short-term economics is not a factor.

Short-term economics is one of the primary factors affecting decision making when a building retrofit is considered, and is a key barrier to wider adoption. While energy prices are likely to rise significantly over the next 30 years, the cost of deep retrofit remains relatively high, and for most building typologies the financial 'payback' is very long (sometimes in excess of 20 years). The upfront costs are considerable, and commercial loans do not typically encourage this investment. While KfW bank in Germany supports the refurbishment of existing residential properties through grants (up to €30,000 where energy consumption is less than 55 kWh/m^2/a) and loans depending on the predicted performance of the building, this is not widely replicated.[6] Failure of the Green Deal scheme in the UK showed among other findings the impact of high interest rates on decision making by homeowners.

Education and skills are an essential ingredient in the successful delivery of deep retrofit. To achieve the scale of retrofit necessary to meet carbon reduction targets, we need to rapidly increase the size of the contractor supply chain and retrain our existing workforce to the higher standards required. While the skills necessary to install double-glazing and loft installation are quite basic and involve only one 'trade', the skills to properly deliver a whole-building deep retrofit (installing solid-wall insulation, MVHR systems and airtightness membranes, etc.) are neither simple nor standalone trades. Unless we can train a new generation of 'poly-competent' tradespeople in the skills necessary to deliver these elements, it will require the coordination of at least two or three trades for each deep retrofit project. This means additional time, cost and coordination. While training in whole-building deep retrofit is available for both contractors and consultants through organisations such as the Passive House Academy and the Retrofit Academy, these organisations would require rapid expansion to meet demand if deep retrofit is to become mainstream.

Long-term political policy in the UK is clearly set out in the Climate Change Act of 2008, and buildings will need to achieve 80% carbon reduction targets by 2050. However, the short-term targets necessary to deliver this have not been achieved, and the flagship Green Deal policy failed to deliver the anticipated uptake in domestic retrofit. Since 2008, a series of stop–start initiatives including CERT, CESP, ECO and Green Deal have offered limited short-term funding for partial measures, with no monitoring during construction or of energy performance in use. Deep retrofit is not on the UK government agenda, and legislation (building regulations Parts L1B and L2B) is either weak or non-existent. In the EU the forthcoming nZEB requirement (Article 7: Existing buildings) is likely to drive increased deep retrofit, although the focus is still primarily on new buildings.

Consumer demand is also regarded as a key barrier to deep retrofit. In the UK, levels of home ownership are relatively high (although declining), and with average ownership at only ten years per property, residents are often disinclined to invest in retrofit, as they are unlikely to receive the full benefit of the works. Despite government attempts to increase awareness of energy efficiency, the uptake has been low and retrofit is not seen as a priority. Where retrofit has been undertaken and contractor performance has been poor, it has eroded some public trust in the ability of the industry to deliver. Residents and building owners know that construction projects are typically noisy, messy and disruptive, especially where they remain in occupation during the works. They also know that they can sometimes become extended and costlier due to unforeseen issues.

However, residents and building owners are often willing to undertake construction projects to increase floor area and/or financial value. Unfortunately, there is currently limited evidence to demonstrate that retrofit increases financial value and it does not typically increase floor area; indeed, internal insulation can reduce floor area. While retrofit can dramatically improve thermal comfort and air quality, this is not yet widely known or understood.

The fragmented nature of the building supply chain does not currently provide effective retrofit on a consistent basis. The consumer is not offered a one-stop shop for deep retrofit. There is no quality-assured package of design, construction and post-completion performance monitoring. As a result, there is a lack of consumer trust and buy-in.

Every building is different, in typology, occupation and condition, and the construction industry does not provide an affordable bespoke solution to meet these variables. There is a tendency to regard retrofit as simply an opportunity to 'sell a product', whether external wall insulation, windows or ventilation systems, without considering the potentially adverse impact of limited measures. If there has been no survey of the existing building this can be further exacerbated when applied to buildings with pre-existing defects. The role of the retrofit coordinator is not widely known, and yet this individual has the potential to provide independent guidance to building owners and orchestrate the various parties and products involved. The retrofit coordinator is typically an architect or surveyor with additional training on the coordination issues of deep retrofit. However, as noted, the necessary retrofit skills in both design and construction are often lacking, and quality control suffers as a result. Highly skilled consultants and contractors delivering effective deep retrofit remain in the minority. Simply, the capacity to deliver effective whole-building deep retrofit at the scale required to meet UK carbon reduction objectives is not yet available.

Practical installation issues can cause significant cost and delay if not thoroughly planned. Retrofit is typically more challenging than newbuild, and careful coordination is required. Deep retrofit is often intrusive and can have a significant impact on the existing building. Understanding the size, typology and condition of the existing building is crucial. This is particularly true in non-traditional building types which may be prefabricated, requiring a detailed structural assessment of both the existing condition and its suitability to receive retrofit measures. In more conventional building types there are still issues to be resolved, whether in the condition of building elements, the coordination of services or in the timely receipt of statutory approvals. In smaller buildings space constraints may restrict opportunities to insulate elements or route services, resulting in compromised layouts or details. In occupied buildings the disruption to building users must also be minimised, access arrangements should be carefully planned, and the impact of noise, dust or other by-products of construction reduced.

As a result of these factors, the performance of building retrofits is often compromised and, even where there has been effective design and construction, the actual performance may be lower than anticipated. This can be due to the human impact of building users operating the building inefficiently. However, it can also be affected by the previous usage of the building. For example, in a building which may have been poorly heated (perhaps due to fuel poverty) the actual financial and carbon savings will be much less than a theoretical model might suggest. This is because the building users can now afford to heat the building to a comfortable temperature. Performance is also affected by our ability to measure and, as noted previously, the statutory energy performance tools available in the UK do not accurately represent actual energy performance. This is especially true for buildings that have achieved a deep retrofit to the EnerPHit standard where thermal bridging is much lower than UK norms and ventilation efficiency is much higher.

Pilot projects themselves have also become a barrier to wider adoption of deep retrofit. While the nature of pilot projects is to understand the challenges, this has caused some clients to consider deep retrofit as too difficult or expensive for widespread application. Although there have been successful deep retrofit projects, these have generally been smaller schemes and the results have not been widely disseminated.

Where larger retrofit projects have been undertaken (such as Green Deal), the administrative challenges have proved even larger than the technical obstacles. As a result, the uptake of deep retrofit schemes has been far too slow to achieve the carbon reduction targets set out in the UK Climate Change Act of 2008. Although average SAP levels have continued to increase steadily, this has largely been due to the impact of new buildings and the modest retrofit measures (cavity wall and loft insulation, etc.) undertaken to the remaining uninsulated properties, and is not expected to continue at the rate required.

In addition to the eight barriers listed above, the legal obstacles to retrofit are also relevant in the leasehold and private rented sectors. In these situations, the owner may not be able to upgrade the external envelope of the building without the agreement of both the freeholder and other leaseholders, who must agree to the measures via a 'Section 20' process. Under UK Leasehold Law, there is typically no provision for upgrade or 'betterment', and leasehold contracts usually allow for repairs only. Even when all parties agree to the works, this often means there is no way of recovering the cost of any measures that go beyond building regulations. As such, EnerPHit or indeed any thermal upgrade is not legally enforceable when maintenance is not already required. This barrier has until recently not been widely recognised, although there are important studies covering this subject in more detail.[7]

3.4: THE SPECIFIC CHALLENGES OF HERITAGE BUILDINGS

It is estimated by the Sustainable Traditional Buildings Alliance (STBA)[8] that up to 25% of UK buildings (approximately 6 million) are solid-wall construction and pre-date 1919, with approximately 4.4% (1.2 million)[9] in conservation areas and 1.4% (378,000) listed.[10] Traditional buildings built before 1919 tend to be of solid-wall masonry construction, and perform quite differently from those designed and built in the post-war period, as illustrated in Fig 3.1.

While the application of piecemeal, unplanned retrofit measures can cause significant problems in

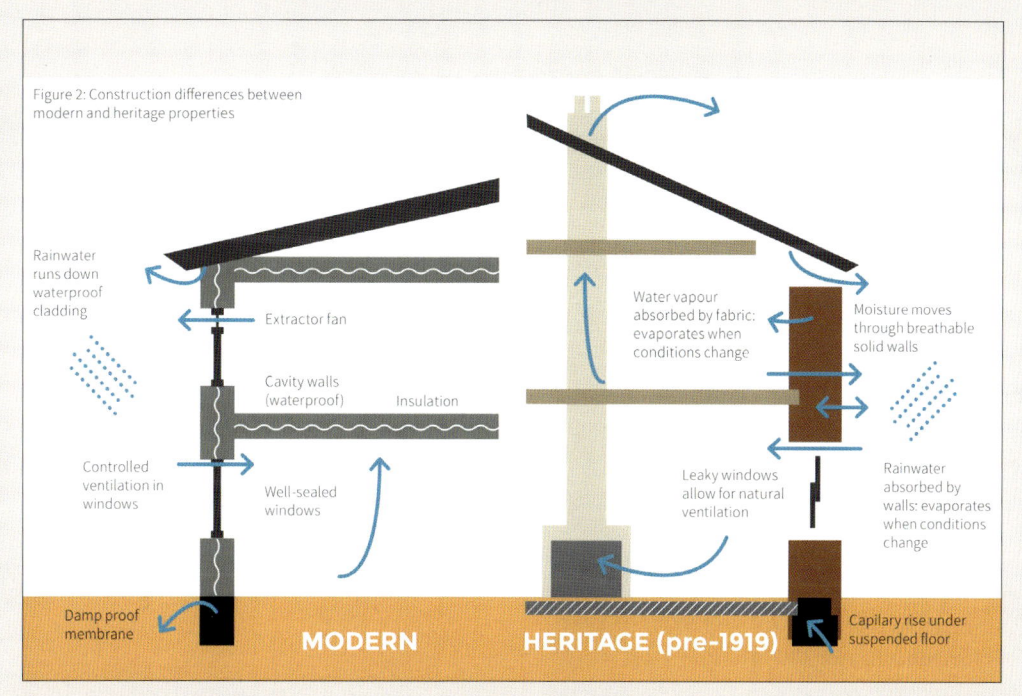

Figure 2: Construction differences between modern and heritage properties

Fig 3.1: Comparison of the performance of modern and traditional buildings[11]

any building, the impact on traditional buildings can be much more severe. A BRE report[12] identified 19 unintended consequences when retrofitting solid-wall properties:

- Overheating (temperature above 28°C in the summer months)
- Increased relative humidity, and associated damp and mould growth
- Negative effect on neighbouring dwellings
- Shifting of thermal bridging to new points
- Increased risk of dry or wet rot to timbers
- Increased risk of insect attack on timbers
- Increased risk of dust mites, bed bugs, clothes moths and other insects within the home
- Increased radon risk
- Rotting of internal floor and roof timbers
- Damage to the external wall structure, or failure of internal finishes, due to water fill and frost damage following internal insulation
- Increased interstitial condensation
- Short-term reduction in air quality following installation of solid-wall insulation (formaldehyde and other VOCs)
- Long-term reduction in air quality following solid-wall insulation (CO, CO_2 levels)
- Aesthetics
- Property value
- Daylighting
- Durability and maintenance, and repair consequences
- Disturbance
- Fire safety

There are clearly significant risks to be addressed when retrofitting solid-wall heritage buildings, which require careful consideration and bespoke solutions. In its 12 recommendations (see Fig 3.2) the Building Research Establishment (BRE) proposes many of the measures already required by the EnerPHit standard, such as the use of certified products, accurate weather files, condensation risk analysis, on-site quality controls and accurate modelling of thermal bridging.

The challenges of EnerPHit

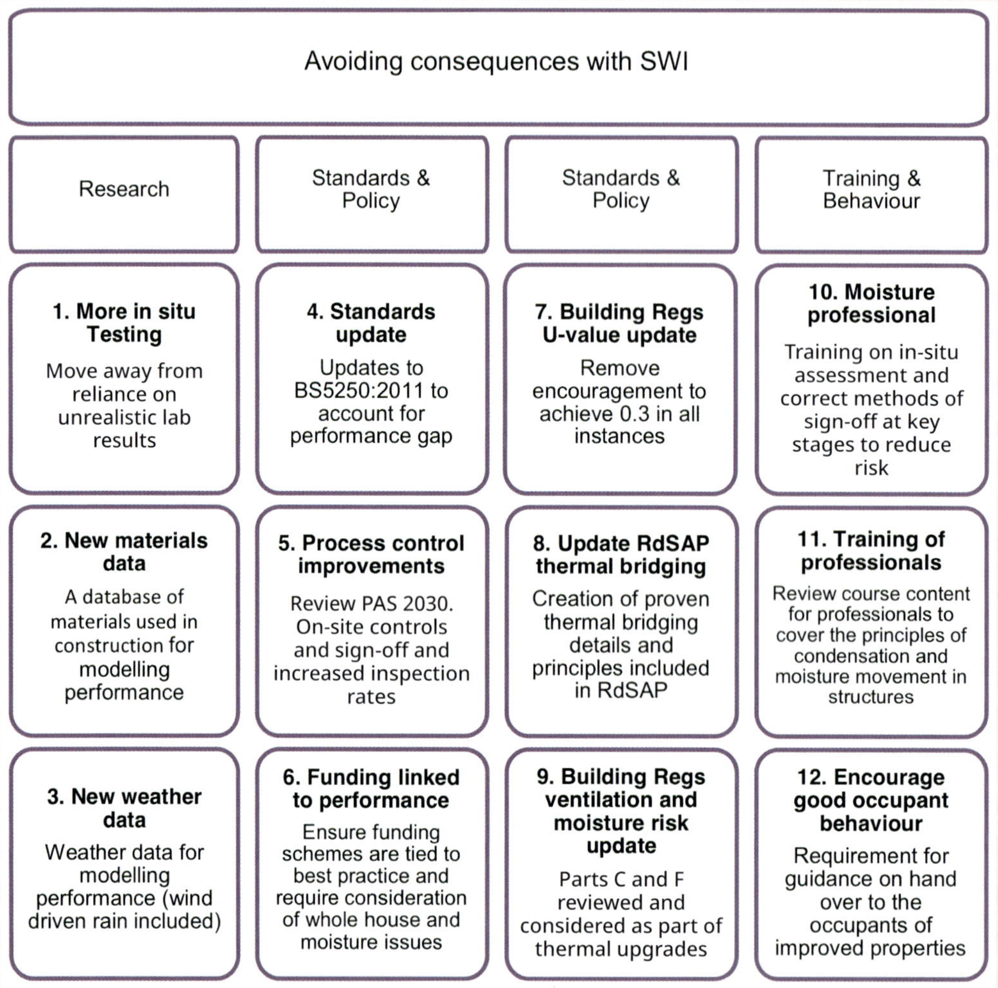

Avoiding consequences with SWI

Research	Standards & Policy	Standards & Policy	Training & Behaviour
1. More in situ Testing — Move away from reliance on unrealistic lab results	**4. Standards update** — Updates to BS5250:2011 to account for performance gap	**7. Building Regs U-value update** — Remove encouragement to achieve 0.3 in all instances	**10. Moisture professional** — Training on in-situ assessment and correct methods of sign-off at key stages to reduce risk
2. New materials data — A database of materials used in construction for modelling performance	**5. Process control improvements** — Review PAS 2030. On-site controls and sign-off and increased inspection rates	**8. Update RdSAP thermal bridging** — Creation of proven thermal bridging details and principles included in RdSAP	**11. Training of professionals** — Review course content for professionals to cover the principles of condensation and moisture movement in structures
3. New weather data — Weather data for modelling performance (wind driven rain included)	**6. Funding linked to performance** — Ensure funding schemes are tied to best practice and require consideration of whole house and moisture issues	**9. Building Regs ventilation and moisture risk update** — Parts C and F reviewed and considered as part of thermal upgrades	**12. Encourage good occupant behaviour** — Requirement for guidance on hand over to the occupants of improved properties

Fig 3.2: Avoiding unintended consequences of solid-wall insulation[13]

3.5 OVERCOMING THE PRACTICAL CHALLENGES OF ENERPHIT

There are other practical challenges to the wider adoption of EnerPHit, and these must be addressed both nationally and locally. National challenges involve the removal of institutional barriers – both political and legal; the increase of skills in design and construction; and measures to encourage consumer uptake. Local challenges involve addressing the site-specific issues inherent in each existing building and reconciling these with the brief needed to deliver EnerPHit within the available budget and timescale.

In chapters 6 and 7, there are case study examples of projects across a wide variety of building types and countries delivered to, or near to, the EnerPHit standard. However, in all projects there were a series of practical challenges to overcome which required careful planning and attention to detail. Many of these issues were common to all schemes (achieving airtightness), while others were generated by the design issues specific to the project. In each case, important lessons can be learned which will inform clients, designers and contractors on future deep retrofit projects.

3.6: OPTIMISING THE THERMAL ENVELOPE: EXTERNAL WALLS

Perhaps one of the most important issues to address in any EnerPHit project is the treatment of the thermal envelope and whether the insulation should go on the inside or outside of the external wall. While there is not a fixed U-value to achieve EnerPHit, it can be assumed for most buildings that the external wall U-value should be not less than 0.15 W/m^{2}K. This is not significantly better than current newbuild regulations (L1A and L2A), which require 0.18 W/m^{2}K; however, the treatment of thermal bridges is significantly more rigorous. The range of insulation types is wide and includes both natural and synthetic products, which can be broken down into two main types: capillary open (breathable) and capillary closed (non-breathable).

Capillary open products include mineral wool and 'natural' products such as hemp and sheep's wool. Capillary closed materials tend to be oil-based products such EPS, XPS or phenolic boards. The lambda value of the latter is generally lower, which means that a thinner profile may be used to achieve the same thermal performance. However, oil-based products tend to have high embodied carbon for Passivhaus/EnerPHit buildings (with low operational carbon). The embodied carbon can represent a significant proportion of the whole, and the designer may wish to consider natural, recyclable or low-carbon insulation options wherever possible. In the wake of the Grenfell Tower disaster, there is also doubt around the combustibility of oil-based insulation types. In recent years new high-performance insulation types have been used on certain building retrofit projects where reducing thickness is a key concern. An example of this can be seen in case study 6.6 (Gloucester Place Mews) where aerogel insulation is used as internal wall insulation (IWI). As a capillary open product this is suitable for use as IWI; however, the cost of this product currently prevents its widespread use. Other high-performance insulation types include vacuum insulated panels (VIPs), which come from the refrigeration industry and have ultra-low lambda values. These panels are both expensive and vulnerable to damage, and must be protected during construction and in use.

Internal wall insulation

IWI is typically used where it is not possible or desirable to change the external appearance of the building. Three of the selected case studies use IWI of various types in conjunction with high-performance components (e.g. triple-glazed windows) to provide a relatively continuous thermal envelope. The use of IWI is often problematic, as it is extremely disruptive to the normal use of the building and it is unlikely that the building users will be able remain in situ during the works. This is particularly true in residential properties where both services and fixtures and fittings are located on the internal face of an external wall. This can include staircases, sanitary ware, kitchen appliances and units, boilers and soil pipes.

IWI also reduces floor area and, if incorrectly specified and installed, can cause interstitial condensation that damages the building fabric. To reduce the impact on floor area, high-performance insulation such as aerogel can be used. To avoid the risk of interstitial condensation capillary open (breathable) insulation should be used, and detailed analysis should be carried out on each elevation using WUFI software[14] to establish the dew point and condensation risk. This allows the designer to determine the condensation risk for the specific building materials and locations, and is particularly useful where IWI is to be applied to traditional buildings or in areas of high rainfall. Walls facing the prevailing wind and rain in high rainfall areas are particularly vulnerable, as shown in Fig 3.3.

The porosity of the existing external face is also a key factor affecting moisture content. For example, London stock brick is typically porous and would be unsuitable for use in exposed locations, whereas engineering brick or slate tiles would be much less vulnerable. Care should also be taken when insulating around joists, as the 'cold' end of the joist which is traditionally built into the wall may be more prone to degrade (as an exposed thermal bridge) if not correctly detailed.[15] Wherever possible, existing joists should be cut and rehung on joist hangers within the thermal envelope, although this is costly and disruptive.

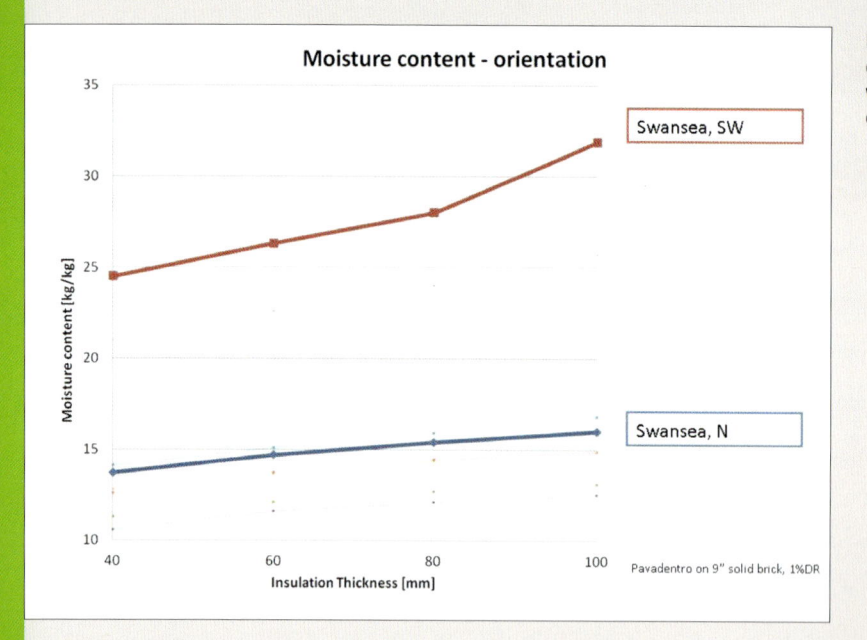

Fig 3.3: Moisture content in external walls by location and orientation[16]

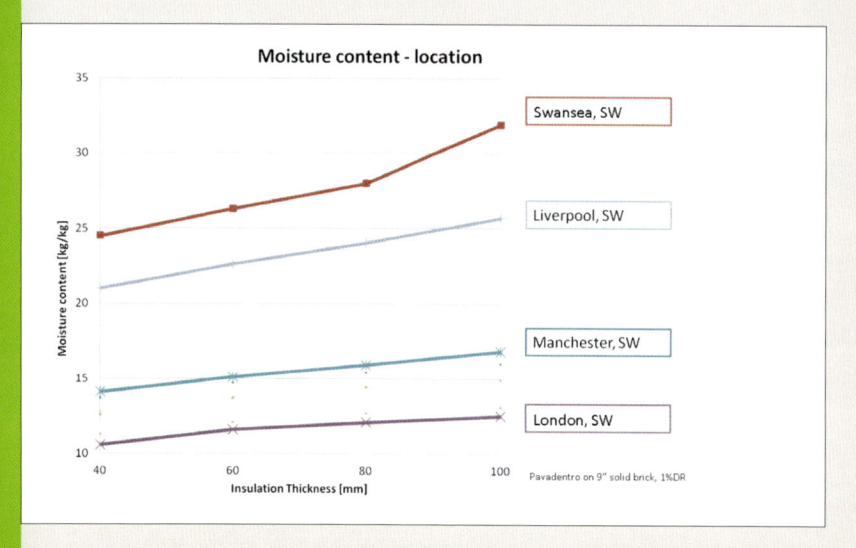

Achieving a continuous thermal envelope is much more challenging when insulating internally, and it is likely that, even in EnerPHit projects, some limited thermal bridges may remain. However, unlike a standard retrofit, the Passivhaus/EnerPHit methodology requires the heat loss from all thermal bridges to be calculated using THERM (2D) or TRISCO (3D), and from this condensation risk can be established and detailed analysis undertaken using WUFI software (see Fig 3.4). In summary, IWI should be undertaken with care using appropriate risk modelling tools, and is only realistically possible in unoccupied buildings.

External wall insulation

External wall insulation (EWI) offers a more comprehensive and simpler means of insulating the thermal envelope with reduced thermal bridging and lower associated risk, and is typically used wherever possible. However, even EWI can be prone to defects if not correctly detailed and installed at openings and junctions such as windows, eaves and ground. All services (statutory service boxes, rainwater pipes, external soil stacks, satellite dishes, etc.) must be removed and brought in front of the insulation zones to maintain a continuous thermal

Fig 3.4: Condensation risk analysis (WUFI)[17]

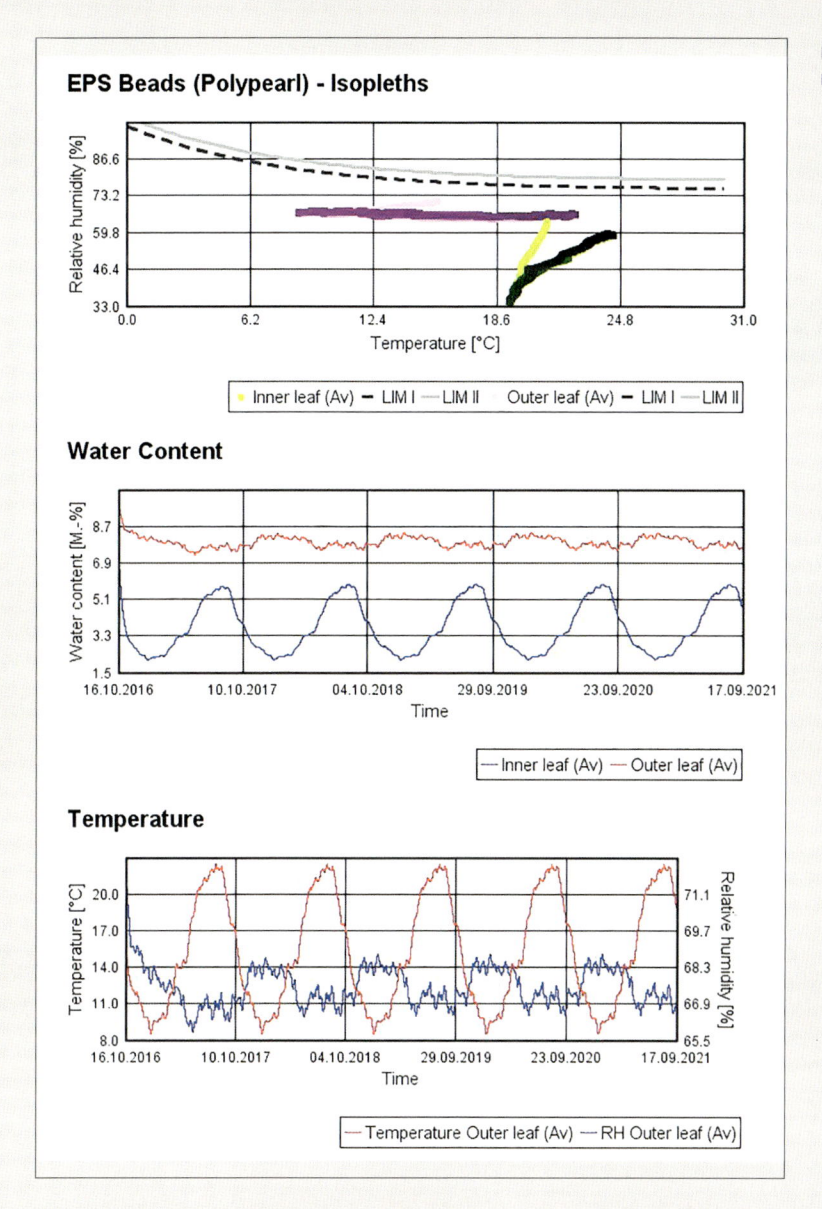

envelope. Window sills should be extended to ensure rainwater is kept clear from the face of the wall. At ground the damp-proof course (DPC) should be brought forward and a rigid insulation used below the DPC to a depth of at least 1 m to suit adjacent ground levels around the perimeter of the building, creating a 'thermal skirt'. Detailing at boundary and party walls can be challenging, and these should be detailed to minimise thermal bridging wherever possible. For example, a garden wall should be disconnected from the building to enable a continuous wrap of insulation. Similarly, a party wall is also a heat loss area and, assuming it is not possible to insulate externally, this should be done internally with IWI, overlapped by up to 1 m where possible. The external treatment of EWI can be designed to suit the architectural proposals or wider context, and might include anything from brick or stone cladding to a timber or render finish, subject to local fire safety regulations.

The challenges of EnerPHit

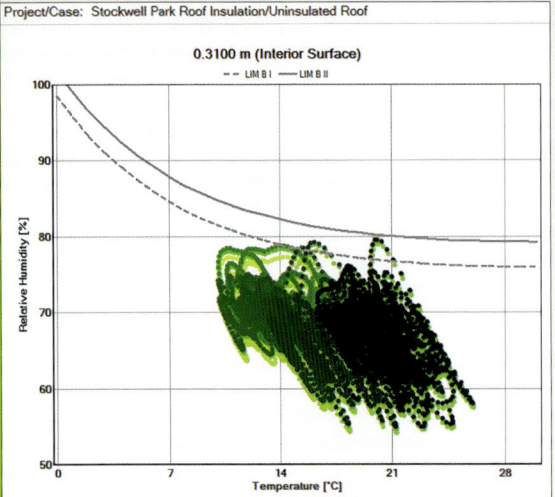

Fig 3.5a: Uninsulated roof (concrete)

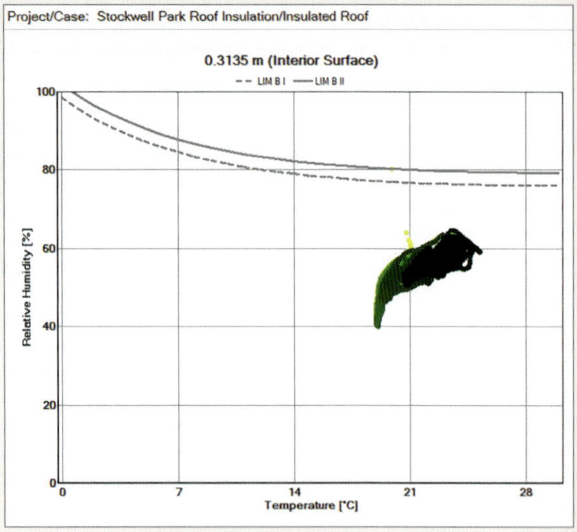

Fig 3.5b: Insulated roof (concrete) mould growth risk analysis (WUFI Pro)[18]

3.7: OPTIMISING THE THERMAL ENVELOPE: GROUND FLOOR

In occupied buildings it is usually impossible to insulate the ground floor. It can also be challenging to insulate the ground floor in unoccupied buildings, as it is usually necessary to maintain the same or very similar floor height to avoid clashes with doors, staircases and other elements which are not easily moved. In larger buildings the size of the ground floor in relation to the rest of the building envelope can be quite small, and the impact of heat loss from this element may not be significant overall. However, in smaller buildings with a relatively large footprint this heat loss can be considerable, and therefore any attempt to achieve EnerPHit should consider some form of insulation to the ground floor. For solid-floor properties the only realistic option is to overlay a bonded insulation to a new floor deck. An aerogel or similar high-performance material can be used to optimise thermal performance. Suspended timber floors require careful detailing and, depending on the existing condition, the designer may wish to replace either the whole floor or the finish. In which case, it would be better to insulate in between and over the existing joists, ideally rehanging these within the thermal envelope at the external wall. If the existing floor is in good condition, this can be disruptive, costly and wasteful, and the designer may wish to consider other innovative tools such as Q-Bot.[19] This semi-autonomous robot can install insulation to the underside of suspended timber floors, and recent trials suggest it may be an important tool in improving the thermal performance of ground floors in occupied buildings while maintaining sufficient ventilation to the structure.

3.8: OPTIMISING THE THERMAL ENVELOPE: ROOF

The roof is typically a straightforward element to insulate, especially if a 'cold' roof solution is used, with insulation laid or sprayed over the existing ceiling. The key issues to address are thermal continuity and maintaining sufficient ventilation at the eaves. While there is no specific U-value requirement under EnerPHit, the designer should assume a target U-value of not less than 0.1 W/m²K using an appropriate insulation to suit the location. Insulating the roof, whether at ceiling level or following the roof pitch, can typically be done with building users in situ. However, the contractor should ensure safe access and weather protection to the building where roof finishes are temporarily removed.

3.9: OPTIMISING THE THERMAL ENVELOPE: WINDOWS AND DOORS

To achieve EnerPHit, it is typically necessary to replace existing windows, as they are extremely unlikely to meet the performance requirements of 0.8 W/m^{2}K (installed). The 'installed' performance of a window is not widely reported in the UK construction industry, and suppliers prefer to state the performance of the window in isolation (or even the glass), as this will be a higher figure. However, the Passivhaus methodology requires the designer to account for the heat losses around the frame, which ensures the model more closely matches reality. Windows can be replaced with building users in situ; however, they should ideally be replaced at the same time as external wall insulation is applied. This ensures that the new windows can be located within the insulation zone to provide a continuous thermal envelope, improving the 'installed' value. This usually means that windows need to be hung off the existing structure, and the designer should ensure that the appropriate fixings are supplied and installed.

3.10: OPTIMISING THE THERMAL ENVELOPE: SOLAR GAIN/SHADE

Passivhaus and EnerPHit buildings aim to achieve an optimum balance between solar gain and solar shade, with considerable attention paid in PHPP to the orientation of the building and the size, shape and properties of both windows and shading devices. In temperate or cold climates, it is desirable to allow winter sun at low levels to provide passive heat,

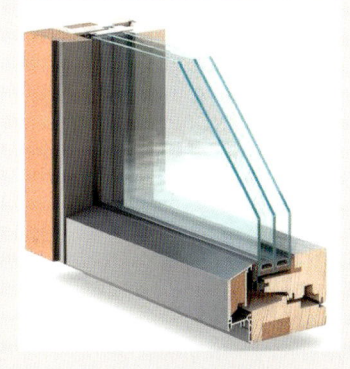

Fig 3.6: PH-certified triple-glazed window[20]

Fig 3.7: Solar shading devices. Sparkasse Bank, Gross Umstadt, Germany[21]

The challenges of EnerPHit 41

whereas it is necessary to prevent overheating in the summer. There are tools available to the designer, including external brise-soleils, shutters and glazing specifications modelled in PHPP to optimise performance. The designer should be aware of the limitation of PHPP for overheating analysis on complex buildings, and may wish to carry out multi-zonal analysis targeting a lower overheating threshold – lower than the 10% of total hours stated in PHPP (as this accounts for more than one month in a year). Further useful guidance on this subject can be found in a recent Passivhaus Trust publication.[22]

3.11: OPTIMISING AIRTIGHTNESS

While the EnerPHit standard accepts a slightly lower performance level of 1.0 air change per hour (ach) at 50 pascals (n50) compared to 0.6 ach n50, it remains a very challenging target in an existing building. When preparing design proposals, it is essential to identify the location of the proposed airtight layer and ensure that any penetrations through this are minimised and properly sealed and recorded, with interim tests carried out. An airtight layer can be a suitable airtight board (Smartply Propassiv, or similar), a plastered wall or a membrane to suit the relevant location with appropriate tapes at all junctions, such as window openings. To optimise airtightness it is important to sequence a series of interim tests during the works to ensure the project is on track to meet performance requirements. Airtightness works can in theory be carried out with building users in situ, as the tests are relatively low pressure and are not harmful to human health. However, the practicalities of doing this on large multi-occupancy residential buildings can be extremely challenging (as explained in the Wilmcote House case study in chapter 6).

3.12: OPTIMISING VENTILATION SYSTEMS

All Passivhaus/EnerPHit schemes incorporate high-efficiency MVHR. PH-certified MVHR units are measured in a series of real-world tests to determine performance against a range of measures, including thermal comfort, heat recovery rate (efficiency), power consumption, airtightness, balancing and adjustability, sound insulation, air quality and frost protection. This is significantly more rigorous than current UK standards require under Appendix Q of SAP, and the designer should ensure that the most appropriate PH-certified product is specified to suit the size and occupancy levels of the building.

The effectiveness of the ventilation system is not simply reliant on the efficiency of the MVHR unit but also its location, type, shape and routing of ductwork, both within the building and to the perimeter air intake and extract. There are simple rules to follow when considering the schematic layout of an MVHR installation which should ensure that the system will be reasonably efficient. For example, the air intake duct from the external wall to the MVHR should be relatively short and sufficiently insulated to prevent heat loss. The length of ductwork should be minimised, and rigid, circular profiles used wherever possible, ideally in metal. While acoustic attenuation is required between rooms this should be used only where necessary to avoid further reduction in efficiency. The MVHR unit should be accessible for maintenance and ideally located within the thermal envelope, typically adjacent to a corridor. However, due to space restrictions, some have been successfully installed outside the envelope in a loft space. In these cases the ductwork from the house must be sufficiently insulated to prevent heat loss. These factors are measured in the PHPP and a final, more detailed review can then be undertaken to optimise performance.

The installation of MVHR systems in existing buildings can be challenging, especially when users remain in occupation. In smaller residential properties with limited storage space, it may difficult to accommodate the MVHR unit in a suitable place. The routing of ductwork also needs to be carefully considered to avoid excessive reductions in ceiling height or bulkheads. In larger buildings the routing of ductwork can compromise fire compartmentation if not carefully detailed, and this can prove particularly challenging; in some cases it may be necessary to route the ductwork externally (see case study 6.4).

Fig 3.8: Achieving airtightness[23]

3.13: OPTIMISING THE BUILDING FORM

The complexity of the building form can have a significant impact on heat loss where the wall-to-floor ratio is high. Many post-war buildings are particularly complex, with numerous exposed elements arising from unusual forms of plan and section (such as large cantilevers and uninsulated soffits). In some building types it can be possible to simplify the form and reduce overall heat loss while improving the architectural appearance of the building. The case studies for Ērgli Secondary School, University of Innsbruck and Wilmcote House offer good examples of what can be achieved.

3.14: SUMMARY

EnerPHit is undoubtedly a challenging target to apply on a large scale, and there needs to be greater focus on achieving this target within government and the building industry. The national and local barriers are significant, and the achievement of deep retrofit to the EnerPHit standard has so far been restricted to pilot projects.

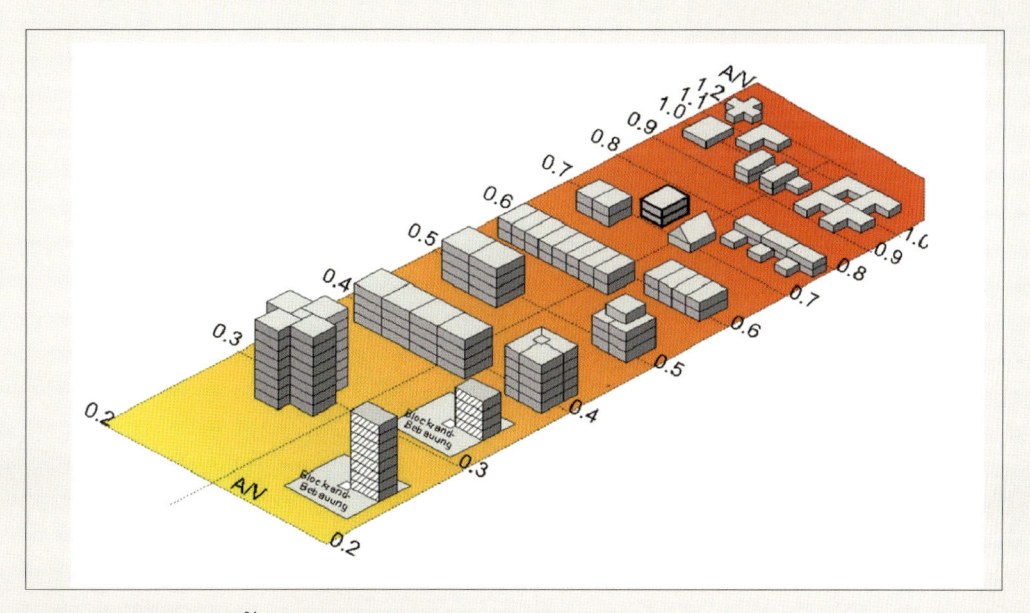

Fig 3.9: Building form factor[24]

The challenges of EnerPHit

4.0: Step-by-step to EnerPHit

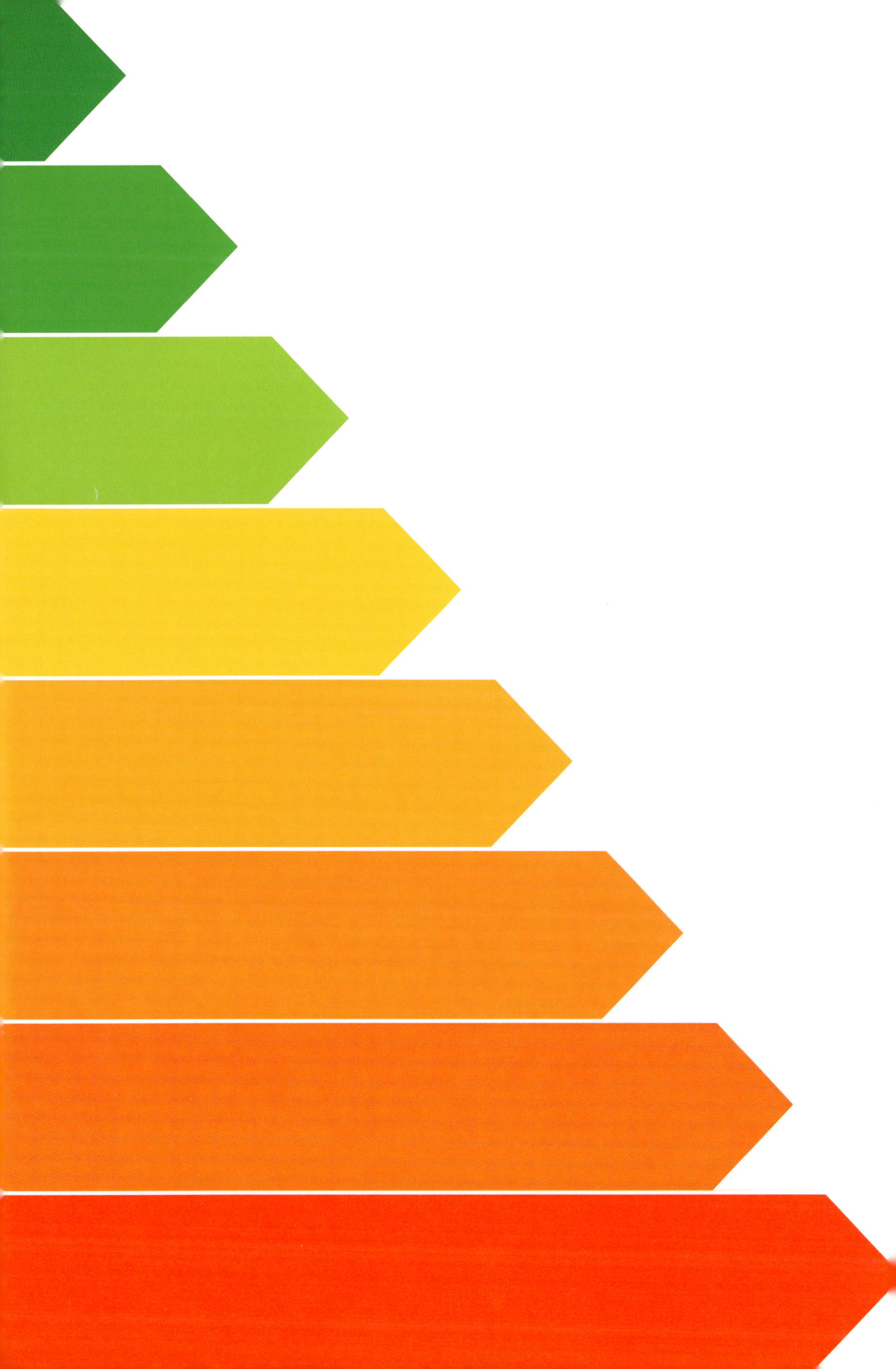

4.1: A BACKGROUND TO PLANNED MAINTENANCE

Building maintenance is not a glamorous subject. The aim is essentially to carry out the necessary repairs to restore the building to its original condition on a responsive, cyclical or planned basis. This does not necessarily improve either the appearance or the performance of a building. However, it is an extremely important process as the deterioration of a building can result in its demolition, if the scale of repairs outweighs the cost of replacement. In the meantime, the deterioration of the building will have a negative impact on the building users, the value of the building and the appearance of a wider area, which can cause a vicious cycle of decay.

Responsive repairs tend to be minor works arising from specific faults such as leaks, whereas cyclical repairs tend to be more extensive, including the internal or external redecoration of a building. Planned maintenance tends to be of a much larger and more intrusive nature, incorporating the replacement of key building elements, such as kitchens and bathrooms, boilers, re-wiring, replacement windows or roofs and, in more recent years, the installation of loft and cavity wall insulation.

On commercial buildings or large multi-occupancy residential buildings (or those that are part of a wider estate or portfolio), maintenance is typically managed by an estate management team, who may also carry out repairs in-house or subcontract specialist works as necessary. Alternatively, the repairs may be carried out in whole or part by a facilities management (FM) team contracted to undertake the necessary repairs to the building. This contract can include the day-to-day operations of the building, including energy management.

For private residential dwellings, maintenance tends to be carried out on an ad hoc basis arising from faults. Otherwise it will be done in preparation for a sale or in connection with improvements or extensions. It may include changes which improve the thermal performance of a building, such as loft conversions where insulation is added at rafter level. Alternatively, it may include changes where the thermal performance is reduced by the addition of a conservatory. Where this is not separated from the rest of the property, it can result in increased heat loss in winter and increased risk of overheating in summer (reducing thermal comfort and increasing fuel bills).

If we disregard responsive and cyclical maintenance as being of a minor nature, the decision to undertake planned maintenance for both commercial and residential properties is an important milestone, which has typically been budgeted for as part of a long-term investment in capital expenditure (capex). Whether the money invested is a result of savings or borrowings, there will typically be an expectation of increased value, amenity or comfort, especially where the works result in increased floor area. However, the investor will also recognise that the works will result in some degree of disruption depending on their scale and nature, and whether the building user remains in occupation for their duration. For planned maintenance to proceed the investor will need to decide that the value of improvements outweighs the associated disruption.

The timing of works being triggered will vary across commercial and residential sectors to suit the drivers for each building owner and investor. Having overcome the barriers of financial investment and disruption, the owner/investor undertaking planned maintenance may also consider other complementary energy-efficiency improvements alongside the 'anyway' cost already budgeted for. Understanding these specific triggers provides an important opportunity to improve the performance of a building as part of a long-term plan.

4.2: FUNDING RETROFIT: THE DANGER OF POLITICAL CHANGE

In the UK, retrofit for energy-efficiency measures has been funded by a variety of government departments and agencies via a series of short-term initiatives over the last 25 years. The type and specification of these measures has varied significantly, although performance has generally been delivered to minimum threshold levels with installation carried

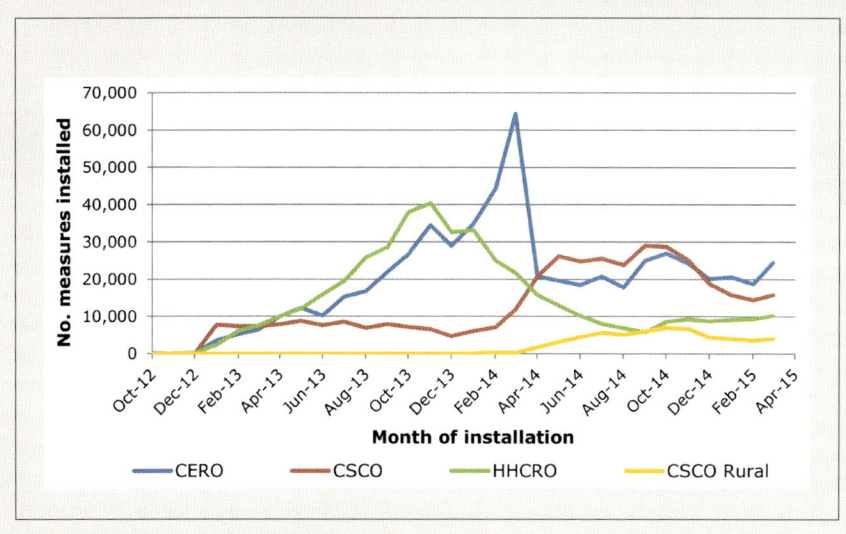

Fig 4.1: Installation of energy-efficiency measures under ECO1 and the impact of political decisions[1]

out by multiple contractors. Since 2008 alone these initiatives have included Carbon Emissions Reduction Target (CERT), Community Energy Saving Programme (CESP), Energy Company Obligation (ECO) and Green Deal. Setting aside the quality-control issues, and assuming these will be resolved by improved guidance and enforcement, we must consider the role of funding in determining output.

ECO is the current funding route for building retrofit. It was launched in 2013 and is currently in its third phase (ECO3), running from 2018–22. This obligation requires energy companies to reduce their carbon emissions by purchasing energy-efficiency measures carried out by contractors.

ECO had three distinct obligations, initially conceived as:

- the Carbon Emissions Reduction Obligation (CERO) focused primarily on the installation of insulation measures in hard-to-treat properties with a target of 20.9 MtCO$_2$ lifetime savings;
- the Carbon Saving Community Obligation (CSCO) focused on low-income areas with a target of 6.8 MtCO$_2$ lifetime savings, 15% of which was to be delivered in rural areas to consumers on certain types of benefits (the rural sub-obligation);
- the Home Heating Cost Reduction Obligation (HHCRO) focused on reducing heating costs for consumers on certain types of benefits as a way of targeting vulnerable households. The HHCRO target was £4.2bn lifetime savings.

In many cases, the energy companies have acted as contractors, offering building owners retrofit measures and reduced energy bills with single-point responsibility. While this has proved popular with many housing landlords, there have been quality-control issues on certain schemes and there has been a reduction in the number of measures installed on 'hard-to-treat' properties with a loosening of eligibility criteria (see Fig 4.1) due to political lobbying from energy companies.[2]

While ECO1 (2013–15) ultimately exceeded its carbon reduction targets, this was largely due to the loosening of eligibility criteria that allowed loft and cavity wall insulation to be included in CERO. This resulted in a significant reduction in the number of 'hard-to-treat' solid-wall properties. Many landlords discovered in early 2014 that energy companies were no longer able to offer acceptable levels of funding for this type of retrofit. This change had a dramatic impact on the retrofit supply chain, with many subcontractors badly affected by the stop–start nature of the work.

4.3: FUNDING RETROFIT: THE DANGER OF MODEST GAINS

ECO provides 'deemed lifetime scores' for a variety of measures implemented on different property types to a range of specifications. These scores represent carbon savings, which are traded via an ECO brokerage. For example, a brick solid-wall property (one-bed flat with three external walls) with an existing gas boiler which received 100 mm insulation (reducing the estimated U-value from 2.1 to 0.35 W/m^{2}K) would save 25.64 tonnes of CO_2 with an associated cost saving of £8,277. The same property receiving the same retrofit measures but using existing electric storage heaters would save 65.376 tonnes of CO_2 with a cost saving of £23,465. If the same property (gas-fired boiler) were to receive cavity wall insulation (thermal conductivity of 0.027 W/m^{2}K) it would achieve a saving of 16.086 tonnes of CO_2 with a cost saving of £5,352. Given the significant cost difference between installing external wall insulation (say £15,000 for 100 mm EWI on a typical semi-detached house) compared to cavity wall insulation (say £500 for 100 mm CWI on a similar property), as well as the relatively small difference between estimated carbon saved, it is not surprising that energy providers and retrofit contractors have focused on cavity wall insulation, loft insulation or boiler replacement. These are easier and cheaper solutions, and the providers have targeted properties using less efficient heating systems, such as electric storage heaters. However, the number of cavity walls and lofts which are not adequately insulated is now relatively low, at 30% and 31% respectively,[3] and it is widely recognised that the 96% of 'hard-to-treat' uninsulated solid-wall properties need to be tackled. As yet, there is little evidence of change. In ECO3 there is an increasing emphasis on fuel poverty and the need to tackle the worst-performing properties (Bands E, F and G) with ECO funding to support the MEES legislation, which is targeted at the most energy-inefficient part of the housing industry – the private rented sector.

While ECO rewards improved efficiency, it does not recognise excellence or reward deep retrofit. For solid-wall properties the highest benchmark for wall insulation is 0.18 W/m^{2}K, while the U-values of roof and floor insulation are not specifically measured. While draught-proofing is included, there is no performance criteria for airtightness, and there is no allowance for triple-glazed windows. There is no financial incentive for deep retrofit in the main source of grant funding for retrofit, and it is therefore not surprising that the majority of retrofits undertaken in the UK to date have achieved relatively modest improvements.

However, this strategy should not be applied to solid-wall properties. There is increasing awareness of the dangers of locking-in modest improvements on buildings. This is particularly acute for those

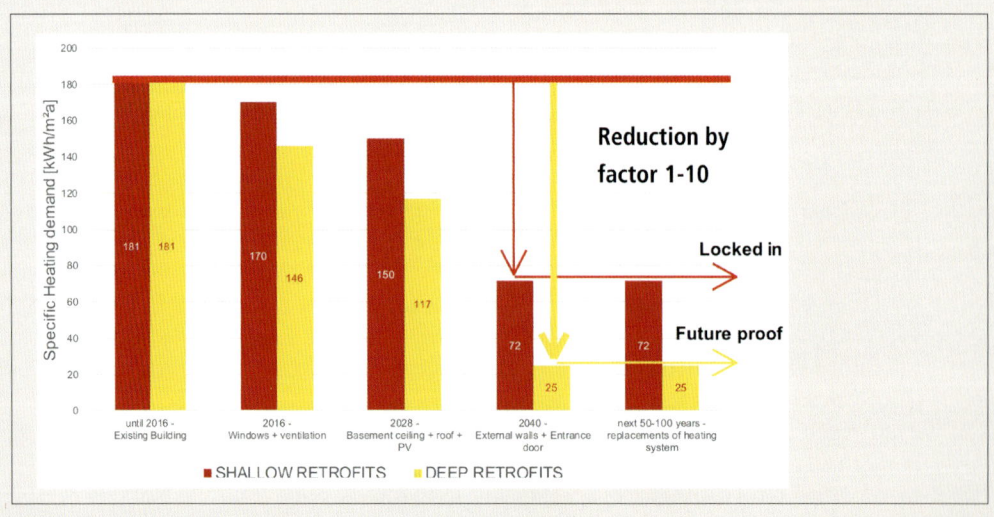

Fig 4.2: The impact of shallow retrofit on preventing future deep retrofit[4]

48 **EnerPHit:** A Step-by-Step Guide to Low Energy Retrofit

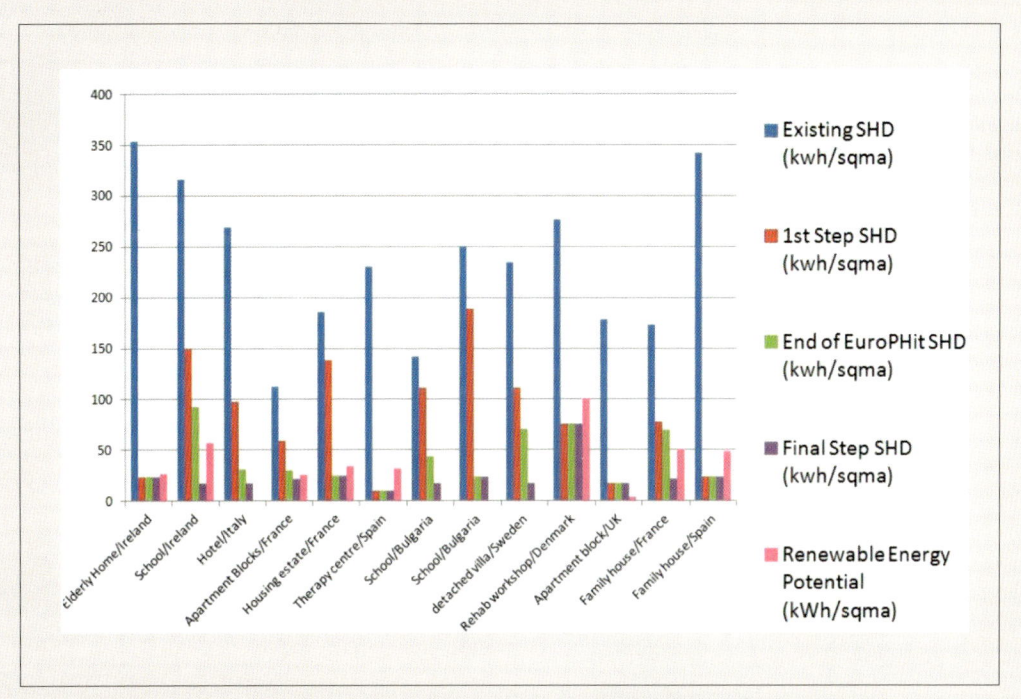

Fig 4.3: EuroPHit case study projects – performance targets for space heating demand (SHD)[5]

building elements which are not regularly maintained or improved, such as external walls. Fig 4.2 shows the impact of shallow retrofit on external walls where EWI has been applied at a 'standard' depth. While this has achieved a significant reduction in energy consumption it has also prevented the future improvement of deep retrofit necessary to achieve longer-term goals. This issue is particularly relevant to building owners who are seeking to futureproof their buildings and reduce their energy consumption but who may not have the necessary finance available to fund deep retrofit in a single project.

4.4: THE EUROPHIT PROJECT: AIMS AND OUTCOMES

Recognising the need to support building owners to achieve deep retrofit to the EnerPHit standard and the forthcoming nZEB requirements, the PHI launched the EU-funded EuroPHit project in 2014. The project sought to build capacity and break down some of the barriers to deep retrofit, providing a model for incremental improvement to the EnerPHit standard. Implemented across 20 pilot projects in nine EU member states, it included the development of a long-term planning tool and certification scheme. It offered guidance and support to those in the industry looking to develop suitable products, and engaged with the financial industry to study best practice for investment and funding of future deep retrofits. While building retrofit would ideally be carried out in a single project, partial retrofit steps are more common, completed on a building over time – also known as step-by-step retrofits. Indeed, 80–90% of all retrofits undertaken are retrofit measures rather than complete, one-time deep retrofits.[6]

4.5: THE ENERPHIT RETROFIT PLAN AND INCREMENTAL IMPROVEMENT

The planning tool developed to support this process is the EnerPHit Retrofit Plan (ERP), which is part of the updated PHPP (version 9.6 onwards). The ERP comprises three parts:

- Cover letter
- Scheduler of measures
- Overview of measures

The overview tab provides the following output:

- **Chronological sequence of the steps**
- **Measures necessary in any case, and resultant energy-saving measures**
- **Characteristic values of building components**
- **Building parameters**
- **Achievement of EnerPHit criteria**
- **Investment and energy costs**

This update also enables comparison of retrofit options in terms of energy saved and cost benefit. This can also be used to show the impact of planned incremental steps towards EnerPHit (see Fig 4.4), enabling the Passivhaus designer to provide guidance on the suitability and compatibility of particular measures and how these might be best installed over a number of phases. Fig 4.5 shows a typical scheduler output from an ERP describing the proposed measures and the sequencing of the works.

Select the active variant here >>>>>>>	Units	Active 3-2nd Step (2018)	Comparison worksheet variant "Poorer energy efficiency"	Existing Building	1st Step (2015)	2nd Step (2018)	Final Step		
		3	0	1	2	3	4	5	6
Heating demand	kWh/(m²a)	36.7		214.0	49.5	36.7	24.0		
Heating load	W/m²	18.9		63.5	22.5	18.9	13.3		
Cooling & dehum. demand	kWh/(m²a)								
Cooling load	W/m²								
Frequency of overheating (> 25 °C)	%	0.0		0.0	0.0	0.0	0.1		
PER demand	kWh/(m²a)	101.0		398.9	121.9	101.0	79.0		
EnerPHit Classic?	yes / no	no		no	no	no	yes		

Fig 4.4: Incremental steps to achieve EnerPHit at Stella Maris House using the 'variants' tab in PHPP v9[7]

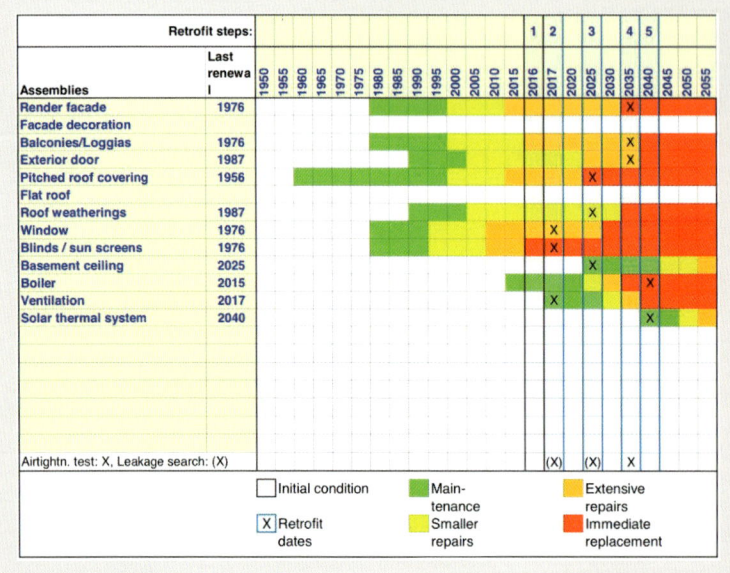

Assemblies	Last renewal	1950	1955	1960	1965	1970	1975	1980	1985	1990	1995	2000	2005	2010	2015	1 2016	2 2017	2020	2025	3 2030	2035	4 2040	5 2045	2050	2055
Render facade	1976																				X				
Facade decoration																									
Balconies/Loggias	1976																			X					
Exterior door	1987																			X					
Pitched roof covering	1956																X								
Flat roof																									
Roof weatherings	1987																	X							
Window	1976															X									
Blinds / sun screens	1976															X									
Basement ceiling	2025																			X					
Boiler	2015																					X			
Ventilation	2017															X									
Solar thermal system	2040																					X			

Airtightn. test: X, Leakage search: (X)   (X) (X) X

	Initial condition		Main-tenance		Extensive repairs
X	Retrofit dates		Smaller repairs		Immediate replacement

Fig 4.5: Typical ERP

50 **EnerPHit:** A Step-by-Step Guide to Low Energy Retrofit

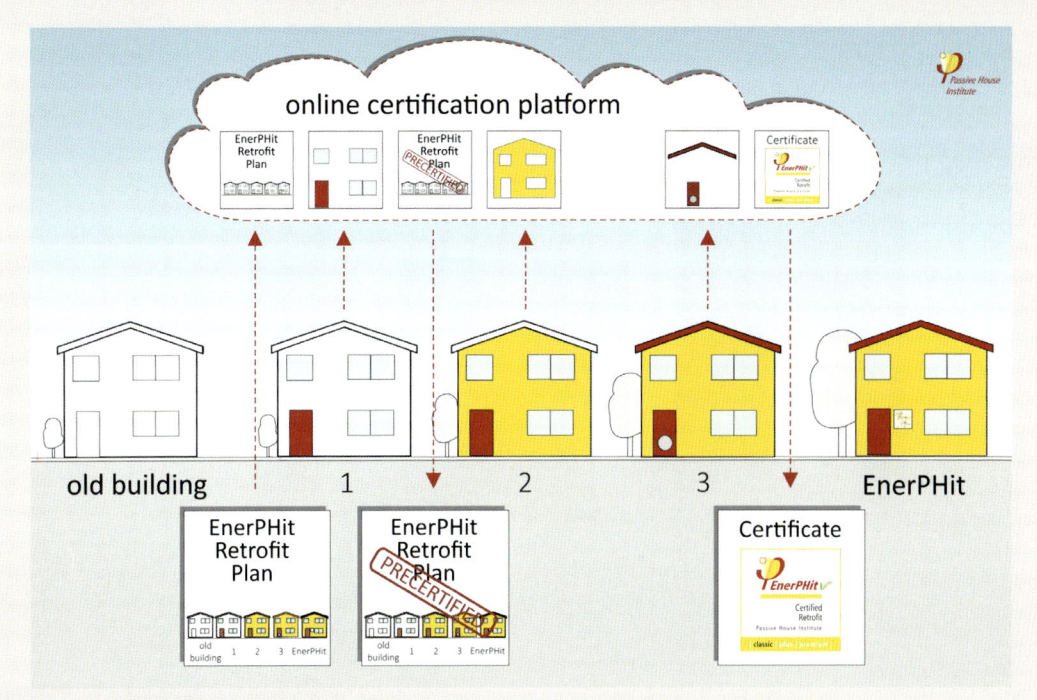

Fig 4.6: Online certification platform[8]

4.6: PRE-CERTIFICATION FOR STEP-BY-STEP RETROFIT

To ensure long-term compliance via a step-by-step route, a pre-certification route is provided for quality assurance that allows the building owner and designer to plan, measure and monitor performance over time. Pre-certification includes a thorough check of the ERP as well as the detailed design documents for the first step. The certifier checks for compliance with EnerPHit criteria and checks sequencing and compatibility of the proposed works. In this way, lock-in effects and unnecessary investment and energy costs can be avoided. After approval of the ERP by the certifier, the first set of measures can be implemented. This will also be checked by the certifier for compliance with the plan. If this is the case, and energy savings of at least 20% are achieved with the first step, the building owner will receive a pre-certificate for the building. An online platform (see Fig 4.6) facilitates and structures the data exchange and communication between energy consultant and certifier. The pre-certification gives planners and building owners the certainty that the desired energy standard will be achieved after the last step has been completed.

4.7: ALIGNING PLANNED MAINTENANCE AND STEP-BY-STEP RETROFIT TO ENERPHIT

The triggers for planned maintenance can vary depending on ownership, management and building typology. However, all buildings require some degree of planned maintenance during their lifetime. This maintenance might include renewal of cladding systems, the replacement of windows or the overhaul of existing services. Each building element has an anticipated lifespan depending on its typology, durability, location and use.[9] For example, the structure of a commercial building might typically last the full life of the building (say 60 years), while the cladding might last 30 years. The mechanical and electrical (M&E) services or windows might last 20 years, while the finishes might only last 10 years. Understanding the replacement cycles for each element is essential when planning step-by-step retrofit to avoid duplication and ensure that the 'anyway' maintenance cost is incorporated within each retrofit. For example, it may be necessary to renew a cladding system that is failing or otherwise unsuitable or unattractive (see case study 7.4). This work should be coordinated with the installation

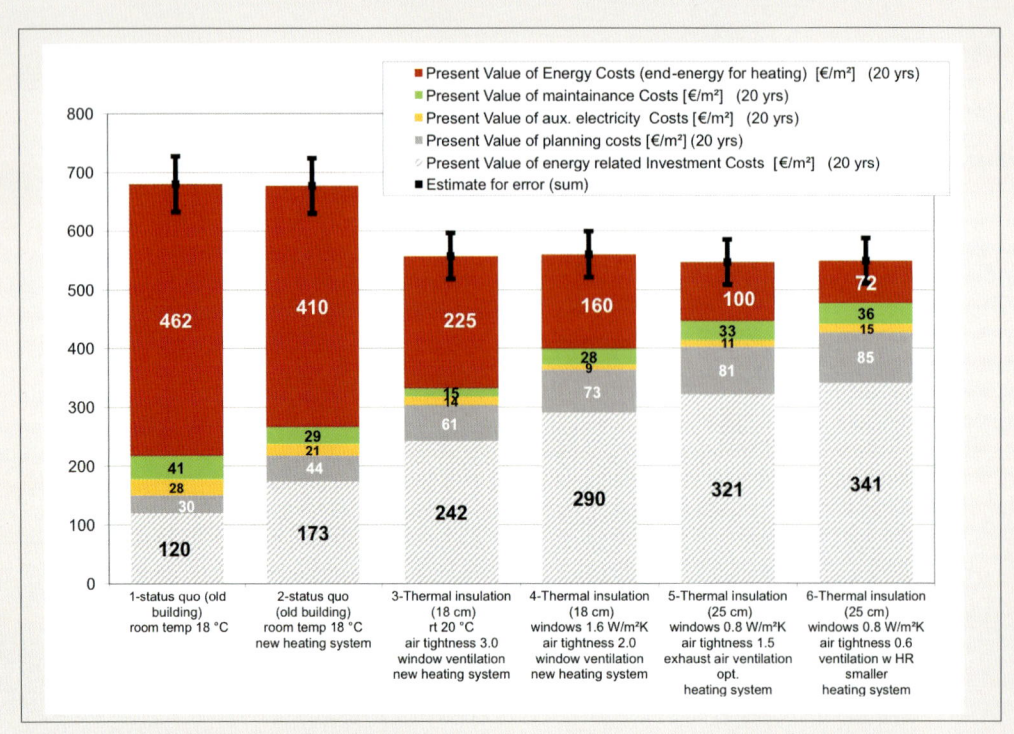

Fig 4.7: Example showing the total life-cycle costs for different modernisation variants – cash/present value for the cost of a single-family house of 156 m² (German construction costs as at 2016)[10]

of EWI of a depth necessary to meet the EnerPHit standard, as this building element is unlikely to be upgraded again within 30 years. In this way, planned maintenance and deep retrofit can be aligned, and the cost of additional scaffolding, cladding and preliminaries can be avoided, significantly reducing the energy consumption. Doing this may make it possible to achieve a net positive financial outcome, as described below.

4.8: THE ECONOMICS OF STEP-BY-STEP RETROFIT

The ERP considers the cost of implementing deep retrofit over time and includes the capital cost of the works, the revenue cost saved, and any additional maintenance cost incurred. It considers the specific measures proposed and discounts the 'anyway' costs that would be required (as identified by the building owner) under a normal maintenance regime. For example, it may be necessary to replace an existing boiler or windows at a given time, and the cost of this is discounted against any additional cost for a better-quality boiler or windows. The comparative cost can be calculated using PHPP v9 in the PHeco tab. The typical output from this can be seen in Fig 4.7.

This output makes important assumptions about the cost of the works and the ongoing cost of energy:

- Interest rate: 2% (alternative interest rate may be used).
- Energy price 0.1 €/kWh as an average price throughout the entire consideration period. An energy price increase exceeding the general inflation rate is not assumed.
- Consideration period is 20 years.
- Average useful lives of different components are predefined in the PHPP. These can be adjusted by the user if required.
- If the useful life of a component or the

average useful life is known and it is longer than the consideration period, a residual value of the measure after 20 years is automatically calculated in the PHPP. This is deducted from the investment costs in the economic efficiency analysis.
- For simplification, in the economic efficiency analysis it can be assumed that all measures are implemented at the same time (present value), although they may be implemented over several years in the case of a step-by-step modernisation. This simplification makes sense for reducing the calculation procedure and the input required in the PHPP.
- If these exist, subsidies can be taken into account in the economic efficiency analysis by decreasing the costs accordingly.

Several correction factors can also be applied to boundary conditions to allow for user difference and improve accuracy. For example, the 'normal' PHPP assumption of 20°C for internal room temperatures can be reduced to 18°C for the existing uninsulated building, as occupants may not be able to afford the cost of heating their uninsulated home to a comfortable level. Planning fees are identified separately and can be set at a percentage of the investment cost to suit the project (say 10%). This allows for the cost of employing an architect or engineer, and would typically be included in the 'anyway' costs; however, if there are additional studies or services needed to achieve deep retrofit (e.g. avoiding thermal bridging), this should be included in the energy-efficiency costs. The comparative costs in Fig 4.7 do not include the 'anyway' costs of the other associated measures and the residual value (beyond 20 years) of any investment. These should be added to understand the total investment cost.

This example shows that it can be possible to achieve a significant reduction in energy consumption while keeping the capital cost of additional energy-efficiency savings within the revenue savings achieved from the energy-efficiency measures. This assumes measures are carried out in a coordinated manner alongside appropriate 'anyway' measures.

4.9: A CASE STUDY IN STEP-BY-STEP ENERPHIT: STELLA MARIS HOUSE

Stella Maris House is a two-storey owner-occupied residential property on the edge of Wicklow Town, Ireland, originally extended in 1995. Situated on a steep slope, it enjoys excellent views to the sea and nearby mountains to the north, while to the south it faces the slope. The existing house has multiple external wall types, with a large oversailing roof

Fig 4.8: Stella Maris House (pre-retrofit)[11]

Fig 4.9: Stella Maris House: EnerPHit in four steps[12]

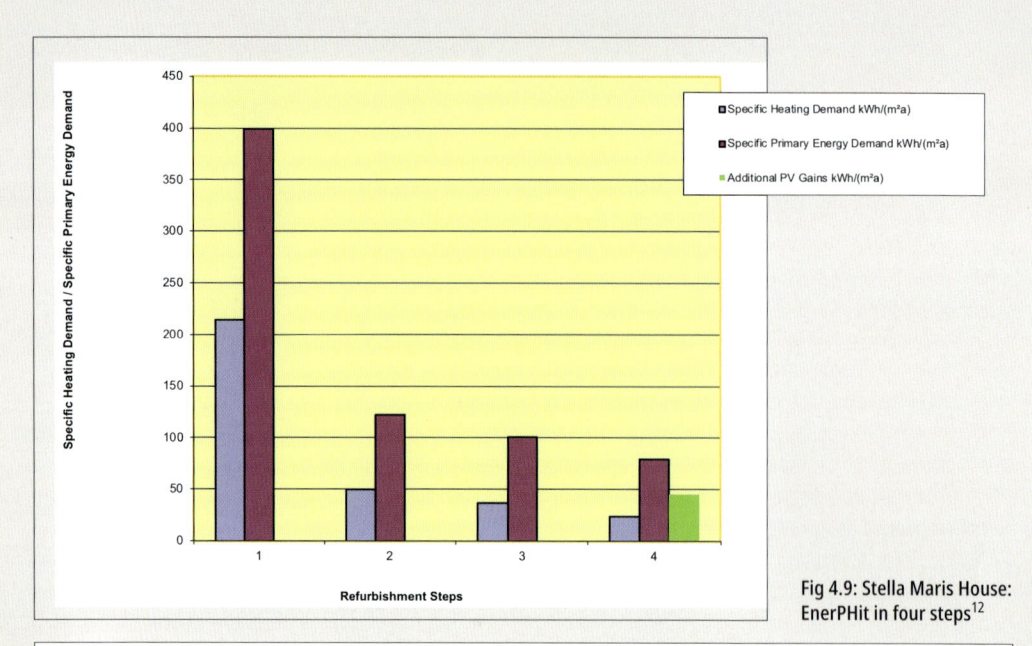

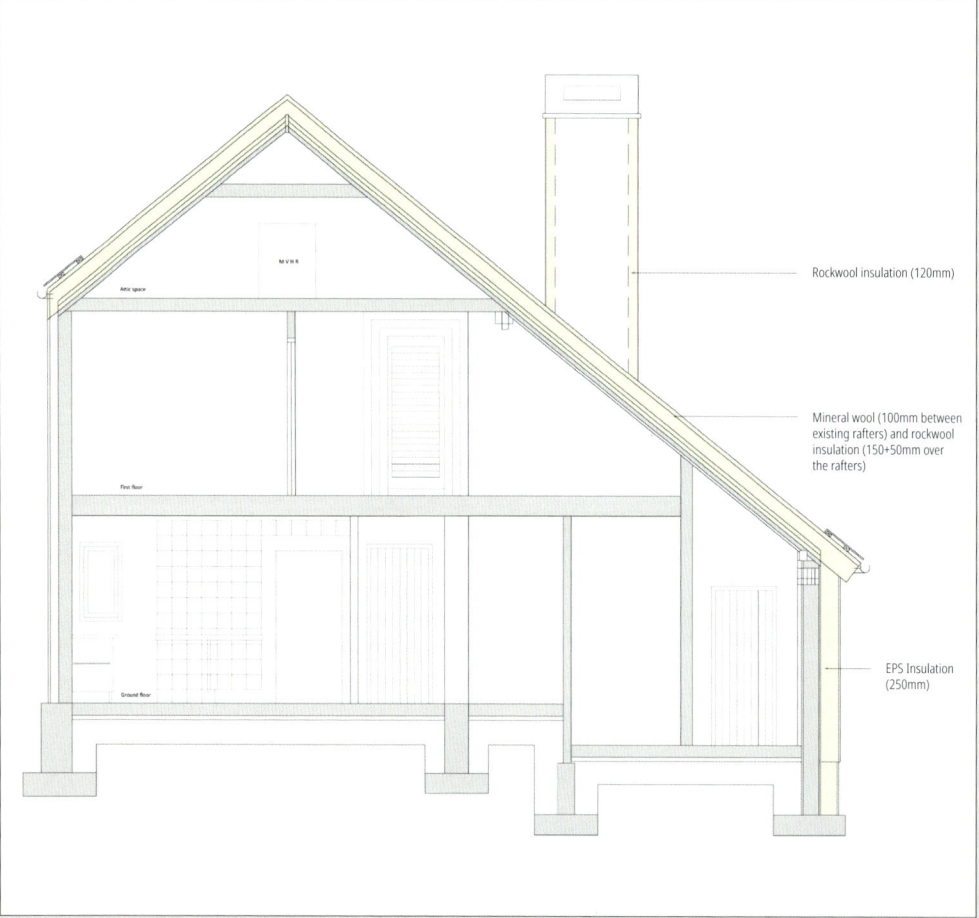

Fig 4.10: Roof + north elevation + MVHR[13]

Fig 4.11: Avoiding thermal bridging at DPC[14]

Fig 4.12: 150 + 50 mm insulation laid over airtight membrane with 100 mm below[15]

which forms one of the largest building elements. The property suffered from extreme air leakage from the roof, which resulted in high levels of heat loss. The residents could not afford to carry out the necessary measures to achieve EnerPHit in a single step, but wanted to ensure this was possible over time so that they could retire in a low-energy, low-cost building.

An ERP was prepared based on a four-stage retrofit process, with the first step being the retrofit of the existing roof to incorporate improved airtightness and additional insulation. Considering the most sensible detailing and sequencing of the works, it was agreed that works to the north elevation should be carried out at the same time. EWI was proposed above and below DPC to a depth of 250 mm and overlapping adjacent elevations by 400 mm to allow for future phases. Rigid insulation was extended down to foundation level, and the metal base rail at DPC was brought into the insulation zone, preventing a thermal bridge at ground level (see Fig 4.11). To simplify detailing, the windows and doors in the north elevation were also replaced with high-performance units, and the adjacent wall insulation extended 40 mm over the frames to improve thermal continuity. An insulated threshold detail was also used at the base of the door to further improve thermal continuity.

The designers originally intended to fill the 175 mm rafter zone in the roof with loose mineral wool and lay an airtight membrane over this before installing 150 mm rigid insulation above, achieving a U-value of 0.121 W/m^2/K. However, it became clear that this would have resulted in increased risk of interstitial condensation (one-third to two-thirds R-value ratio rule). A revised design comprising 100 mm insulation between rafters and 150 + 50 mm above was therefore installed, achieving a U-value of 0.129 W/m^2/K. The upper level of insulation was staggered over the rafters to further reduce thermal bridging, and the membrane fully taped to ensure airtightness. Insulation was also extended at the verge to allow for the junction to insulation at the gable walls in a future phase.

The existing roof included four rooflights installed in the 1990s. Although double-glazed, they were a significant source of heat loss and thermal bridging. These were replaced with high-performance units which comprised five panes of glass within a frame and could be installed in the insulation zone, improving thermal continuity. The existing chimney was a significant thermal bridge in the envelope, and it was decided to sleeve the full height of the stack with 120 mm Rockwool to ensure fire safety and provide thermal continuity with the newly insulated roof.

Building services are normally upgraded in later phases; however, the existing building started with an airtightness of 5.8 ach n50. It was likely that the proposed works would significantly improve this to the extent that mechanical ventilation would be required. A PH-certified unit with 93% efficiency was installed using spiral-mounted ducts with insulated and vapour-tight intake and extract ducts to the gable wall. The designers recognised that the interface with the wall would need to be modified in

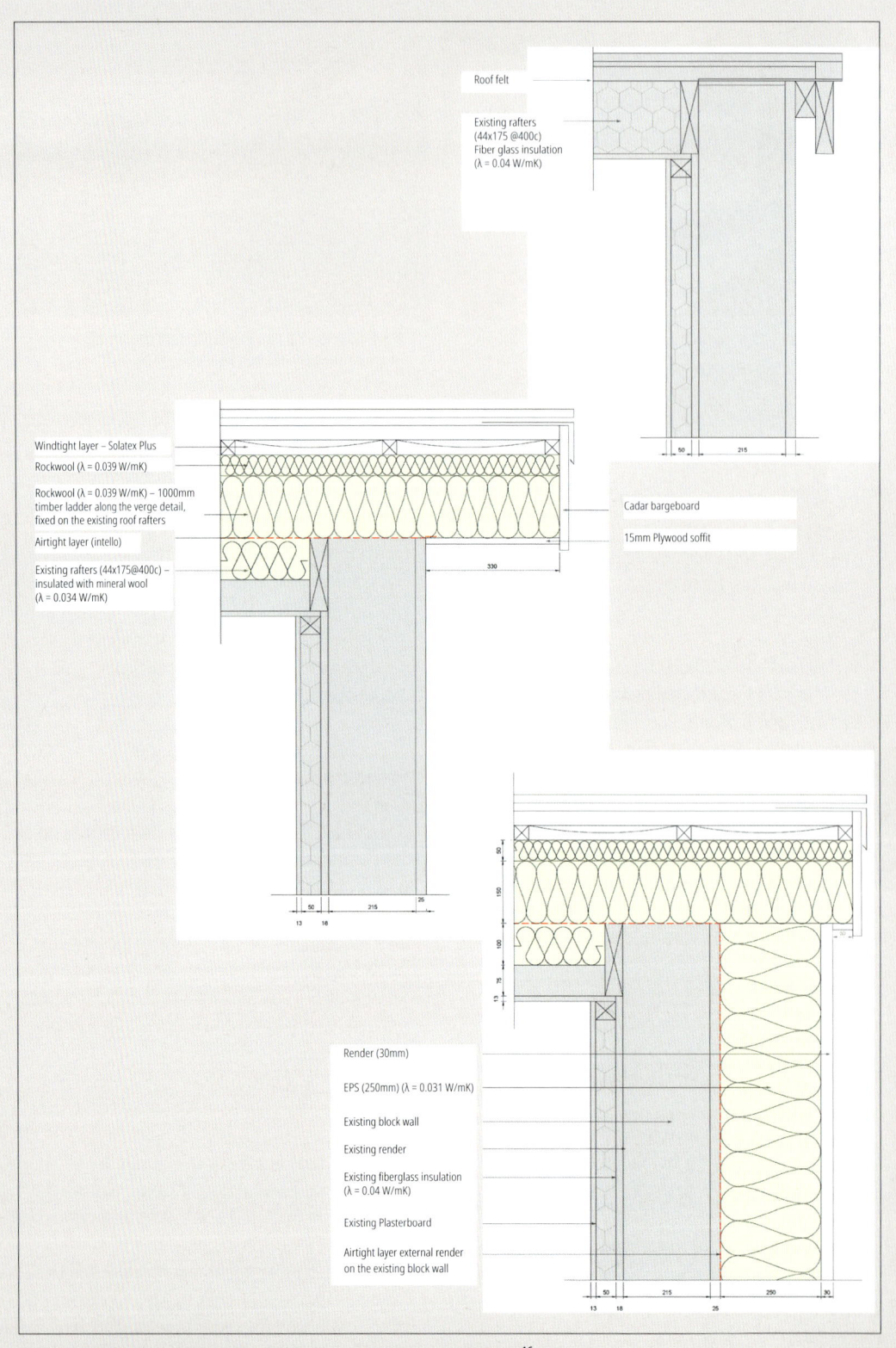

Fig 4.13: Roof overhang at verge to allow for future insulation to gable wall[16]

56 EnerPHit: A Step-by-Step Guide to Low Energy Retrofit

a future phase to allow for insulation to be installed on the gable walls. The airtightness test result at the end of the first step achieved 2.4 ach n50. The same test at the end of the second step has not yet been carried out, but the designers anticipate further improvement.

In summary, the ERP comprised four phases, with the first phase completed in 2015, the second phase completed in October 2018 and the third phase to be completed by 2029.

- Phase 1 has reduced space heating demand by 68% from 214 kWh/m^2/a to 49.5 kWh/m^2/a, with a dramatic reduction in draughts, increased heat retention and improved air quality. The existing heating system remains, with a high-efficiency gas condensing boiler serving radiators and hot water supply that is augmented by solar thermal panels.
- Phase 2 comprised the extension of the MVHR to serve the whole property (this could be seen as a sub-phase, i.e. 1a) and the inclusion of an independent air source to the wood-burning stove for combustion. The building owners also decided to bring forward the insulation works to the gable walls on the east and west elevations and part of the south elevation from the third phase in order to improve thermal comfort in the whole house. This was particularly challenging, as the existing wall build-ups included significant variations.
- Phase 3 will comprise the remodelling of the south elevation and replacement of existing glazed screens with high-performance windows and a small extension to increase accommodation and improve amenity. An airtight wood log stove will replace the existing wood log stove. The gas boiler heating system will be replaced with a more sustainable heating system, which has not yet been decided on.
- Phase 4 will include the installation of PV panels on the roof, reducing the primary energy demand by 22 kWh/m²/a.

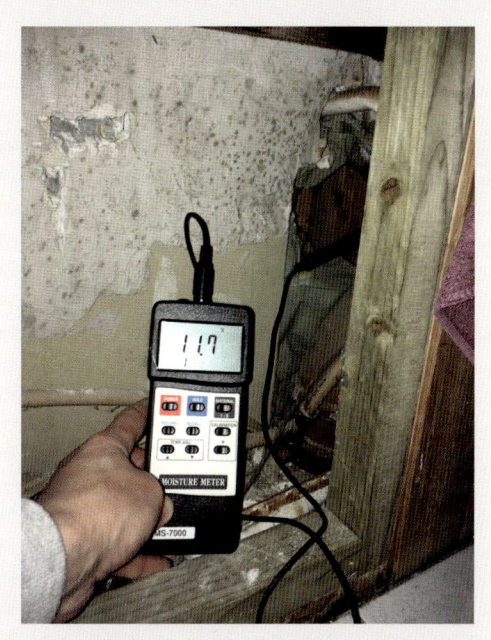

Fig 4.14: Checking existing moisture levels in wall

Lessons learned so far include giving building owners flexibility of phasing to bring forward or push back certain works as priorities and funding change, as long as sequencing is not compromised. It is important to consider the risk of interstitial condensation in all details, even when insulating externally. The use of manufacturers' 'standard' details should also be questioned when they compromise thermal integrity. For example, the use of an aluminium starter rail on an EWI system can be a significant thermal bridge if not separated from the existing wall. It is essential to analyse the existing fabric, and check for any existing interstitial condensation or mould growth in the existing fabric prior to any retrofit. Humidity sensors were used to check the timber frame wall to assure that the existing fabric had no condensation issues (see Fig 4.14). The MVHR should be the latest model, incorporating an integrated pre-heater, as this can affect both efficiency and thermal comfort. While the new windows incorporated larger frames, existing daylight levels were generous and these could generally be accommodated within existing structural openings. However, in one location an existing window also served as a means of fire escape, and the size meant that the existing structural opening had to be increased. Finally, as with all retrofit projects, there is a need to ensure contractors are

Fig 4.15: Extending flues while maintaining airtightness (gable: masonry part)

Fig 4.16: Installing windows in the insulated zone (gable: masonry part)

Fig 4.17: Installing windows in the insulated zone (gable: timber frame part)

Fig 4.18: Gable wall detailing

experienced or else fully trained in deep retrofit to avoid delays and increased risk of non-compliance.

While funding for retrofit was available from Sustainable Energy Association Ireland (SEAI), the owners chose not to pursue this as the funds were modest and unsuited to incremental improvement. Excluding the MVHR installation (requiring a new ceiling bulkhead), the works have generally been carried out externally, reducing the impact on the residents. The cost of Phase 1 was €95,000, with Phase 2 being €85,000. Energy savings of 164.5 kWh/m^2/a and 13 kWh/m^2/a respectively were achieved, resulting in an annual energy saving of approximately €3,722. While the financial saving is important, the much greater achievement is in thermal comfort, with all rooms achieving this with minimal heating. As the residents intend to live in the property through their retirement, they expect to recoup the capital cost through energy savings at a time when their income will reduce and their need for thermal comfort will increase.

Fig 4.19: Stella Maris House in context

Fig 4.20: Phase 2 completed: view to entrance

4.10: IMPLICATIONS FOR BUILDING MANAGEMENT

Having shown that deep retrofit can be achieved over the life cycle of a building at no additional cost, what other barriers might remain, and what are the implications for building management? To achieve a cost-neutral (or indeed cost-positive) outcome, it is essential to align planned maintenance with deep retrofit. This requires building managers or those responsible for the maintenance of their building(s) to take control of their assets and develop a long-term view of their capital investment and running costs. Ideally this person (or people) would be responsible for both parts of this equation so that investment in retrofit can easily be recovered in savings in energy bills. Where this isn't possible, there may still be good reasons for investment in deep retrofit, such as fuel poverty. Another issue for building owners to consider is the current and future value of their building(s) if retrofitted or not. There have been relatively few studies in this area, and further research is required; however, it is clear from the case studies presented in this book that it is not

Step-by-step to EnerPHit 59

simply energy efficiency which has been improved. Deep retrofit offers an opportunity to dramatically improve both the architectural quality and amenity of buildings, and this can increase the financial value of the asset. However, if implemented poorly, retrofit also includes a risk of lower performance and reduced value. In recent years many housing landlords in the UK have focused on the piecemeal short-term grant funding of insulation measures (CERT, CESP, ECO, etc.), to the detriment of long-term building performance. To avoid this risk, building owners must ensure they understand the retrofit measures proposed and are satisfied that this risk has been mitigated.

In seeking to align planned maintenance and deep retrofit there is an underlying assumption that all building owners understand their future maintenance needs and can therefore plan to incorporate deep retrofit in stages over a 20- or 30-year period. However, for both residential and commercial property owners there are reasons why this may not be the norm. In the residential domestic sector, the owner-occupier may intend to live in the property for a long period (as in the Stella Maris House); however, the average turnover of residential properties in the UK is approximately 10 years, and therefore a long-term plan may not be of interest to all. For larger, more complex buildings in both the residential and commercial sectors there may be issues with the suitability, accuracy or lack of building information. Following the Grenfell Tower disaster, the subsequent Hackitt review[17] included a recommendation that all high-risk residential buildings (HRRBs) should require a digital record in a non-proprietary open format. Housing landlords in the UK have traditionally managed properties using stock condition surveys, but these documents are basic spreadsheets which do not adequately describe the size, shape, complexity or condition of the building, and in many cases this information has been cloned from similar property types. The quality of information held by commercial landlords varies enormously; there is no single format, with landlords holding a variety of paper and digital records which rarely offer sufficient information to adequately plan for deep retrofit.

4.11: BIM AS A TOOL FOR STEP-BY-STEP RETROFIT

Building Information Modelling (BIM) Level 2 has been mandated on all UK government projects since March 2016, and is increasingly common in the construction sector for new buildings and infrastructure both in the UK and globally. It provides a coordinated 3D model of the proposed building (see Fig 4.21), incorporating information from all members of the team, and enables the design team, contractor and client to interrogate the design (typically via a web portal) and improve project delivery and cost certainty. It also provides a wealth of manufacturers' data on the construction materials and components used, which is available not only to the designer and the contractor, but critically also to the building owner on completion. This data incorporating information on life cycles and maintenance requirements is held in an open-source COBie (spreadsheet) format which can be easily accessed for the life of the building, enabling the building manager to quickly understand future maintenance needs. However, the increasing quality and ease of access of information available from BIM projects is in stark contrast to the generally poor quality of information held for existing buildings.

We might ask how the quality of information for existing buildings can be improved within a BIM environment. What are the costs of modelling our existing buildings in BIM, and what level of detail is required? Fortunately, BIM can also be applied in a step-by-step process and can be tailored to the needs of the building owner. BIM models are generated to a specific level of detail (LOD) that reflects the RIBA stages of work, and the cost of generating a model is closely linked to the LOD required. For example, LOD 1 (equivalent to RIBA Stage 1) for a house might be a simple box describing the number of storeys, number of rooms, location, orientation, year of construction and construction type. At LOD 2 the same model might incorporate windows and doors, with an outline specification for the wall, floor and roof build-up and a description of services and key components. At LOD 3 the same model would typically include all finishes such that a planning application could be submitted. At LOD 4 the model would include all

Fig 4.21: Typical 3D BIM (Level 2) model[18]

necessary information for construction, including a full specification of all elements and components. At LOD 5 the model would include as-built information, with all relevant detail on the future maintenance of the building.

Applying this methodology to an existing building on a step-by-step basis can be started with a LOD 1 model of the entire building, adding sufficient levels of detail for specific parts of the building as required. For example, a commercial building with a leaky roof might require a model of the roof and the top floor in a much higher LOD than the rest of the building. In future years, the building owner might want to update the LOD for the rest of the building when undertaking other works on the lower floors. Ultimately, the building owner will end up with a complete picture of the size, shape and condition of their building asset in a common format that is easily accessible. This enables better management of the building. In this way, BIM (like deep retrofit) can be aligned with future construction or maintenance projects so that the 'anyway' cost of design is not duplicated.

4.12: SUMMARY

EnerPHit can be achieved on an incremental basis, and the tools exist to ensure this happens. Step-by-step retrofit can be cost-neutral or even cost-positive, if the building owner is able to recover the cost of future energy saved. Step-by-step deep retrofit requires long-term planning to ensure that the necessary measures are aligned with other essential maintenance works to avoid duplication. Planning for maintenance and deep retrofit is made easier where accurate information is available for the existing building. Where this is not present, the BIM methodology can be aligned to the incremental process of step-by-step retrofit to ensure that the building owner has an accurate record of their building and can plan future maintenance as required.

5.0: Targeting EnerPHit

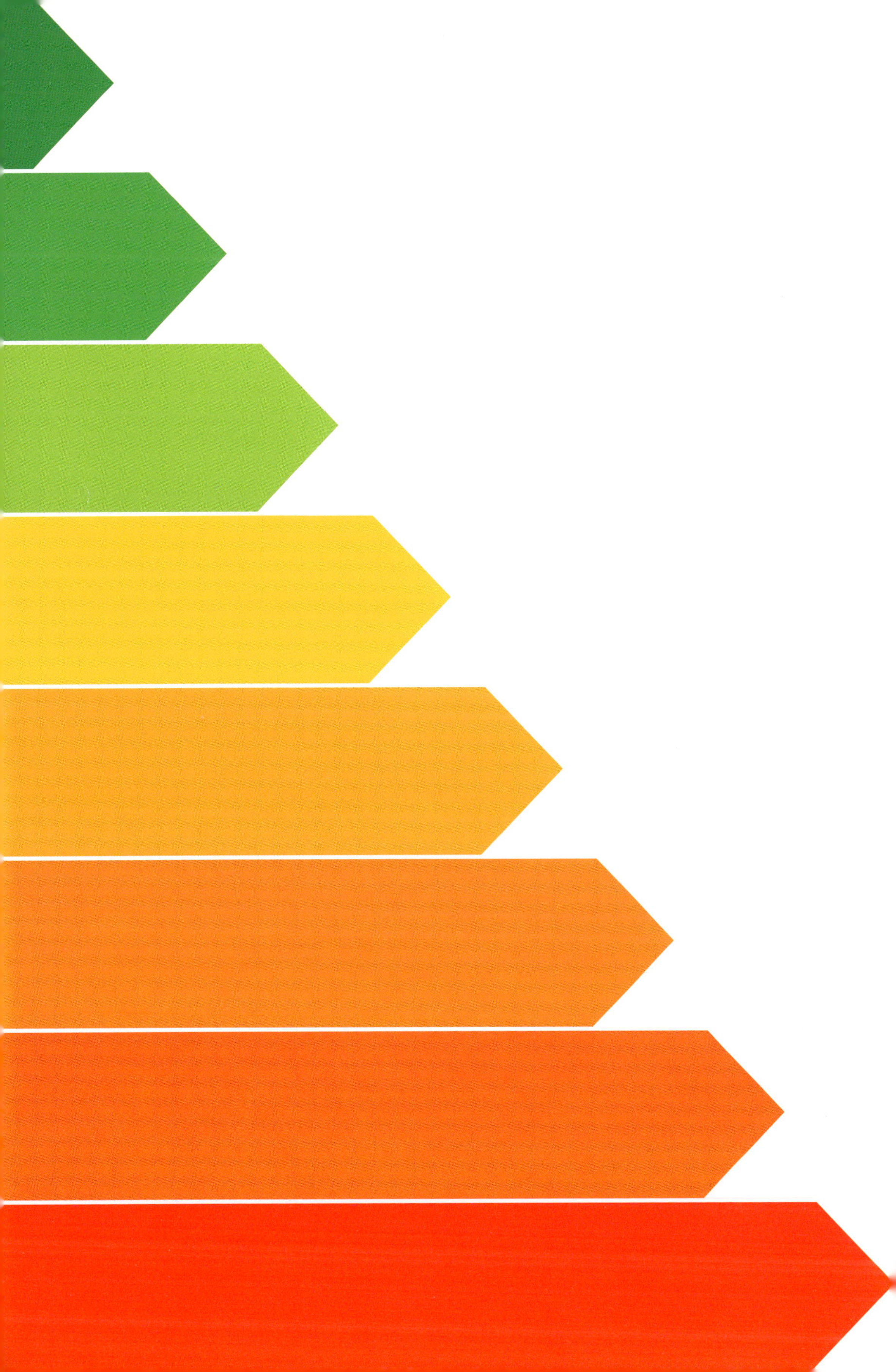

5.1: DOES RETROFIT MATTER?

Improving building fabric is not the only means of reducing carbon emissions, and buildings are increasingly integrated elements within a network of energy supply and consumption. For example, can the increasing supply of clean energy via the grid or district heating fuelled by waste heat, coupled with the likely growth of battery storage, completely negate the need for building retrofit?

Building Performance Institute Europe (BPIE) describes a future where buildings operate as part of micro-energy hubs, with energy saved, generated, stored and used where people spend most of their time – in buildings. Its report[1] identifies 10 interrelated principles for the creation of these micro-energy hubs:

- Maximise the buildings' energy efficiency first
- Increase on-site or nearby renewable energy production and self-consumption
- Stimulate energy storage capacities in buildings
- Incorporate demand-response capacity in the building stock
- Decarbonise the heating and cooling energy for buildings
- Empower end users via smart meters and controls
- Make dynamic price signals available for all consumers
- Foster business models aggregating micro-energy hubs
- Build smart and interconnected districts
- Build infrastructure to drive further market uptake of electric vehicles

While these measures can be undertaken in any order, the first principle of maximum energy efficiency should be achieved before consideration of other measures. The reason for this is two-fold. First, the laws of thermodynamics mean that space heating can be achieved using relatively cheap 'low-grade' energy (e.g. burning fuel) and consumption can be dramatically reduced by better energy efficiency. Meanwhile, electrical 'high-grade' primary energy is inherently more expensive and less efficient to produce (say 30% of the efficiency of typical power stations) and distribute (say 10% distribution losses) and its use should therefore be restricted to high-grade consumption, such as for appliances. Second, the requirement for space heating in the winter period coincides with the period of lowest solar gain (approximately seven times lower), which results in both a negative energy balance at building level and reduced electricity production from photovoltaics (PV).

There are two increasingly important factors which may ultimately affect at least one of these principles. The rapid growth of the renewable energy sector and the increasing decarbonisation of the grid will drive improved efficiency (see Figs 5.1 and 5.2). Separately, the deep retrofit of buildings and the incorporation of renewable energy sources could result in the increasing use of electric heating in buildings where ultra-low-energy demand has first been achieved. Where heat pumps are used, electrical efficiency is further improved, and reliance on fossil fuels such as gas for heating and hot water is avoided.

5.2: ENERPHIT AS A RETROFIT TARGET

The current specific heat demand for UK buildings is approximately 140 kWh/m^2/a (see Fig 5.3). If we assume (for simplicity) no change in the current fuel source and we target an 80% reduction in carbon emissions by 2050 (as per UK government carbon budgets), we might therefore suggest a specific heat demand for 2050 of 28 kWh/m^2/a. This closely matches the EnerPHit specific heat demand of 25 kWh/m^2/a, but is significantly lower than the current fabric energy-efficiency demand of Part L1A/L2A for new buildings at approximately 54 kWh/m^2/a. Given that new buildings completed

Fig 5.1: Forecast change in UK electricity sources[2]

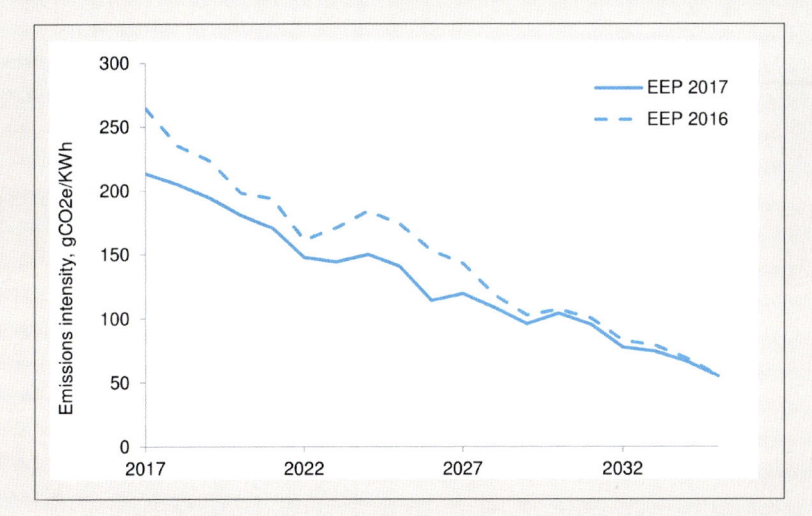

Fig 5.2: Forecast change in UK electricity carbon intensity[3]

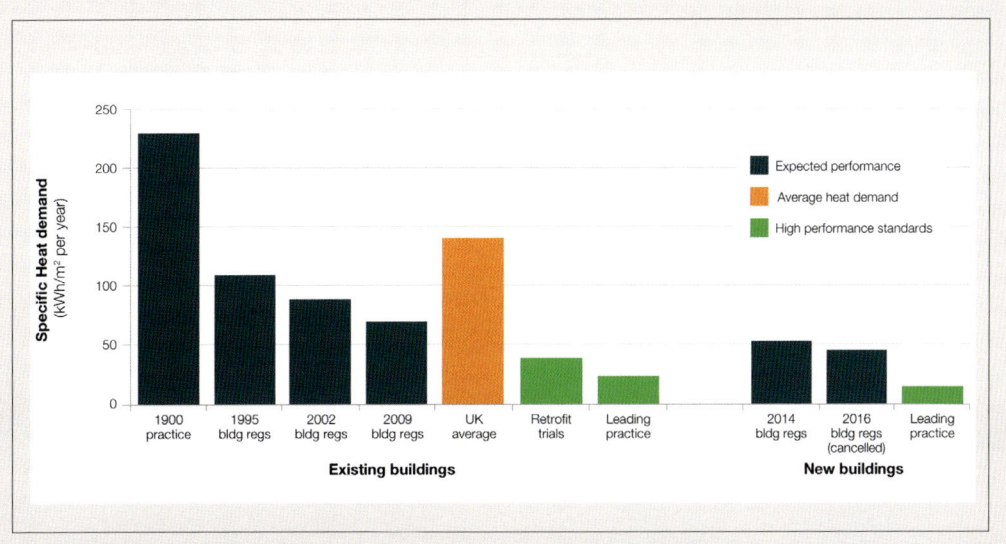

Fig 5.3: Taken from *Heating Buildings: Reducing Energy Demand and Greenhouse Gas Emissions*[4]

Targeting EnerPHit 65

in 2018 are still not achieving the average specific heat demand that we might expect all buildings to achieve in 32 years' time, this might be worrying. Furthermore, as many buildings will be more expensive and harder if not 'impossible-to-treat'[5] we might assume that the target for normal buildings should be lower than 28 kWh/m²/a to compensate for buildings we are unable to fully retrofit. If we then consider the typical performance gap between energy consumption as predicted and actual consumption[6] we might further reduce the target performance to ensure the actual performance is in line with retrofit targets.

When comparing the performance of a typical retrofit scheme delivered to the requirements of Parts L1B or L2B of the UK building regulations, the difference becomes even more stark. These standards, where they are infrequently applied,[7] set limiting factors on the main elements of the building (e.g. an external wall U-value of 0.30 W/m²K) which, assuming typical retrofit performance of other building elements, may result in an approximate Fabric Energy Efficiency Standard (FEES) of 80 kWh/m²/a. In practice this means a typical shallow retrofit specification for external walls in the UK is currently written with an insulation thickness of, say, 100 mm instead of 200 mm. As the lifespan of an insulated external wall is typically 30 years, this means that a building retrofitted in 2018 is unlikely to be treated again until after 2050. Clients become unwittingly locked in to modest improvement and prevention of future upgrades. If this is repeated on a large scale, the potential carbon savings available from retrofitting the UK building stock could be dramatically reduced, jeopardising future carbon budgets and the ability of the building sector to decarbonise by 2050.

The ultra-low-energy consumption offered by EnerPHit could also complement heating from low-carbon electric sources, ideally via high-efficiency heat pumps connected to a central heating system, perhaps augmented by solar hot water panels. Where energy consumption is even further reduced, perhaps by incorporating other renewable sources to achieve EnerPHit Plus or EnerPHit Premium, the building user might simply use basic electric resistant heaters as a secondary back-up to the warm air supplied via the MVHR.

5.3: DISTRICT HEATING SYSTEMS AND ENERPHIT

There are approximately 2,000 district heating networks in the UK, serving 210,000 domestic properties and 1,700 commercial premises plus numerous communal networks, which together supply approximately 2% of UK building heat demand. While the majority of these currently use gas-fired boilers, these could be converted to use low-carbon energy sources. Both the UK government and the Greater London Authority (GLA) are encouraging through policy such as the London Plan the extension of district heating networks and the use of Micro-CHP (combined heat and power). While there are a number of low-carbon alternatives to gas, the most practical solution is to connect these where possible to existing local sources of waste heat, i.e.: power stations.[8] However, the availability of local heat sources and proximity to existing or potential heat networks is relatively limited. While energy from waste incineration is an increasingly important source, it is relatively small. Other alternatives such as using waste heat from rivers are less efficient, and the widespread use of biofuel for heating does not make either economic or strategic sense,[9] as explained in a number of publications.[10] Micro-CHP is effectively a mini-power station located on site, which uses (in the same way as a power station) the waste heat generated by the production of electricity. In theory this could solve the problem of proximity; however, where installed these units have not proved to be particularly efficient or reliable. The typical energy supply is also not suited to modern homes, with too much heat and too little electricity generated. Nevertheless, with improving efficiency and greater scale, CHP can continue to offer a niche supply to industrial or commercial energy users.

It should also be noted that district heating systems require ongoing specialist maintenance, and also require the operator to recharge – through a local energy supply company (ESCO) or similar – multiple building users for the energy consumed. This scenario may not be acceptable to many building owners, but where this can be reconciled, and retrofit can be aligned with district heating in a single charge to the consumer, as per the Energiesprong model, we should consider the compatibility of

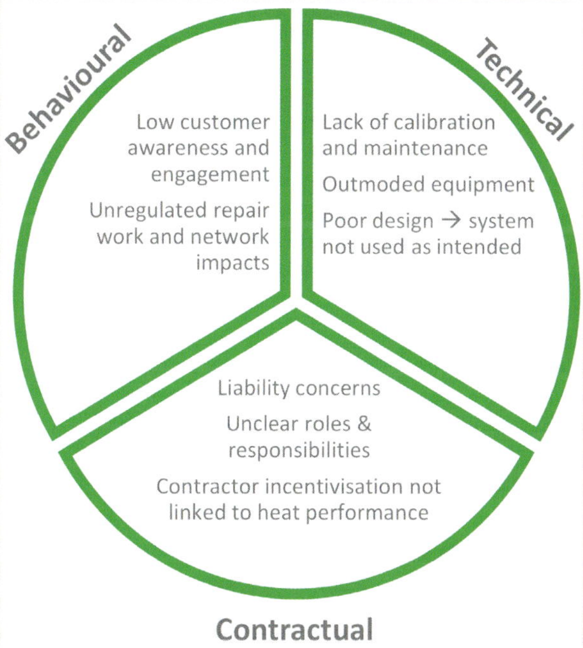

Fig 5.4: Common performance barriers affecting installed heat networks[13]

Behavioural
- Low customer awareness and engagement
- Unregulated repair work and network impacts

Technical
- Lack of calibration and maintenance
- Outmoded equipment
- Poor design → system not used as intended

Contractual
- Liability concerns
- Unclear roles & responsibilities
- Contractor incentivisation not linked to heat performance

EnerPHit with district heating. Before doing so we might consider the performance and efficiency of existing district heating systems in the UK, many of which are over 30 years old. While there is no single database of network performance data available, the CBxchange research[11] suggests that the experiences of engineers, property developers, tenants and others involved with heat networks indicate that many are not operating as efficiently as they could. This can lead to higher bills for tenants and lower overall carbon savings.[12] There are a variety of reasons why this may be the case, ranging from poor design to unanticipated changes to heat load. Fig 5.4 describes the key problems that affect the performance of existing heat networks. While I do not intend to comment on the potential expansion of heat networks, the potential inefficiency of existing heat networks has a direct impact on compatibility with EnerPHit, as described below.

As noted previously, the Passivhaus/EnerPHit methodology results in an ultra-low-energy demand of between 15 and 25 kWh/m^2/a. Unfortunately, communal or district heating systems work most efficiently where there is a significant energy demand. For a typical UK property with a space heat demand of 140 kWh/m^2/a, a district heating system can be an effective source of heat; however, in a Passivhaus/EnerPHit property where the energy demand is typically 90% lower than average this may be problematic. Where an existing system is to be retained, the risk of overheating must be addressed. All pipework should be insulated and the number of heating sources reduced, as shown in case study 7.3 (University of Innsbruck). Nevertheless, the cost of maintaining or upgrading an existing district heating system should be financially justified in relation to the long-term cost of EnerPHit. Although there are newbuild Passivhaus schemes such as Agar Grove, Camden which incorporate (for local authority policy reasons) modern efficient communal heating, even here the risk of heat loss from pipework is problematic.[14] In summary EnerPHit and existing district heating are typically mutually exclusive, and even where new district heating systems are installed there may be challenges which do not warrant the investment.

However, there is an important role for district heating in those buildings where deep retrofit is not possible. Unlike EnerPHit, which generally requires insulation to either the internal or external face of the building, district heating can provide low-carbon heat where deep retrofit may not be

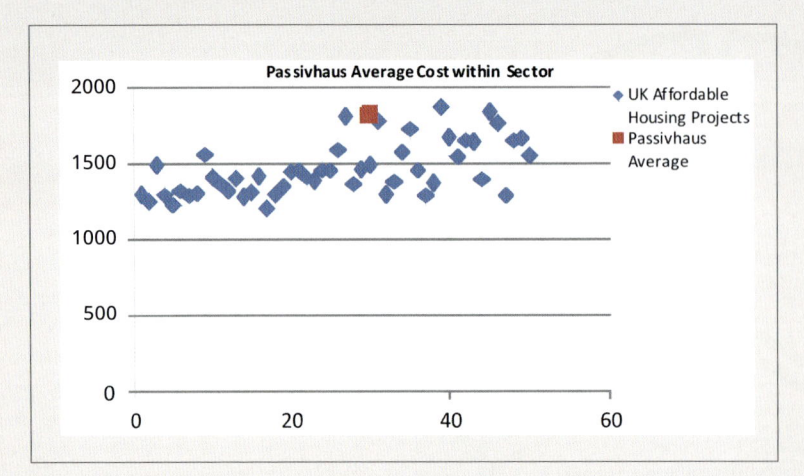

Fig 5.5: Passivhaus average cost within the affordable housing sector[15]

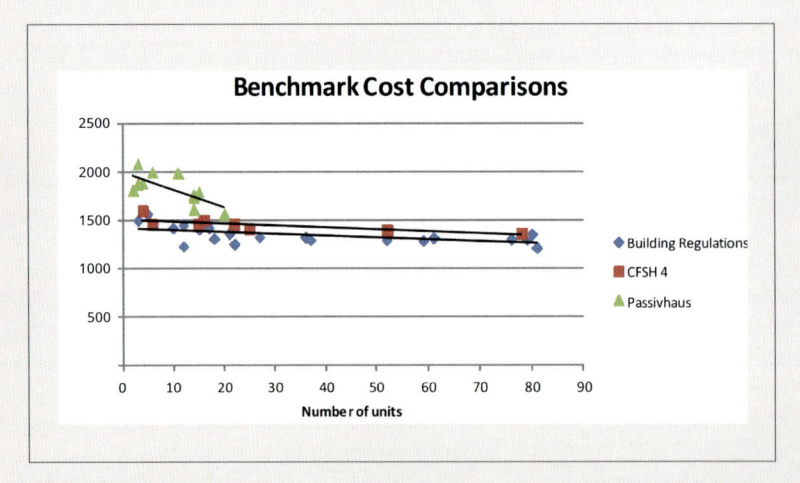

Fig 5.6: Benchmark cost comparisons[16]

possible or desirable, for example in listed buildings with protected internal features. District systems currently provide only 2% of UK heat supply and despite policy incentives (GLA, etc.) this is unlikely to increase dramatically. Nevertheless, as listed buildings represent only 0.15% of the current building stock, the expansion of district heating systems might be targeted to include these 'impossible to treat' properties.

5.4: THE CAPITAL COST OF ENERPHIT

There is much debate in the UK about the capital cost difference of Passivhaus and building regulations. This is partly due to the lack of available data, as well as the increasing performance of newbuild building regulations (Parts L1A and L1B: FEES) and additional local requirements such as the London Plan (Carbon Tax). The only UK cost study of Passivhaus schemes published in 2015 was based on a sample of 11 small residential projects (typically 10 units per site), which suggested a difference of approximately 20–25%.[17] Nevertheless, the cost difference was significantly reduced with an increasing number of units (see Fig 5.6). More recently completed projects suggest that the cost difference has reduced further, and recently completed schemes suggest that the cost difference can be virtually nil where there is sufficient scale and the brief is fixed from the outset.[18] This latter point is particularly important, as there have been projects in the UK where the Passivhaus designer has been brought onto the project at a late stage, which has caused the project to be redesigned at additional abortive cost. Furthermore, the later involvement of the PH designer can often mean that

68 EnerPHit: A Step-by-Step Guide to Low Energy Retrofit

it is too late to incorporate low-cost energy savings (such as orientation, form factor and avoidance of costly heating systems), further exacerbating the cost difference.

There has been little guidance on the cost difference between building regulations and EnerPHit. Although there have been several academic studies,[19] there have been few studies of live projects at sufficient scale to assess the difference. One of the very few projects to calculate this on a larger project is Wilmcote House. In this project the design team considered the cost implications of achieving Part L2B (2010) against the cost of achieving EnerPHit. Using tendered rates (2013) for the EnerPHit comparison and separating the extra over, the project team identified a capital cost difference of 10.1% (total £13 million).

This additional cost is identified across each part of the works (see Fig 5.7). The most significant cost is the MVHR (3.1% extra/over) as the scheme required 111 individual MVHR units to each flat with associated ductwork, although there is a small saving on the traditional extract that would have been required for kitchens and bathrooms. One of the

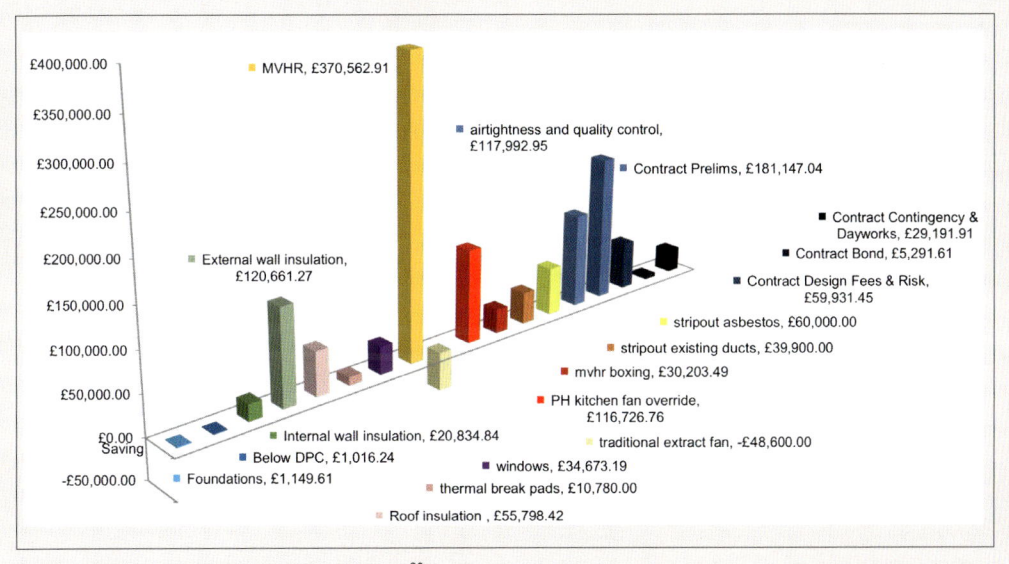

Fig 5.7: Capital cost difference for Wilmcote House[20]

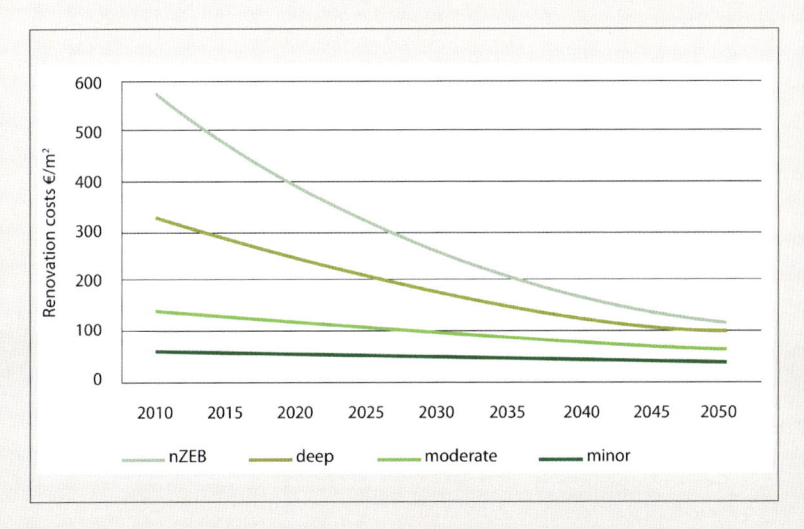

Fig 5.8: Cost reductions for different levels of renovation over time[21]

Targeting EnerPHit **69**

other significant cost differences is for contractors' prelims (1.5%). This includes the additional overhead costs the contractor believes necessary to deliver an EnerPHit scheme. This scheme included contractor design portion (CDP), so this cost would include additional design support and, most importantly, risk (as the first and largest occupied building of its kind to target EnerPHit). Other significant cost differences included additional airtightness testing and QA support (1%), plus the additional external wall insulation needed (1%). Interestingly, perhaps due to the scale of the project, the cost difference for triple-glazed windows compared to standard double-glazed windows is a mere 0.3%.

Nevertheless, this cost difference represents a considerable investment in the building. Research by BPIE suggests that the cost of retrofit to the nZEB standard will reduce significantly over the next 30 years, as shown in Fig 5.8.

5.5: ENERPHIT COMFORT STANDARD

The health benefits of improved thermal comfort are well known. The Marmot review[22] established a direct correlation between cold homes and increased mortality measured in excess winter deaths (EWDs), and increased morbidity measured in worsened health conditions. This was evidenced directly through increased cardiovascular, respiratory and mental health conditions. It also has an indirect effect through educational attainment, emotional wellbeing and resilience in children, dietary opportunities, dexterity, and risk of accidents and injuries. Guidance on the impact of fuel poverty and how to mitigate this has been provided to healthcare professionals.[23] Since then, a few small local studies have shown the positive financial impact of building retrofit on health savings, and the cost-benefit ratio is estimated to be in the order of 1.5:1.[24] On one low-income estate in East London the healthcare costs of people living in 107 homes were compared with those of people living in a similar but 'improved' estate. The average annual health costs of a person living in the unimproved estate were £512, while that of a person living in the improved estate were only £72. Another study looked at 203 adults on one 'unimproved' estate and compared their health to a matched sample from the English Housing Survey. The costs of health services were around 50% higher in the unimproved estate sample. If these results were extrapolated to the 10% of houses in the UK that are considerably cold and damp, the cost to the NHS in 1994 prices would have been around £600 million, or £1.13 billion today.

Air quality is of increasing concern in many cities, with NOx levels in London regularly breaching World Health Organization (WHO) maximum thresholds. While increasing restrictions on the use of diesel vehicles and the growth of electric vehicles might be expected to improve urban air quality, there are other pollutants such as volatile organic compounds (VOCs) that may be harder to treat. The role of mechanical ventilation, providing clean, warmed and filtered air, should be considered as a means of improving indoor air quality and thermal comfort. There is a proven causal link[25] between mould growth, arising from poor ventilation causing moist air to condense on cold surfaces, and increased rates of asthma. Many older properties suffer from excessive ventilation through gaps and cracks, causing draughts which can dramatically reduce thermal performance and comfort. Meanwhile in poorly retrofitted properties, where ventilation has not been properly considered, there may be insufficient ventilation, which can cause increased CO_2 levels and headaches resulting in increased sickness.

The Passivhaus/EnerPHit methodology tackles these issues at source, with continuity of insulation ensuring thermal bridges are prevented, thus reducing the risk of cold surfaces. The significantly improved airtightness coupled with the use of Passivhaus-certified components reduces the risk of unintended air leakage. Finally, the use of an efficient MVHR unit ensures there is always sufficient ventilation which can be boosted as required by the building occupant.

Noise is increasingly recognised as a health issue in urban areas, with over 30% of Europeans living in areas where 55 dB (WHO threshold) is exceeded. EU-funded research has shown this can cause interrupted sleep patterns, which can increase the risk of a range of health problems including type

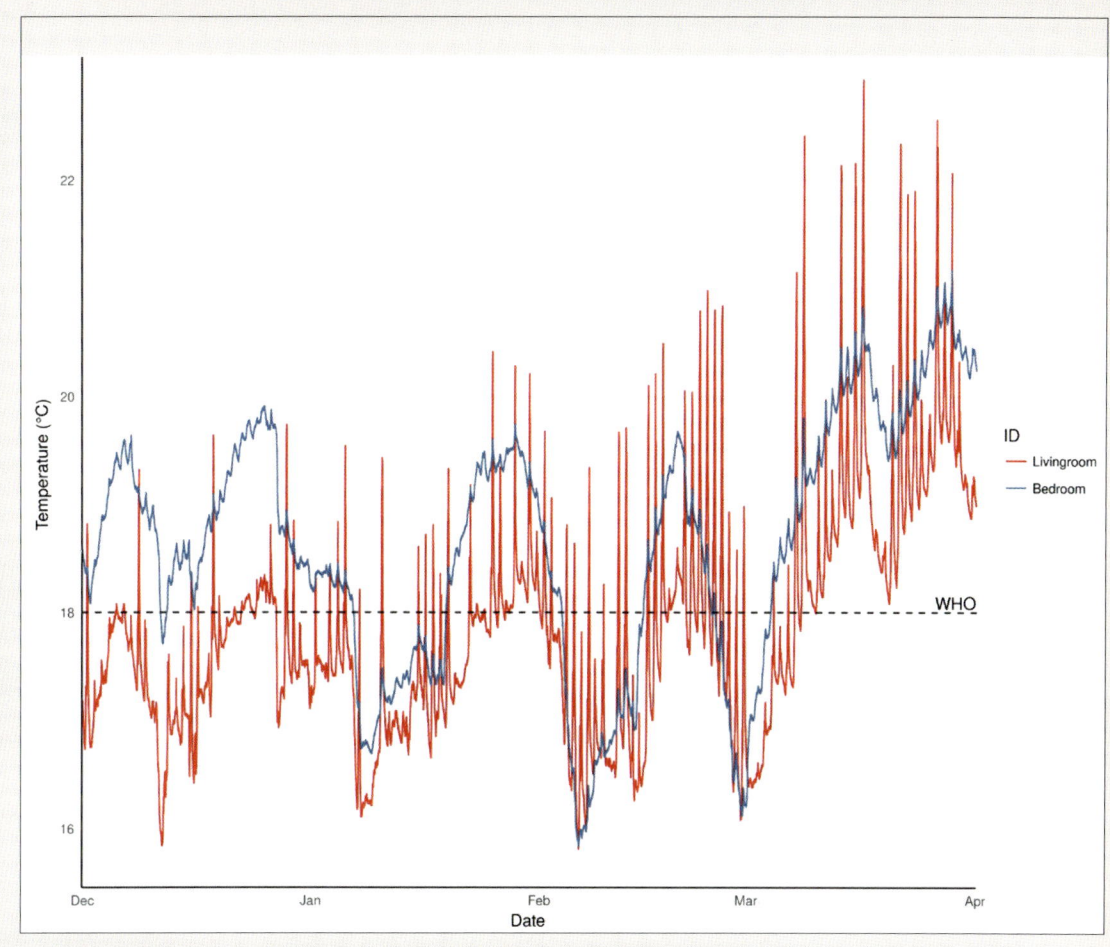

Fig 5.9: Wilmcote House – indoor temperatures in an empty and unheated flat during the extremely cold winter of 2017–18[26]

2 diabetes, and breast and distal colon cancer by up to 11% for every 10 dB increase in background noise.[27] While there has been relatively little research in this area, the acoustic performance of Passivhaus buildings has been shown to reduce background noise by approximately 10 dB (50%) for comparable wall types.[28]

Overheating is an issue common to many buildings, with approximately one in five overheating at current temperatures. Highly insulated newbuild properties of lightweight construction are particularly prone, with insufficient attention paid to this risk in the design phase. While UK building regulations require overheating risk to be modelled and reduced, it is widely known that the SAP methodology (Appendix P) is not a reliable design tool for this purpose.[29]

However, with increasing temperatures resulting from climate change it is estimated that over 50% of UK properties will overheat by 2050. In 2011, England's Health Protection Agency officially described overheating as a public health issue, and subsequent studies have shown that increased mortality occurs where external temperatures exceed 24°C. The heatwave of 2003 resulted in an additional 2,000 premature deaths, and the increasing likelihood of heatwaves will see this pattern repeated. Separately, it is estimated that approximately 3% of UK properties currently have comfort cooling; however, this is set to increase – with associated energy use and carbon emissions – unless passive measures can be used to reduce overheating risk. This problem must be tackled to reduce the impact on human comfort and avoid

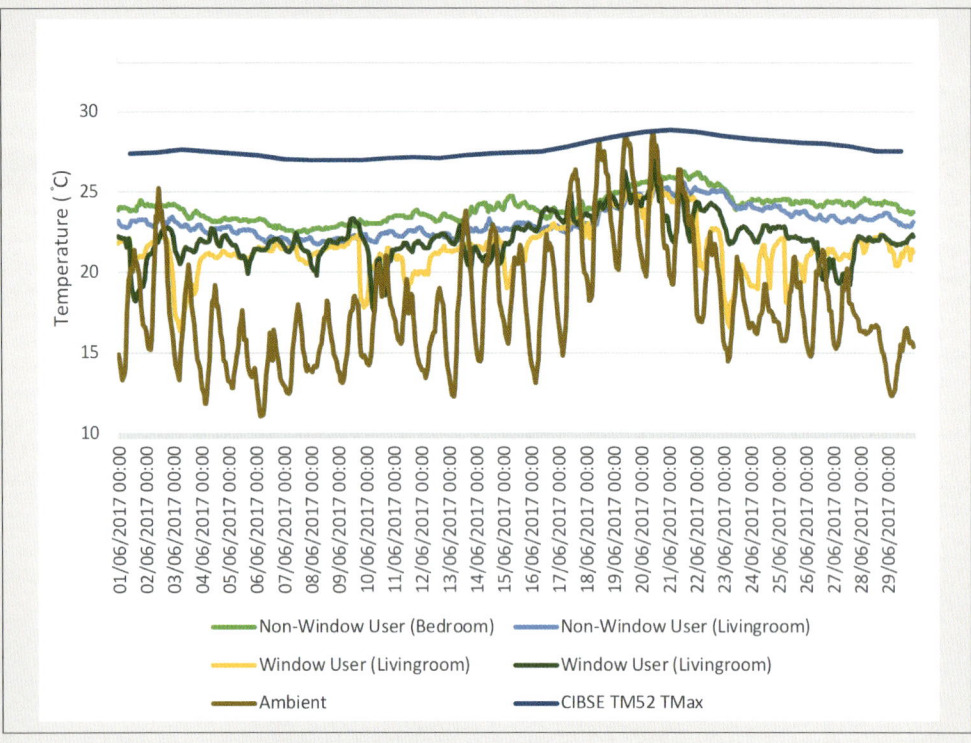

Fig 5.10: Wilmcote House: indoor air temperatures summer 2017[30]

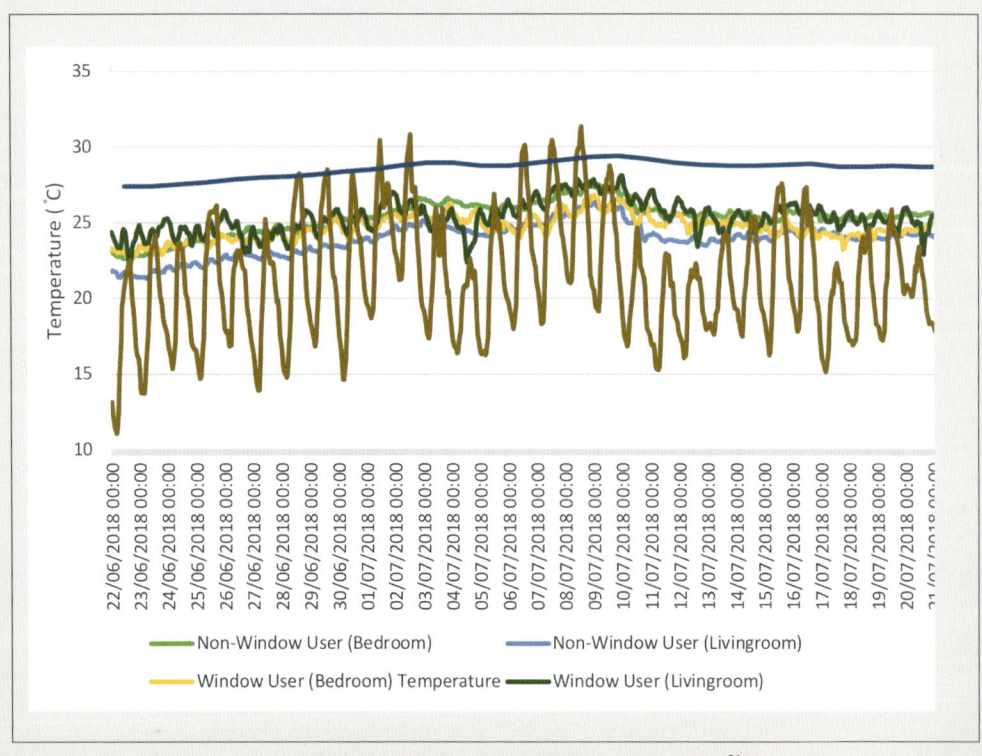

Fig 5.11: Wilmcote House: indoor air temperatures summer 2018 during five-week heatwave[31]

72　EnerPHit: A Step-by-Step Guide to Low Energy Retrofit

the risk of additional carbon emissions arising from comfort cooling. The increasing occurrence of heatwaves (such as that in summer 2018) will cause many properties to overheat, with single-aspect properties in urban areas at greatest risk.

Passivhaus and EnerPHit provide a good indication of overheating risk (steady-state, single-zone analysis) and how to reduce this. The PHPP model incorporates detailed modelling of glazing, shading and insulation coupled with local weather files, which can provide a good understanding of overheating risk. However, unless the boundary conditions can be accurately modelled, this should be augmented by dynamic modelling for more complex or multi-zonal buildings. Passivhaus buildings experience a high degree of thermal inertia, which means they are slow to cool down. Therefore it is particularly important to understand the impact of a warming climate and make the necessary adjustments to ensure that the building continues to provide thermal comfort to 2050 and beyond.[33] The case study for Wilmcote House offers a good indication of overheating risk for both a 'normal' year (2017) and a 'heatwave' year (2018). Figs 5.10 and 5.11 show that the risk of overheating increases but remains below CIBSE recommended threshold levels. Further improvement is possible by opening windows to benefit fom night-cooling.

5.6: ENERPHIT QUALITY STANDARD

Quality control in the construction industry is an increasingly important issue, with several high-profile retrofit failures in the UK alone.[33] The impact of poor-quality retrofit on energy efficiency can be severe, as outlined in the Arbed programme in Wales.[34] Quality control is also an issue in the newbuild sector, with house builders facing increasing criticism for poor performance.[35] Since the Grenfell Tower disaster, building regulations and the approval and sign-off process for design and construction have also come under scrutiny.[36] While there are several quality control issues to resolve in design, construction and delivery of retrofit, as outlined in the Bonfield review,[37] there are encouraging signs (e.g. PAS 2030: 2017) that if implemented PAS 2035: 2018 would offer a more comprehensive methodology for retrofit in the future. The impact of BIM on existing information would also

improve the ability of building owners to accurately predict future maintenance, and would hopefully further raise the standard of design, construction and handover of information.

Improvements to design and construction methodology require appropriate performance benchmarks to ensure the right targets are set and achieved. These benchmarks must provide clear, unambiguous, independent building performance outputs that are based on real-world findings and designed to suit the location and the building. These outputs can then be compared against similar building types to determine the success of the project. These benchmarks cannot be offset against other criteria or downgraded to suit short-term political requirements, but must offer a fixed standard that is either achieved or not. Only by providing clear signals to industry with appropriate guidance can performance improve, and costs reduce.

5.7: EIGHT REASONS TO TARGET ENERPHIT

Given the benefits outlined above, there are eight main reasons why EnerPHit should be considered as our performance target for retrofit of most building types:

1. **The EnerPHit standard offers clear outputs in a widely understood metric ($kWh/m^2/a$) providing the drastic reduction in energy consumption and carbon emissions that are required by 2050.**

2. **The EnerPHit standard provides significantly improved thermal comfort to building users with associated benefits to health and wellbeing.**

3. **The EnerPHit standard offers the necessary quality control measures built into design and delivery, which ensures actual performance more closely matches design performance.**

4. **The EnerPHit standard is built on the internationally tried and tested**

Passivhaus methodology over 25 years with rigorous performance requirements and scrutiny.

5. The EnerPHit standard can be applied on an incremental basis as part of a long-term retrofit plan.

6. The EnerPHit standard offers a futureproof solution, avoiding the risk of lock-in caused by modest, unplanned retrofit.

7. The EnerPHit standard significantly reduces the risk of unintended consequences such as condensation and mould growth from poor-quality retrofit.

8. The EnerPHit standard can offer a cost-neutral (or indeed cost-positive) outcome if coordinated with existing planned maintenance and future energy savings are recovered (see the case study for Wilmcote House).

5.8: DOES ENERPHIT CERTIFICATION MATTER?

EnerPHit certification requires the project team to follow the processes outlined in detail in the *Building Certification Guide*.[38] Unlike many other standards there are fixed performance criteria designed to suit the local climatic conditions, and the project team cannot ignore the poor performance of one part of the scheme and rely on the good performance of another part (offsetting). The project team are also required to prove to the certifier the actual performance in use rather than rely on assumptions or 'rules of thumb' (e.g. thermal bridging) common to many national standards, including those in the UK. The certifier is an independent third party that has a duty (to the PHI) to uphold the standard and requires evidence that the project seeking certification has met all relevant criteria. This requirement to prove performance to a third party ensures the outcome is far more likely to resemble the design. Provided this is written into the contract, it gives the contractor a very clear set of performance criteria, and the client an assurance of clear scrutiny.

Where EnerPHit cannot be achieved in a single refurbishment, the step-by step process provides a clear pathway to achieve the standard over the long term with pre-certification and agreed incremental targets. Alternatively, for complex, challenging projects EnerPHit(i) can be targeted using Passivhaus-certified components (see the Heinsberg Church case study). However, as described previously, due to various constraints EnerPHit may not be possible on all buildings (even in the long term), and the low-energy building standard described in chapter 2 is offered with certification at a slightly lower standard of 30 kWh/m^2/a. In the UK the AECB standard requiring 40 kWh/m^2/a can also be used, although this comes with caveats when applied to retrofit projects.

If the building owner doesn't regard EnerPHit certification as important, does it still matter? To ensure the quality control benefits of achieving this benchmark (as described above), the short answer might be yes. If the building owner wants to target a broader definition of sustainability and include factors such as water consumption, travel, pollution, etc., and compare this against other buildings using BREEAM or LEED, EnerPHit certification may not be a priority. Nevertheless, the rigorous nature of the PHPP calculation methodology offers the building owner and designer a far more reliable indication of current and future performance than other statutory certification tools. Coupled with plug-ins such as designPH (using SketchUp) or Passivlink (using Revit), PHPP is an effective design tool that shows the designer and client the immediate impact of early design decisions. It also shows the steps necessary to reduce energy consumption to EnerPHit and Passivhaus levels, if the building owner decides this is a priority. Whether these benchmarks are required, PHPP still provides a good indication of potential performance. Without certification, the difficulty may be enforcing design intent and converting potential to actual performance.

5.9: FINANCING ENERPHIT

If a building owner wishes to pursue EnerPHit and would prefer to achieve this in a single phase (perhaps due to vacant possession) but does not have sufficient finance, how can this be resolved? The UK public sector has access to very low interest rates (approximately 2% over 10 years) via the Public Works Loan Board (PWLB) and could in theory borrow against future energy savings if these can be recovered by the landlord. However, UK local authority landlords are typically restricted by central government from borrowing to retrofit, which means that retrofit projects are generally self-financed and augmented by whatever grant funding (ECO or similar) is available at the time.

In the private residential sector there are a few initiatives such as that run by KfW bank in Germany, which supports the refurbishment of existing residential properties through grants of up to €30,000 and loans depending on the predicted performance of the building, but since the closure of the Green Deal there have been no other major sources of private-sector funding for retrofit. However, two recent projects funded under the EU Horizon 2020 programme suggest how future funding for retrofit might be secured against future energy saved in both the private and public sectors.

- **EuroPACE is the European arm of a US initiative which has over 50 schemes in development in the US across 20 states with $4.7 billion invested. It offers 100% funding to all parts of the private sector (including residential) for a range of measures, including heating/ventilation, lighting, insulation, water pumps, renewable energy systems, motors and controls. Loans are typically for up to 20 years and (like Green Deal) remain with the property, transferring to the new owner on sale. Unlike Green Deal the interest rates are more commercially attractive. It should be noted that PACE requires property laws to be amended, although at the time of writing 33 US states have already passed the necessary legislation to allow the recovery of investments. EuroPACE does not specify a performance standard, but the measures installed are required to achieve sufficient savings to cover the investment. Given the strong correlation between designed and actual performance, EnerPHit is a good fit with EuroPACE financing.**

- **Energiesprong is a Dutch initiative which has successfully retrofitted several hundred homes in the Netherlands. The offsite modularisation of retrofit is described in chapter 3, but the financing of the project from future energy saved plus the increased value of the property offers an attractive solution which several public-sector landlords in the UK (e.g. Nottingham City Homes) are pursuing. However, while Energiesprong reduces carbon emissions through deep retrofit and use of low-carbon technologies, it does not target the ultra-low-energy consumption of the EnerPHit standard. It also does not offer third-party certification of quality, relying instead on a long-term performance agreement for energy supply. Like EuroPACE it requires the energy savings to be recovered directly by the energy provider, which may not be possible on all projects. Nevertheless, Energiesprong may offer a credible alternative for many public-sector landlords who wish to pursue deep retrofit.**

5.10: IMPLEMENTING ENERPHIT FOR ALL

A number of local authorities around the world have adopted Passivhaus as a standard for newbuild development, including Oslo, Vancouver, New York, Dún Laoghaire, Dublin, Brussels, Exeter and Norwich, plus numerous cities in Germany. However, this is not typically a mandatory requirement; it is instead encouraged as a means of achieving or exceeding other local regulations such as nZEB. Unlike statutory tools, PHPP provides the designer with the information necessary to make informed design choices with a single metric of performance that can be applied to all building types. As a result, the early uptake of Passivhaus has largely been driven by design professionals rather than policymakers. The success of the Passivhaus/EnerPHit standard

Fig 5.12: Impact pathway map[39]

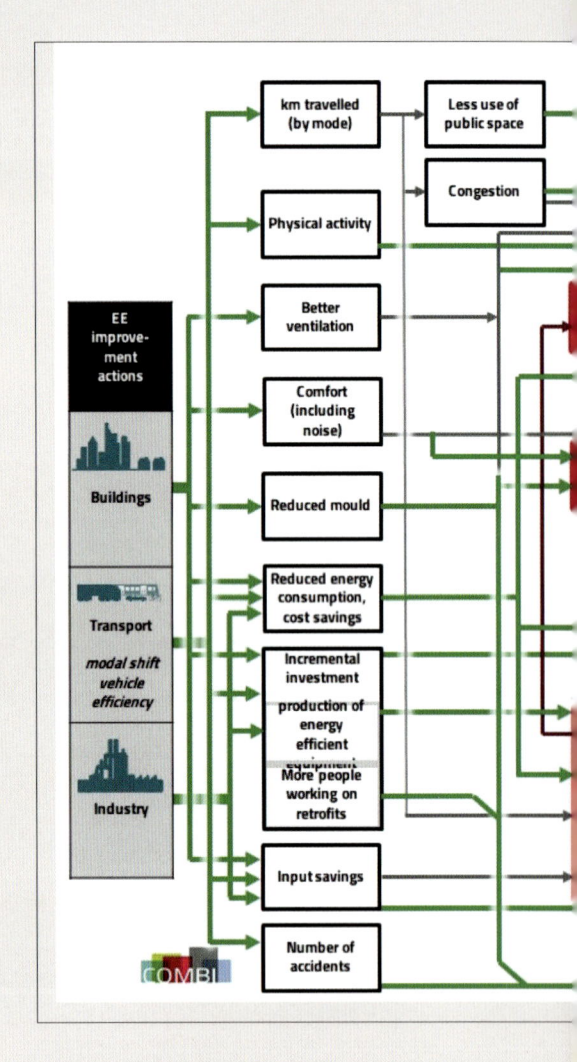

is perhaps due to its independence from political influence. It should be offered as a long-term strategy for improving the comfort, efficiency and performance of buildings that can be phased to suit the requirements of the building owner.

5.11: SUMMARY

Looking at the recently completed EU-funded COMBI project,[40] which considered 21 key energy-efficiency improvements (EEIs) and the multiple impacts of their implementation in all sectors across all member states, this study was extremely wide-ranging and improvements to buildings were only one aspect of many issues considered (see Fig 5.12). In each case the political, economic and societal benefits of each measure were considered, covering issues such as air pollution, resources, social welfare, macro-economic impacts and energy security.

The refurbishment of buildings in both the residential and commercial sectors offers some of the biggest opportunities for energy efficiency and economic growth (see Fig 5.13).

COMBI impact pathway synthesis

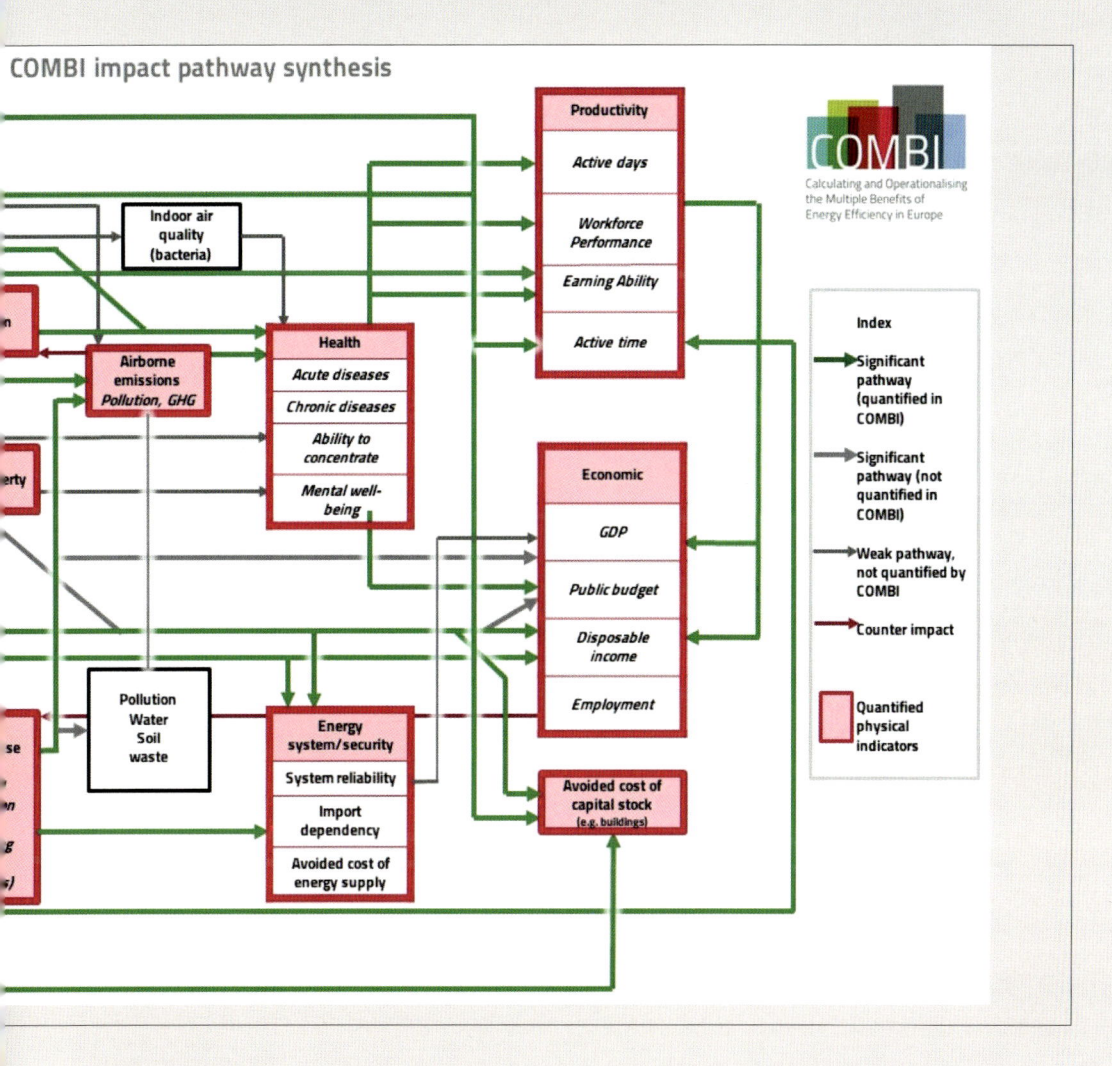

Fig 5.13: Energy savings (all fuels EU28) in TWh/year in 2030 by EEI action[41]

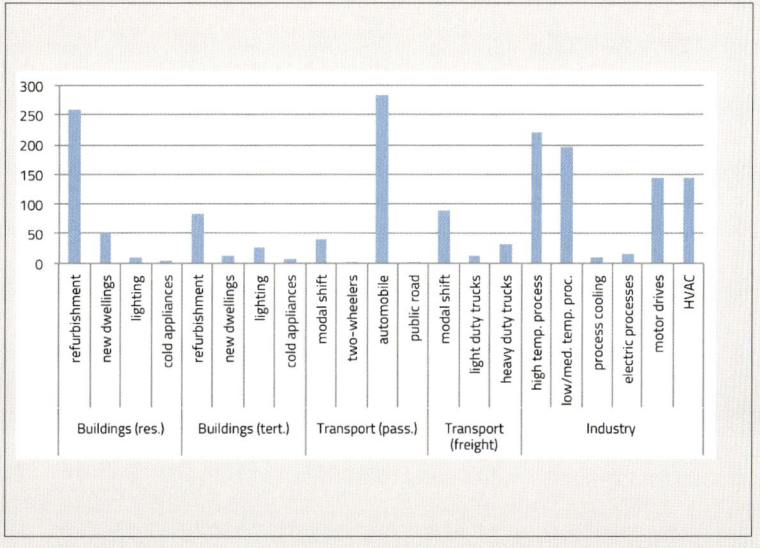

Targeting EnerPHit 77

6.0: Residential Case Studies

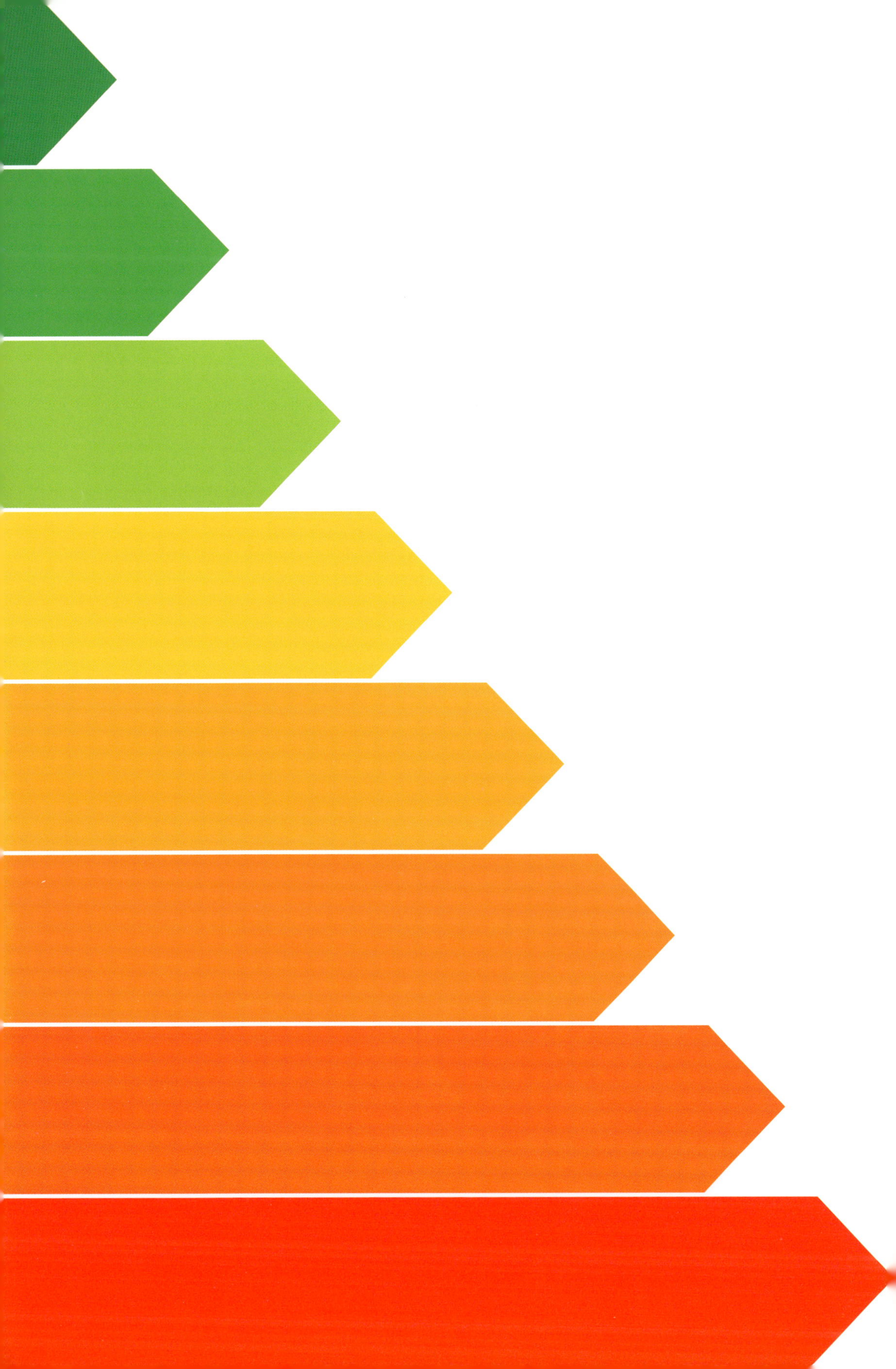

6.1: ACHIEVING ENERPHIT IN THE RESIDENTIAL SECTOR

The housing sector represents the single biggest energy consumer in the UK (approximately 29%)[1] and is a major contributor to carbon emissions (approximately 14%).[2] In the residential sector emissions are closely linked to building performance, with space heating forming the largest contributor to carbon emissions at over 40%, as shown in Fig 6.1.

As a result of government policies, especially since 2008, there has been progress in some parts of the domestic sector, and the overall SAP rating has improved. However, the simplistic methodology (RdSAP) used to generate EPCs for existing domestic buildings may be underestimating the scale of heat losses. As shown in Figs 6.2 and 6.3, the majority of cavity walls and lofts are now insulated, but there is still a huge proportion of solid-wall properties that remain uninsulated. These properties are typically pre-1918 and private sector (95%), and as such are often labelled as 'hard to treat'. If these properties were a small proportion of the total they could perhaps be ignored. Similarly, if the energy consumption of these properties were not significantly worse than modern dwellings we might accept the lower performance and trade-off against improved performance elsewhere.

Unfortunately, the number and performance of these older properties results in disproportionately high carbon emissions, and taken together with pre-1945 properties (many of which are also solid-wall) represent approx 48% of UK domestic carbon emissions (see Figs 6.4 and 6.5).

The average SAP results across pre-war UK housing hide the ultra-poor performance of many older detached properties, which are among the worst performing in Europe (see Fig 6.6). Note the scale difference between the UK and other countries.

Until 2008, energy-efficiency improvements were restricted to piecemeal measures such as double-glazing, loft insulation and cavity wall insulation. These measures were generally installed at relatively low risk by small local contractors without any requirement to consider the wider implications of their work. Since 2008 UK government policies have

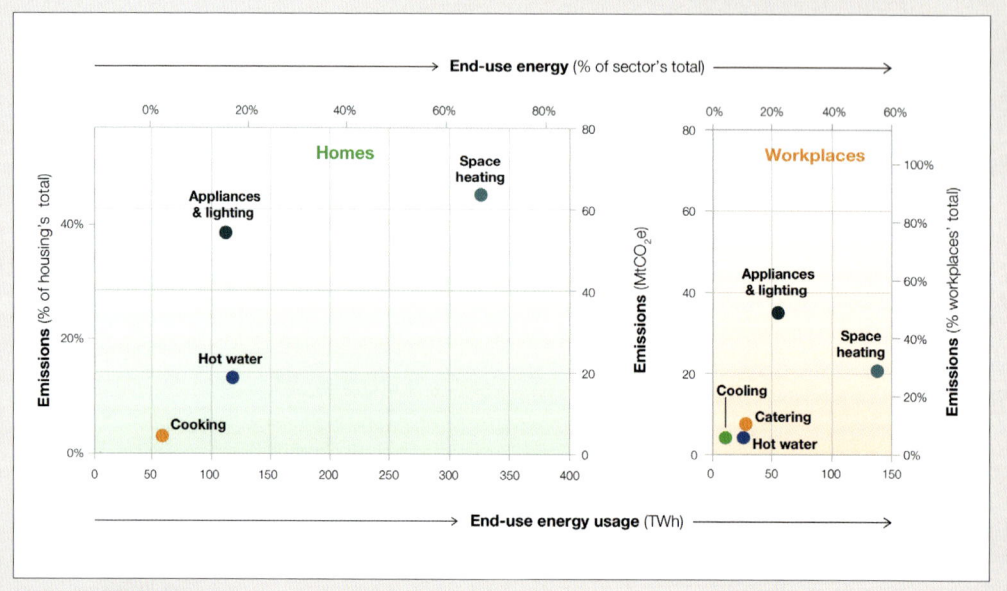

Fig 6.1: Proportion of carbon emissions and energy consumption from buildings in the residential and commercial sectors[3]

80 EnerPHit: A Step-by-Step Guide to Low Energy Retrofit

Fig 6.2: Remaining potential to insulate the housing stock in Great Britain, April 2013

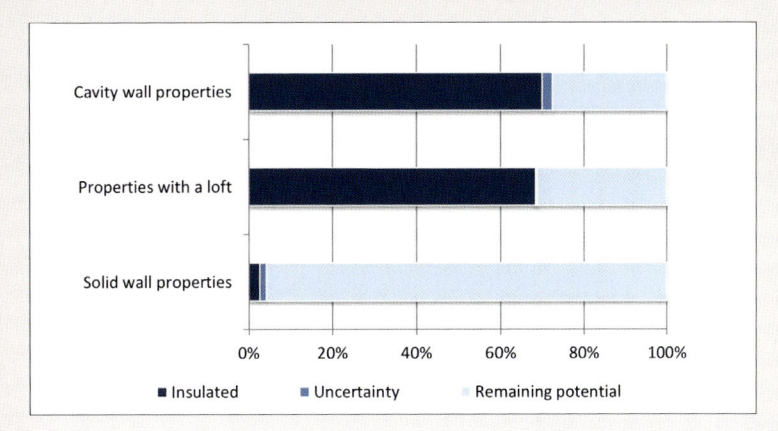

Fig 6.3: Insulation measures undertaken in Great Britain (2002–12)[4]

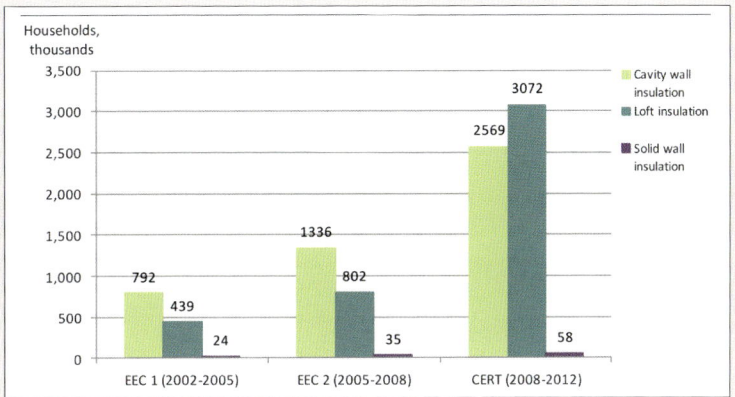

Fig 6.4: Proportion of UK dwellings by age[5]

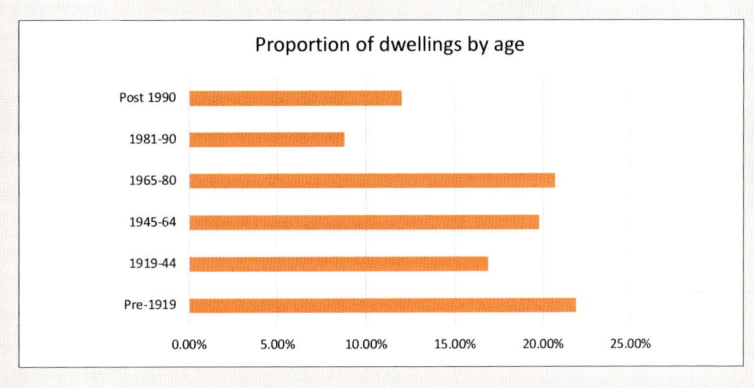

Fig 6.5: Proportion of UK domestic CO_2 emissions by dwelling age[6]

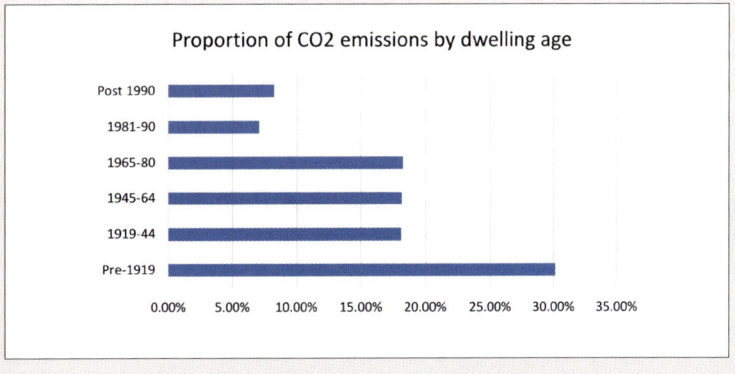

Residential Case Studies 81

Fig 6.6a & 6.6b: Average final consumption levels for heating (kWh/m^2/a) of single-family homes by construction year[7]

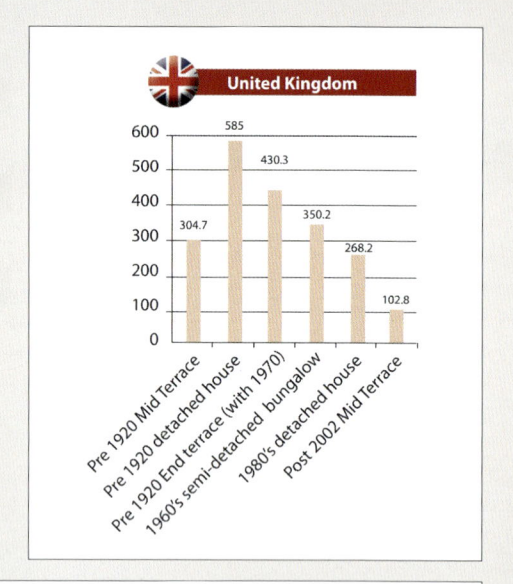

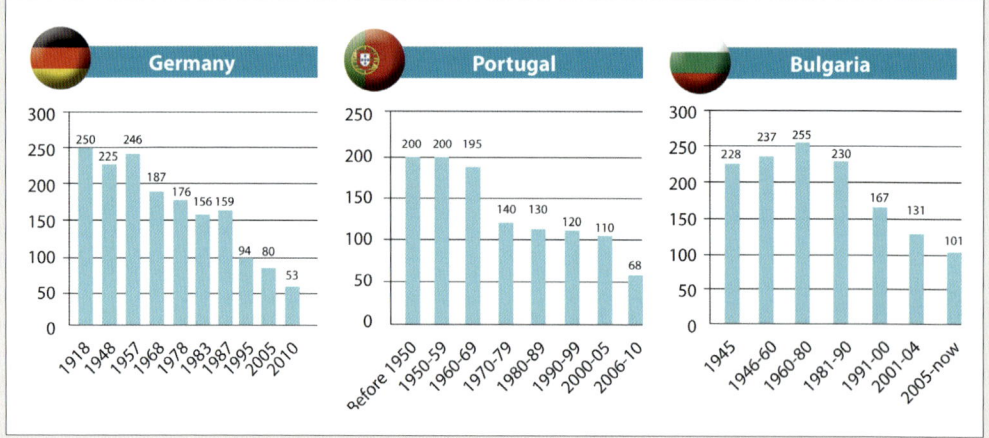

encouraged deeper retrofit with important pilot projects (as described in chapter 3). There has been some success insulating solid-wall properties in the affordable housing sector, but the private sector (which represents 95% of the older stock) remains largely uninsulated (see Fig 6.8). In translating this to widespread application (such as the Green Deal programme) there have been key failures, with poor value, poor customer service and poor technical delivery resulting in limited uptake.

At the same time UK government funding of building retrofit has been extremely inconsistent, causing frustration among both building owners and contractors. A number of important publications have since been produced which consider what went wrong[8] and why,[9] and what needs to be done next.[10]

The next generation of deep retrofit must consider buildings in a holistic way, and retrofit solutions must be tailored to the specific requirements of the building. Retrofit solutions must also target the appropriate benchmark, with sufficient quality control to achieve long-term savings and prevent the lock-in of partial measures. EnerPHit implemented on a step-by-step basis offers the best long-term solution and should be considered as part of a new national residential retrofit programme.

Housing is perhaps the only universal building typology which everyone requires from cradle to grave. Everyone needs a roof over their head, and the luxury of that 'roof' will be determined by the ability of the person to pay. However, the implications of a very poor-quality 'roof' are typically very high

Fig 6.7: Energy efficiency (SAP) by tenure[11]

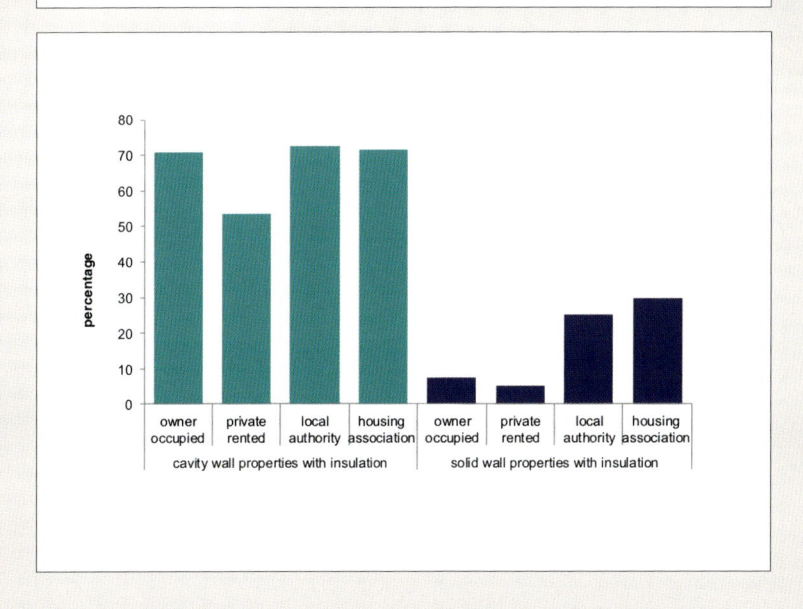

Fig 6.8: Wall insulation by main type and tenure[12]

Residential Case Studies 83

Fig 6.9: Final energy consumption (TWh) by sector (2012)[13]

- Non energy use: 88
- Other: 25
- Commercial and public administration: 197
- Industry: 293
- Housing: 502
- Road transport: 459
- Air transport: 144
- Other transport: 16

Fig 6.10: Projected UK policy savings for final energy consumption (2015–30)[14]

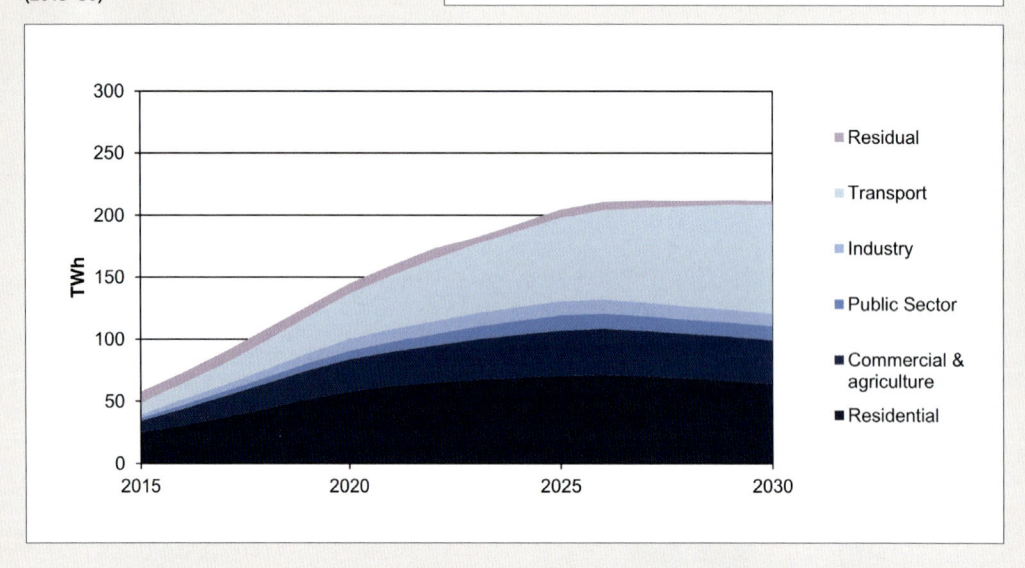

energy costs, which coupled with low income will result in fuel poverty. Fig 6.11 shows that a significant proportion (approximately 34%) of people in England (across all housing sectors) are unable to heat their homes satisfactorily. This fact alone should be reason enough for deep retrofit.

Housing ownership in the UK comes in three main forms, with private owner-occupied properties forming the largest part at approximately 63%; private rented properties represent approximately 20%; the remaining 17% are 'affordable' housing provided by either the local authority or a registered social landlord (i.e. Housing Association). In addition, there are specialist housing typologies to serve needs such as sheltered housing for the elderly and student housing, both of which can be found in the private and public sectors.

The five case studies selected in this chapter reflect these three main forms of ownership and two types of occupancy, with affordable housing, sheltered housing, student housing, private owner-occupied housing and private rented housing. They reflect

84 EnerPHit: A Step-by-Step Guide to Low Energy Retrofit

a wide range of housing typologies with high-, low- and medium-rise flats, a terraced property and a semi-detached listed building. They also reflect the two least energy-efficient forms of housing in pre-1918 properties and post-war prefabricated buildings. Finally, they have been selected to demonstrate that EnerPHit can be achieved across a broad range of locations and climatic zones, with properties in the UK, Ireland, USA and Latvia. All properties have either achieved or are seeking to achieve EnerPHit in a single or step-by-step process. As such they show that EnerPHit can be applied to a wide range of building typologies, ownership and budgets. However, they also demonstrate the challenges that need to be addressed in any deep retrofit project, and how these might be overcome.

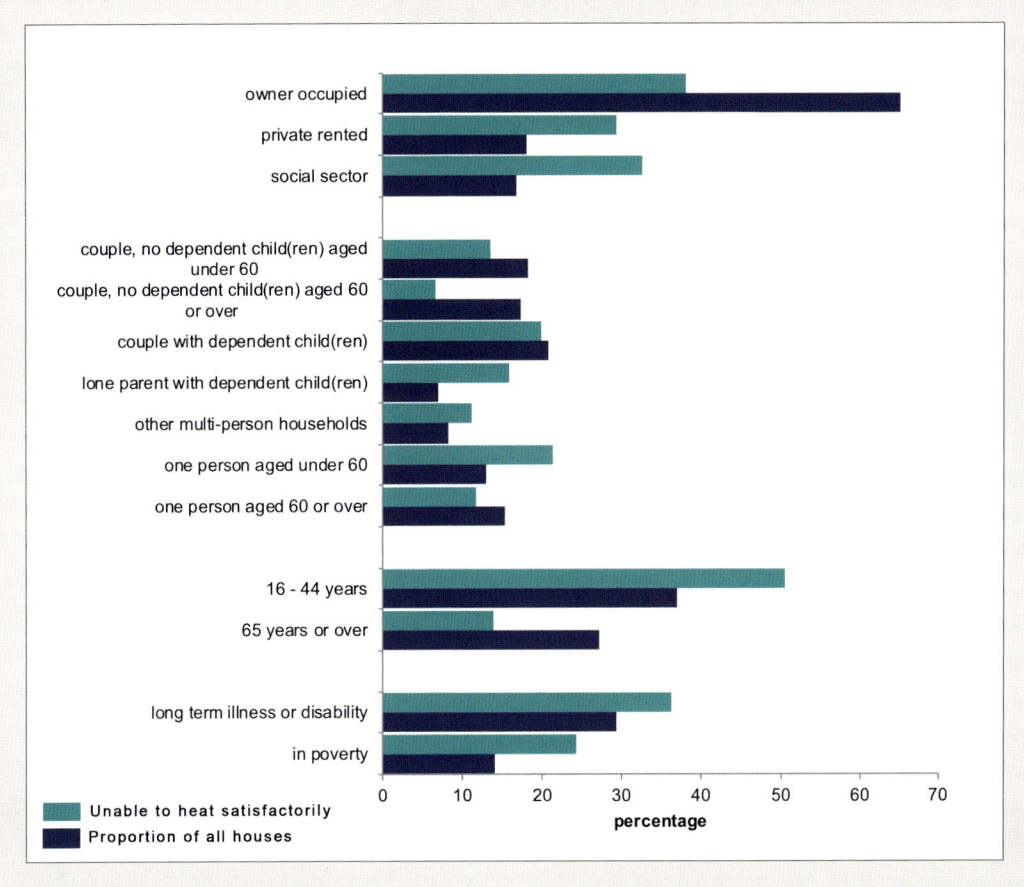

Fig 6.11: English households underheating their home compared to the overall distribution of households (2012)[15]

Residential Case Studies **85**

CASE STUDY 6.2

Affordable Housing
Wilmcote House, Portsmouth, UK

Client:	Portsmouth City Council
Architect:	Energy Conscious Design (ECD)
QS:	Keegans
M&E:	NLG
Structural Engineer:	Wilde Carter Clack
Contractor:	Engie
Contractor Design Team:	GSA Architects; Design Buro; Curtins Engineers

INTRODUCTION

Wilmcote House provides 111 flats of affordable housing for social rent in Somerstown, Portsmouth, and is an 11-storey development comprising three interlinked blocks with a combined treated floor area (TFA) of 10,233 m². It was built in 1968 and is a prefabricated concrete structure of large panel system (LPS) using the Bison Reema system. Following the partial collapse of a similar LPS building at Ronan Point (East London) in the same year, measures were taken to remove gas from all LPS buildings in the UK, and in some cases, carry out strengthening as necessary. As a result, the flats at Wilmcote House were heated by old and inefficient electric storage heaters. The existing concrete panels incorporated a very small amount of insulation, but this was ineffective, and the flats experienced extreme heat loss (see Fig 6.12). While double-glazed windows had been installed in the 1990s, they were relatively inefficient and required replacement.

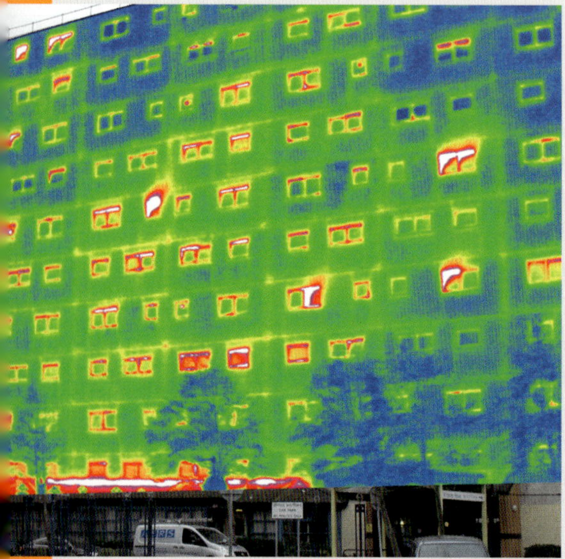

The high degree of heat loss and the expensive, inefficient heating system meant the residents suffered from extreme fuel poverty, as shown in resident feedback (see Fig 6.14).[16] A recent study showed that many residents were underheating their homes well below WHO recommendations, which exacerbated mould growth. As a result of this work and the ongoing deterioration of the block, the client sought options to address these issues. ECD Architects provided two options: the first being the installation of a communal heating system with insulation to the existing envelope in accordance with UK building regulations Part L2B; the second option was to super-insulate externally and simplify the existing envelope to the EnerPHit standard such that a new heating system would not be required. In this option ventilation would be provided by individual high-efficiency MVHR units installed in all flats with triple-glazed windows throughout. This resulted in increased capital cost of approximately 10%; however, the residents would benefit from extra fuel savings, improving their ability to pay

Fig 6.12: Heat loss (pre-retrofit)[17]

Fig 6.13: Heat loss (post-retrofit)[18]

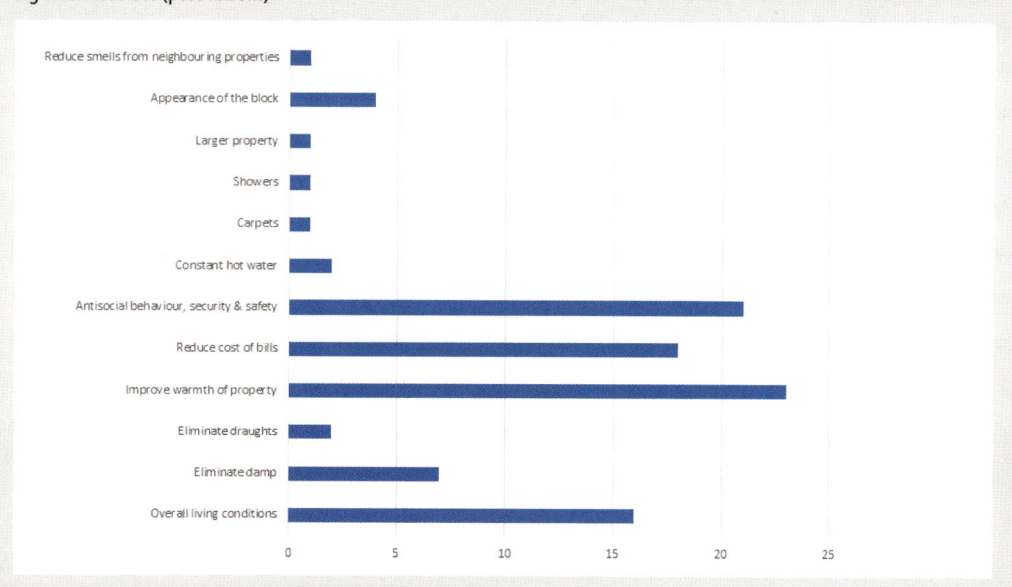

Fig 6.14: Resident feedback on the main purpose of the scheme[19]

Residential Case Studies   87

their rent. This study prompted Portsmouth City Council (PCC) to pursue the second option, and the project was designed to achieve the EnerPHit standard – tendered at £13 million. While this represents a considerable investment per property (£117,000), this was much lower than demolition and replacement costs and will secure the future of Wilmcote House for another 50 years.

KEY CHALLENGES

As an LPS building, the over-cladding strategy required careful coordination with the structural engineer, and it was agreed that all fixings in the existing panels should be avoided, with new structural framing fixed to existing party walls and party floors, as per Fig 6.17 on the road-side elevation. Figs 6.15 and 6.16 show how the thermal and airtightness strategy involved the simplification of the thermal envelope, with a new load-bearing steel frame erected on the garden-side elevation. This allowed the corridors to be enclosed and required the living rooms to be extended to meet the new building line. The residents required protection from the ongoing works, and temporary screens were erected across the affected living rooms, shown in Fig 6.18. During early consultation events, it became clear that residents were concerned about the loss of external space. New internal balconies were provided within the thermal envelope, providing a semi-external space next to the living room. The existing stair cores were refurbished but left uninsulated, and therefore it was necessary to thermally decouple these from the adjacent thermal envelope in blocks A, B and C.

While every effort was made to minimise the impact on residents, the most challenging part of the project was securing access for internal works to the flats, with multiple appointments to install and commission MVHR and complete internal detailing. The delivery

Fig 6.15: Three thermal airtight envelopes and stair cores[20]

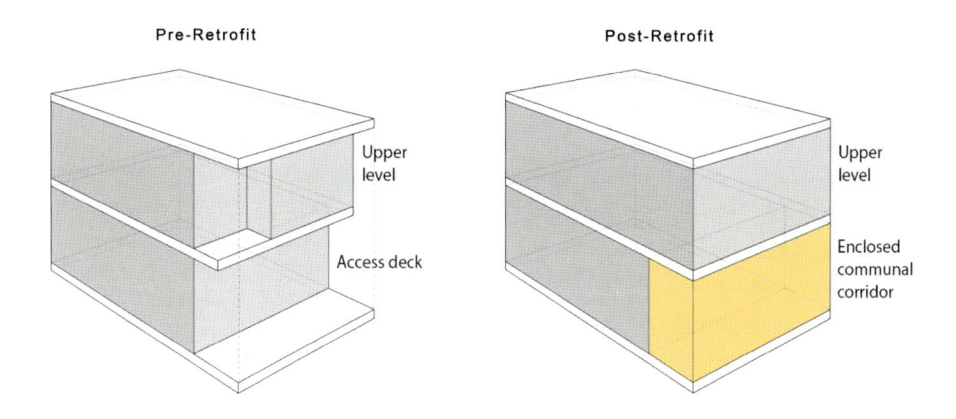

Fig 6.16: Maisonette: extension and enclosure of garden side[21]

of the project with residents in situ proved extremely challenging, and the original project programme of 111 weeks was extended by a further 18 months. This caused frustration on both sides, which in turn caused an unexpected issue at the end of the project, resulting in the inability to obtain access for a full airtightness test. To achieve EnerPHit certification, Wilmcote House will need to resolve this issue and address the PER threshold. Despite anecdotal evidence which suggests that many residents are no longer required to use their heating, the presence of existing electric storage heaters means that a small PV array (approximately 23 kWp) will need to be provided to achieve this standard in due course.

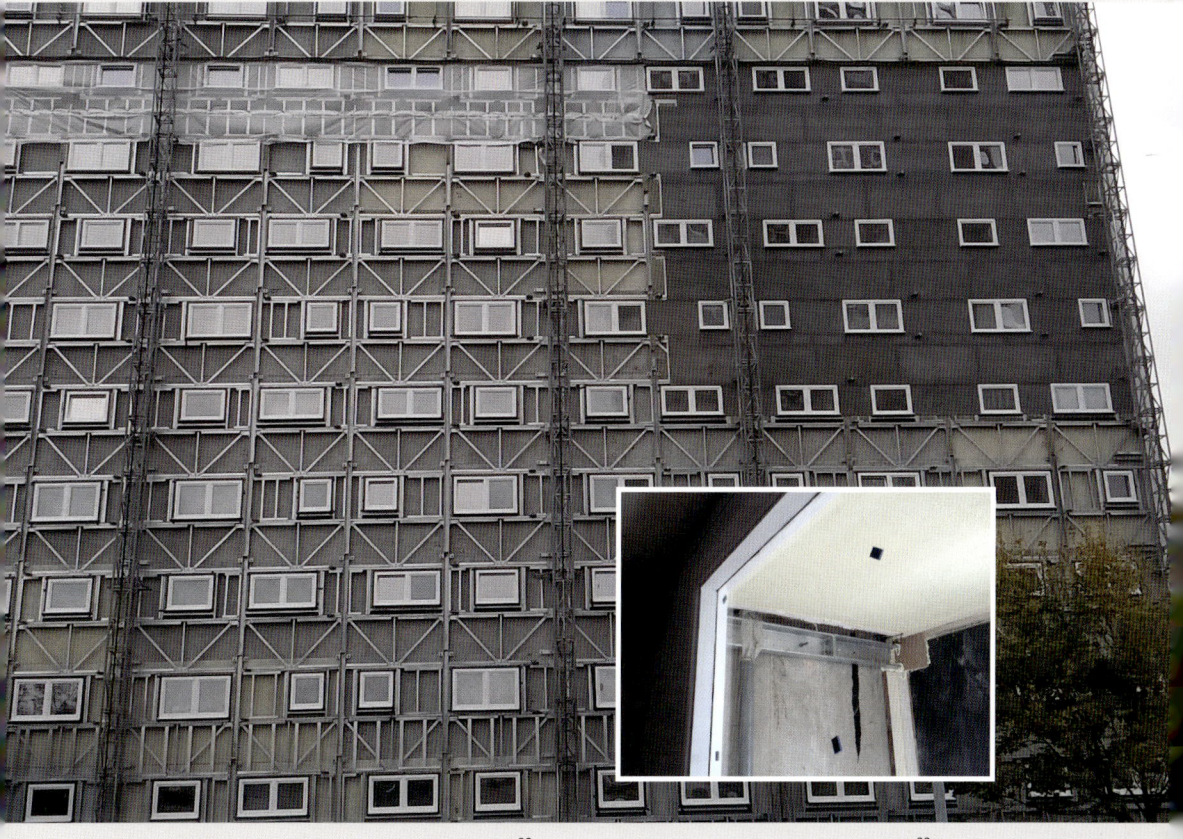

Fig 6.17: Framing to party floors on road-side elevation[22]

Fig 6.18: Temporary protective screens[23]

Residential Case Studies 89

KEY ACHIEVEMENTS

Having selected the EnerPHit option, the client sought to understand the implications of this approach to inform the future refurbishment of its 12 remaining high-rise buildings, and therefore partnered with the London School of Economics (LSE) and Rockwool in a research project which interviewed residents before, during and after the works. Meanwhile Southampton University continued to monitor internal temperatures to determine the impact of the works on winter fuel poverty and summer overheating risk. Wilmcote House was also selected as the UK case study for the EuroPHit project, and the project team benefited from additional support and training provided by the PHI (via BRE) to the client, consultants and contractor supply chain.

Aside from the eradication of fuel poverty and dissemination of the results, the project has achieved its other key objective, which was to radically overhaul the condition and appearance of the building with non-combustible insulation and ensure its long-term safety and sustainability. The thermal performance of the building fabric was radically improved, with the estimated space heating demand reduced from 188 kWh/m²/a to approximately 23 kWh/m²/a, and initial post-occupancy evaluation (POE) data from Southampton University suggests that performance is in line with predictions.

TECHNICAL STRATEGY

Due to the LPS nature of the building and poor-quality, weak concrete wall panels coupled with the very complex arrangement of the garden-side elevation, a bespoke solution was required on both primary elevations (see Figs 6.17 and 6.21). The poor quality of the existing concrete wall panels on the 'simpler' road-side elevation required a new secondary steel frame to be installed with fixings at each party floor (see Figs 6.17 and 6.19). Mineral

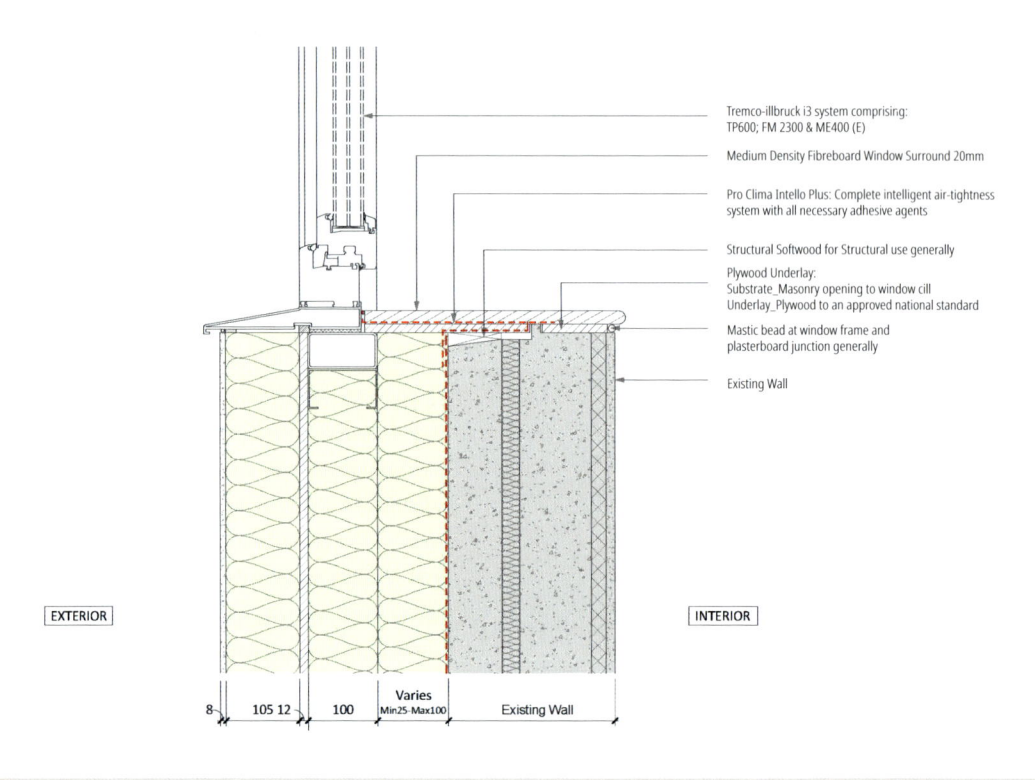

Fig 6.19: Road-side elevation (section detail)[24]

90 EnerPHit: A Step-by-Step Guide to Low Energy Retrofit

wool bats were installed 'full fill' within this frame, and loose mineral wool installed in the 'tolerance zone' of 25–100 mm between the face of the building and the frame. The airtight membrane was then applied with tapes at all openings and junctions, and a rigid board was fixed to the frame. Finally, 105 mm dense mineral wool was applied on top of this (preventing any thermal bridging), which then received an 8 mm render coat.

On the garden-side elevation, the proposal to simplify the complex form and enclose the deck access balconies required a new ground-bearing full-height steel frame to be erected (see Fig 6.21). The 'gap' between the frame and the existing building was then enclosed, and living rooms on all floors extended to meet the new structure. Fig 6.20 shows how the insulation was also applied within the steel frame, which received the airtight layer and rigid board before additional insulation and a render coat were applied.

As an occupied building, it was not practical to insulate the ground floor slab, so a thermal skirt was created below DPC using 200 mm XPS insulation to a depth of 1 m. Passivhaus-certified components were used wherever possible, with triple-glazed windows to all heated areas and individual MVHR units to each flat. The existing roof was poorly insulated and flat, with internal rainwater pipes causing maintenance problems. As a result, the new roof was pitched with new external rainwater pipes and extra-thick insulation filling the large void. The steel structure of the new roof was also decoupled with thermal break pads to prevent any thermal bridging. While most of the components used were PH-certified, there were no certified steel doors available at that time. These were needed for the communal areas, and alternative aluminium doors were not suitably robust. The design team therefore worked with the manufacturer to ensure that these provided acceptable airtightness.

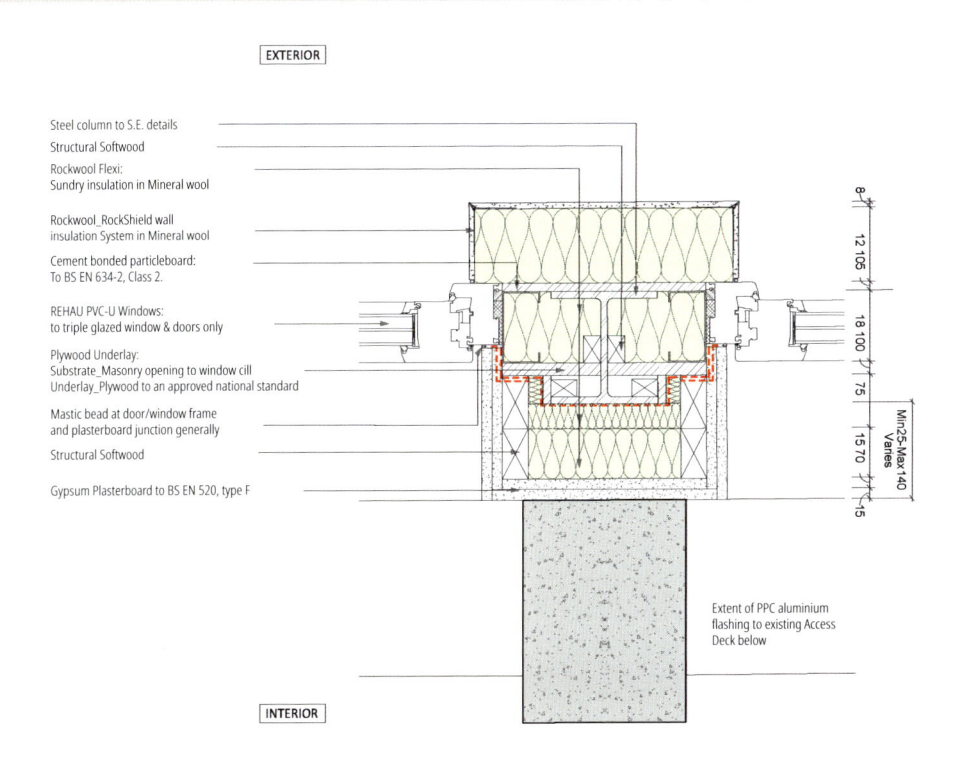

Fig 6.20: Garden-side elevation (plan detail)[25]

Fig 6.21: Garden-side elevation during construction[26]

POST-COMPLETION

As part of the ongoing research projects both the LSE and Southampton University continue to monitor the performance of the building and the satisfaction of the residents. Southampton University results for the winter and summer seasons have shown that the building can provide thermal comfort in winter with little or no active heating, while the risk of overheating in the summer can be reduced. Ongoing research by Southampton University will consider the role of passive 'night cooling' in a warming climate. LSE interviewed residents before, during and after the works and feedback has shown that further support is required to ensure residents understand the ventilation strategy. Although construction works extended well beyond the original completion date, causing frustration to all parties, the completed building is very popular.

Fig 6.22: Garden-side elevation on completion[27]

CASE STUDY 6.3

Sheltered Housing
Rochestown, Phase 2, Dún Laoghaire, Ireland

Client:	DLR Council
Architect:	DLR Council
QS:	Walsh Associates
M&E:	Ramsay Cox & Associates
Structural Engineer:	Hanley Pepper Associates
PH Consultant:	MosArt
Fire Safety Consultant:	John A. McCarthy
Contractor:	Manley Construction

Fig 6.23: Existing building[28]

Fig 6.24: Rooftop extension[29]

INTRODUCTION

This project was also part of the EuroPHit scheme (see Fig 4.3) and, like Wilmcote House, the team sought to achieve EnerPHit in a single phase with a deep retrofit solution for 34 flats with a TFA of 1856 m². The project was tendered in July 2014 and the works started on site in November 2014, completing in August 2016. This project is also the second part of a three-phase scheme for the provision of sheltered housing at Rochestown. Phase 1 is a standard refurbishment, with Phase 3 being a newbuild infill scheme. It was designed by Dún Laoghaire Rathdown (DLR) Council, which owns and manages the facility, and was part of a wider retrofit and downsizing strategy for the council's housing stock of approximately 4,500 units. Unlike Wilmcote House, Rochestown Phase 2 was vacant during the project, which enabled greater access to undertake intrusive works. This was partly due to the fact that as bedsit accommodation the existing flats were unsuitable, so all remaining residents were decanted to the block previously refurbished in Phase 1.

Once vacant, the existing bedsit flats were merged to form one-bed flats (see Figs 6.25 and 6.26) and the block was extended vertically to provide a total of 34 flats (to ensure there was no overall loss of accommodation). Finally the block was wrapped externally (see Fig 6.27). The existing oil-fired boiler was removed, and a new natural gas district

Existing Plan

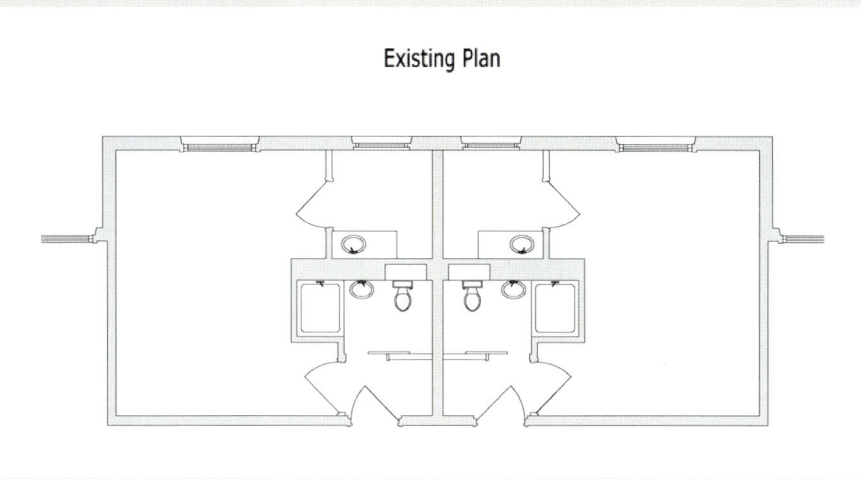

Fig 6.25: Existing bedsit flats (approximately 24m^2)[30]

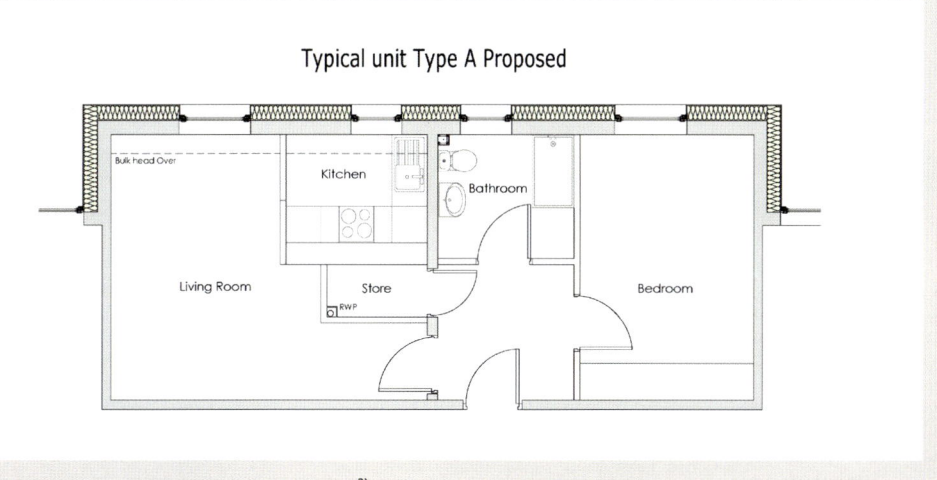

Typical unit Type A Proposed

Fig 6.26: Proposed one-bed flats (approximately 48m^2)

heating system installed. The existing building had no ventilation system and consequently had either poor air quality (windows closed) or excessive heat loss (windows open). New individual high-efficiency MVHR units were installed in all properties to reduce heat loss and improve air quality.

KEY CHALLENGES

Project challenges included the low ceiling heights and the resulting routing of pipework, and the impact this had on airtightness and fire strategies. The project team initially considered a communal ventilation system; however, the low ceiling heights made routing this impossible. Furthermore, the number of fire dampers would have reduced efficiency, and the weight of a single ventilation unit on the roof was problematic. The cost of additional fire dampers and increased risk of these being set off in multiple zones, potentially compromising fire safety, resulted in the decision to provide individual ventilation units to each flat. While it meant annual maintenance access would be required, it was regarded as equivalent to the normal servicing of gas-fired boilers. The position of the airtight membrane in the external wall was relocated from the internal face to the external face to improve coordination of construction trades and reduce the risk of this being damaged (see Fig 6.27). The communal heating system has also brought some overheating challenges in and around the plant room.

Residential Case Studies 95

150mm eps insulation board fixed structure with thermally broken mech fixing & adhesive render

Timber sections fixed with stainless steel angle bracket structural thermal break pads

3mm aluminium drip

3mm ventilated aluminium faced post on breather paper on 50mm eps insulation on plywood

Projecting window to be wbp plywood on continuous treated timber studs, voids filled with rockwool insulation

Timber Window to 0.80 u-value

250mm wide block on flat, 20mm sand cement & skim as airtight barrier

Lintol to engineers specification

Airtight membrane fixed to window frame

Fig 6.27: Airtight membrane on the inner face[31]

Fig 6.28: Windows brought forward into the new insulated zone[32]

Fig 6.29: Achieving airtightness at penetrations[33]

Other lessons learned included the modelling of the overheating risk in single-aspect dwellings. PHPP provides an indicative steady-state assessment of overheating risk for a single-zone building. However, Rochestown (Phase 2) is a multi-zonal building with single-aspect flats and therefore has no cross-ventilation. The risk is exacerbated by the existing east–west orientation of the block, which reduces the effectiveness of shading. While the G-value of the glazing on the west elevation was reduced during the design phase to minimise this risk, several flats on this elevation are experiencing high internal temperatures in the summer period. As a result, the project team are monitoring internal temperatures and may provide localised shading if necessary.

KEY ACHIEVEMENTS

As a result of the work, space heating demand has reduced from approximately 354 kWh/m²/a to 24 kWh/m²/a, and the associated heating cost has reduced from €53,000 per year to €4,000 per year.

Fig 6.30: Main entrance as completed[34]

Residential Case Studies

Fig 6.31: Front elevation as completed[35]

Feedback suggests that some tenants do not feel it necessary to switch on the heating during the winter.[36] Heating controls are very simple, with a single thermostat, and residents can also boost ventilation via a single switch.

The other key achievement has been to provide desirable, affordable and accessible sheltered accommodation of an appropriate size to suit current housing needs, enabling elderly residents in larger properties to downsize. The completed building has transformed the appearance of the development, and with the completion of all three phases will provide a mix of high-quality, futureproof accommodation.

TECHNICAL STRATEGY

Due to engineering constraints the weight of the rooftop extension had to be minimised, so aerated blocks were used with a lightweight metal roof deck. The airtight layer was installed on the exterior by taping the existing concrete panels and extending this up to meet the new blockwork. A parge coat was applied to the blockwork (aerated block on the top floor and new fire escape stairs to the north) to complete the airtight layer, with tapes at all openings and junctions. Typically, 200 mm EPS (150 mm to the timber rainscreen cladding facade on the top level, 200 mm on all the back and side elevations and 250 mm insulation is used on the ground and first floor facades below the timber rainscreen cladding top wall) external walls with 180–120 mm XPS insulation are used below ground. The insulation thickness is reduced at the new top floor in order to

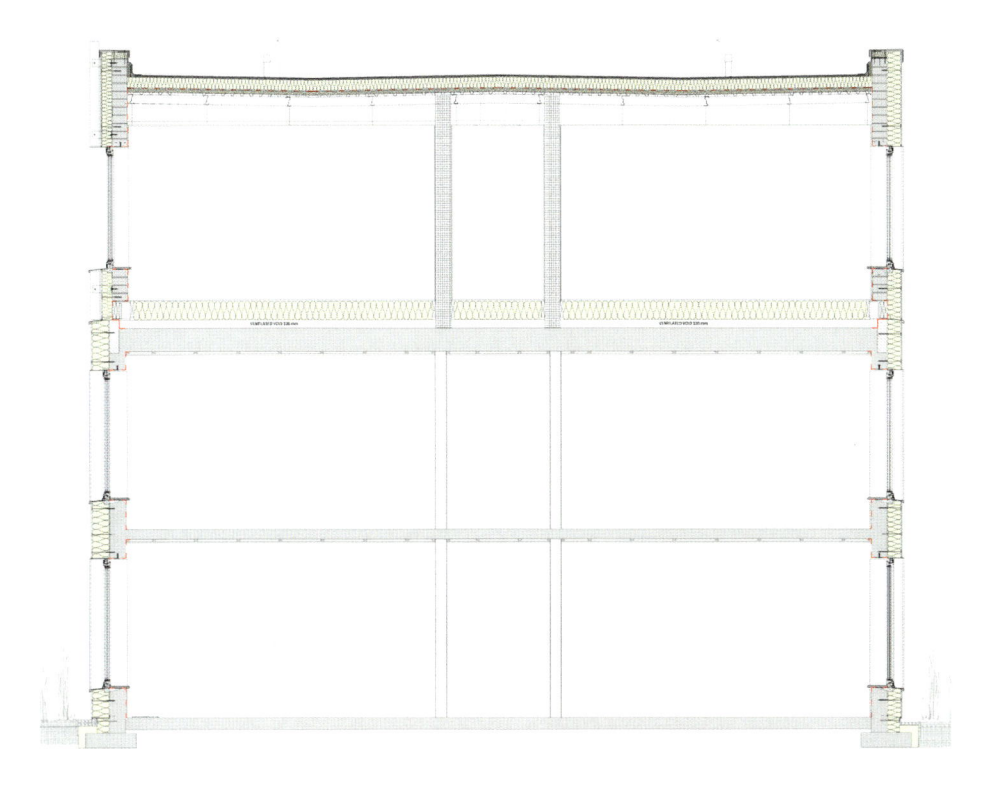

Fig 6.32: Cross-section showing rooftop extension and new insulated envelope[37]

create a flush detail between the render and timber rainscreen cladding above. While this reduced performance, the impact was modelled in PHPP to ensure this did not breach threshold requirements.

A gas-fired Dachs CHP is used, providing 5.5 kW electricity for communal lighting and 14.8 kW for hot water and space heating (via the district heating system and radiators) if required. Given the provision of communal facilities (commercial kitchen, laundry, etc.) and the intention to connect to Phase 3 when completed, a further three gas-fired boilers are also provided as back-up. Insulated pipework for the new district heating system is routed in the sub-floor of the new rooftop extension, and this drops through risers to the flats below. Zehnder MVHR units are provided to each flat and located in a lockable cupboard, with responsibility for maintenance and filter changes given to the local maintenance contractor.

POST-COMPLETION

The project once again provided communal facilities that had been present in the existing building, such as a hairdresser, laundry and community room with a commercial kitchen. These facilities have required mechanical services which would not ordinarily be required for a housing scheme, resulting in additional plant and a full building management system (BMS). At the time of writing these facilities were not in use, although with the completion of Phase 3 it is assumed that they will become operational. Nevertheless, the BMS system enables the team to monitor the ongoing performance of the building, and initial observations indicate that actual performance closely matches the modelled results and is reflected in low running costs.[38]

CASE STUDY 6.4

Student Housing
Ērgļi Vocational School, Latvia

Clients:	The Latvian Environmental Investment Fund, Ministry of Education and Science, Ērgļi Vocational Secondary School
Architect:	Krauklis Grende: Ervins Krauklis, Ilze Prusaka
QS:	Ripess: Andris Pavītols
M&E:	Jevgenijs Lurje
Structural Engineer	Ripess Ltd., Riga, Latvia
PH Consultant:	Mare Mitrevica
Contractor:	Kvadrum

Fig 6.33: Existing uninsulated building[39]

Fig 6.34: Completed building[40]

INTRODUCTION

Ērgļi Vocational School was established in the 1960s. The student housing currently accommodates between 200 and 230 pupils, and has a TFA of 3,521 m². The original five-storey student dormitory building was built in 1972 and was a Soviet-period design with same construction principles as 'Series 103' – a common multi-family flat type found throughout Latvia. The building is one of three occupied buildings on the site, including a teaching block and workshop, all served by a district heating system.

The building was uninsulated and had a calculated space heating demand of 154.8 kWh/m²/a. As a result of the poor thermal comfort of the existing building, the top two floors were unoccupied, as the school could not afford to heat these areas. Students were therefore overcrowded, with up to four students sharing a space of approximately 18 m². Considering this alongside the continuing deterioration of the building fabric, with windows beyond repair and a leaking roof, a decision was required on whether to upgrade the existing district heating and hot water system.

The client had intended to do a standard refurbishment with 75 mm insulation at an estimated cost of €170/m² incl. VAT at 21%. However, this would have required an upgrade to the existing district heating system with a new

Fig 6.35: Base detail[41]

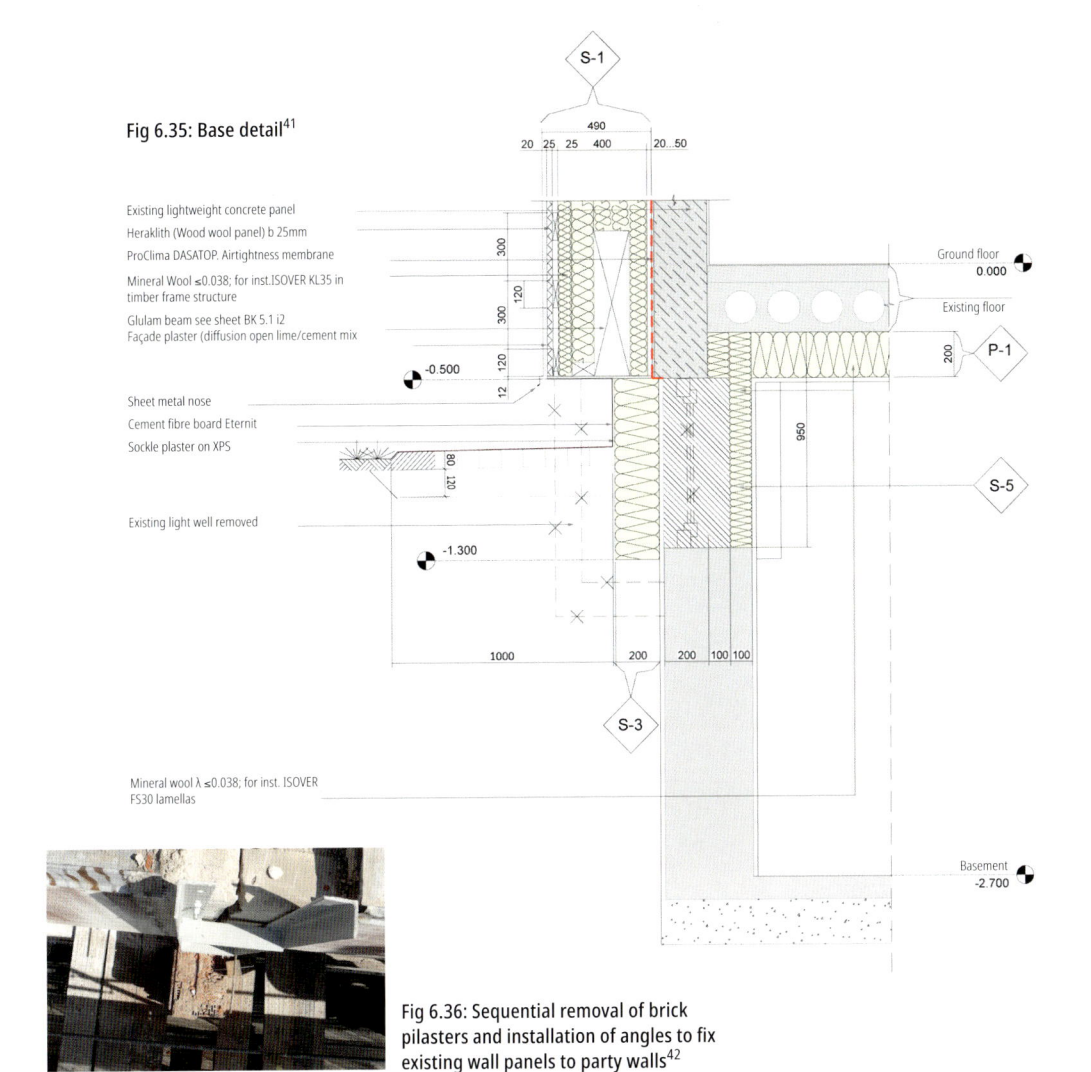

Existing lightweight concrete panel
Heraklith (Wood wool panel) b 25mm
ProClima DASATOP. Airtightness membrane
Mineral Wool ≤0.038; for inst.ISOVER KL35 in timber frame structure
Glulam beam see sheet BK 5.1 i2
Façade plaster (diffusion open lime/cement mix

Sheet metal nose
Cement fibre board Eternit
Sockle plaster on XPS

Existing light well removed

Mineral wool λ ≤0.038; for inst. ISOVER FS30 lamellas

Fig 6.36: Sequential removal of brick pilasters and installation of angles to fix existing wall panels to party walls[42]

boiler plant at an additional cost of €105,000. The EnerPHit refurbishment cost was €240/m² incl. VAT at 21%, but the district heating system cost could be avoided. The project team reviewed the feasibility options and life-cycle costs, and a decision was taken to pursue EnerPHit as the best long-term solution. The project was tendered at €844,740, and the works were carried out during the spring and summer of 2012 to minimise disruption to the school year and provide access to the vacant building. The adjacent workshop with TFA of 2055 m² and room heights from 3.5–5.5 m was retrofitted at the same time, albeit at a lower cost and benchmark standard, achieving 58 kWh/m²/a. This was a considerable improvement on the existing building, which previously required 340 kWh/m²/a and was heated only partially.

KEY CHALLENGES

Challenges included the poor construction quality of the existing building, variations of facade geometry, insufficient load-bearing capabilities of the lightweight concrete panels, thermal bridges and poor airtightness of the existing building envelope, and low ceiling heights (2.5 m) that prevented installation of internal ductwork.

As the building is in a cold climate zone with a heating season of 207 days per year and a design temperature of -23.8°C, it required thick insulation to achieve the EnerPHit standard. As a college the energy costs were managed centrally and therefore a communal ventilation system was acceptable. Given these factors, coupled with the low ceiling height, it was decided to

Fig 6.37: Routing of ductwork within insulated roof [43]

Fig 6.38: Base detail at external wall [44]

locate the ductwork of the heat-recovery ventilation system in the new thermal insulation envelope (see technical strategy, below). The main large-diameter ducts were in the attic insulation (see Fig 6.37), and smaller (100–200 mm) ducts were fitted in the walls. Due to the structural solution of the existing wall (self-bearing lightweight concrete panels) it was only possible to fix the new timber frame to these walls externally. A decision was made to install a 640 x 200 mm glulam timber edge beam at the base, avoiding the risk of thermal bridging caused by a steel connection in the foundation wall (see Fig 6.35).

Among the other key challenges were the 20 existing brick pilasters, which projected beyond the face of the building. In the proposed scheme these would have resulted in a significant thermal bridge, and it was decided that they should be removed. However, the pilasters held the existing wall panels in place, and it was necessary to install angles to tie them back to the structural party walls (see Fig 6.36). This preparatory work took two months of the nine-month programme and, in one of the learnings from the project, the architect has suggested that this could be avoided on future projects by creating a deeper insulation zone and using blown insulation, which would also result in easier distribution of insulation around the ductwork.

KEY ACHIEVEMENTS

Refurbishment of a Soviet-period building with use of PH components had never been done in Latvia. It was a challenge for both the designers and the construction company. The project was important not only for the client, Ērgļi Vocational School, but for the whole country. It demonstrated that refurbishment of Soviet-period building stock with PH components is feasible with local skills and competence, resulting in extremely low heating cost, incomparable thermal comfort and high indoor air quality.

The project took a long time to become a reality, with nearly two years of discussions, preliminary design and cost estimates carried out at risk. Using the findings of the feasibility study the client participated in the state green investment scheme, and was awarded a grant in 2012. Completed at the end of 2012, it remains the biggest retrofit project in the Baltic states to achieve the full Passivhaus standard, with a final space heating demand of 10 kWh/m²/a and airtightness of 0.6 – better than the requirements of the full Passivhaus standard. As a result, it is now possible to use the whole building, which comfortably accommodates one or two students in each room.

TECHNICAL STRATEGY

Airtightness of the existing structure was ensured with Pro Clima Intello membrane. On-site fabricated timber I-beams (400 mm thickness) were mounted on a load-bearing glulam timber beam and fixed to the existing facade panels. The structure was filled with mineral wool. Heraklith boards and lime-cement plaster formed a wind protection layer for the outer walls. A new single-slope roof structure with attic space for blown-in mineral wool (750–1200 mm) was built. Ventilation system ductwork was allowed for in the new thermal envelope, and insulation of the building envelope was also used to insulate the ductwork. To avoid thermal bridges at the ground floor, XPS insulation (200 mm) was used around the perimeter to a depth of 500 mm below ground. As an unheated space the basement ceiling was insulated with hard mineral wool lamellas (200 mm). All existing windows were replaced with 92 mm Timber windows with triple-glazed argon-filled units. The windows were then mounted in the new timber frame structure to ensure thermal continuity.

POST-COMPLETION

Following completion, the project team undertook a detailed POE with Riga Technical University which considered the following issues: energy behaviour, lighting comfort, temperature comfort, acoustic comfort, ventilation comfort, daylight comfort and overall satisfaction. A selection of this feedback is provided below (Figs 6.39a to 6.40b[45]) and it is hoped that EnerPHit will become an achievable target for the remaining 90% of uninsulated Soviet-period buildings in Latvia.

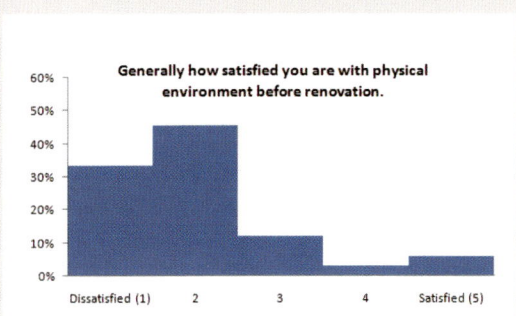

Fig 6.39a: General satisfaction before renovation

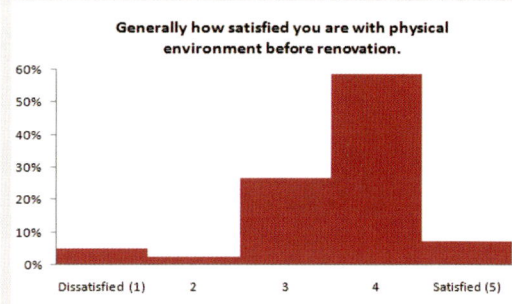

Fig 6.39b: General satisfaction after renovation

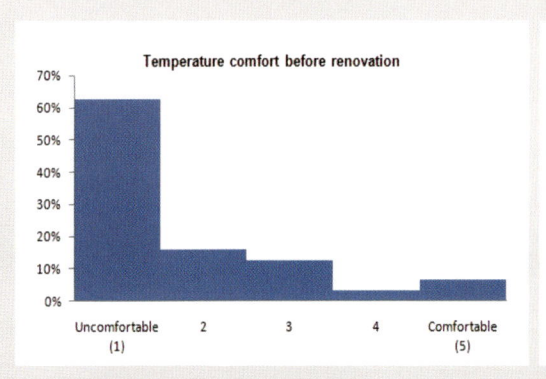

Fig 6.40a: Thermal comfort before renovation

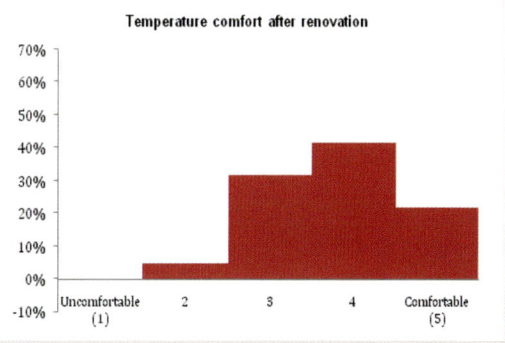

Fig 6.40b: Thermal comfort after renovation

CASE STUDY 6.5

Private Owner-Occupied
105 Willow Street, Brooklyn, New York, USA

Client:	Confidential
Architect:	Baxt Ingui
M&E:	Baukraft Engineering
Structural Engineer:	A Degree of Freedom
PH Consultant:	Baukraft Engineering
Contractor:	Taffera Fine Building
Photographer:	Peter Pierce Photography

INTRODUCTION

This project is a mid-terrace five-storey townhouse with a TFA of 3,793 m^2, built in the early 20th century and a 'Landmark' property in Brooklyn, New York. As such, it was necessary to maintain the visual appearance of the existing building from the road. Internal insulation was used throughout, and attention was paid to the appearance of the replacement sash windows. Although alterations to the rear of the property were possible, this required approval by the Landmarks Preservation Commission (LPC). While the project cost is confidential, the architect noted that Passivhaus projects can be cost-neutral, or even less expensive than equivalent high-value projects. The property was vacant during the works, which enabled the team to undertake extensive improvements to the fabric (particularly the external walls) that would not have been possible in an occupied building. The space heating demand was reduced from 229 kWh/m^2/a to 18.1 kWh/m^2/a with a primary energy demand of 124 kWh/m^2/a. Airtightness was also reduced from approximately 10 ach n50 to a very impressive 0.47 ach n50.

KEY CHALLENGES

One of the initial challenges was the New York City (NYC) approvals process. The local authority building department was sceptical of a proposed building showing a fraction of the typical HVAC tonnage.

Fig 6.41: Front elevation post-retrofit[46]

Painted Mahogany
19mm Exterior Plywood Sheathing
Rigid Foam Insulation
Blown in Dense pack cellulose Insulation

Airtightness tape
Luward opening door

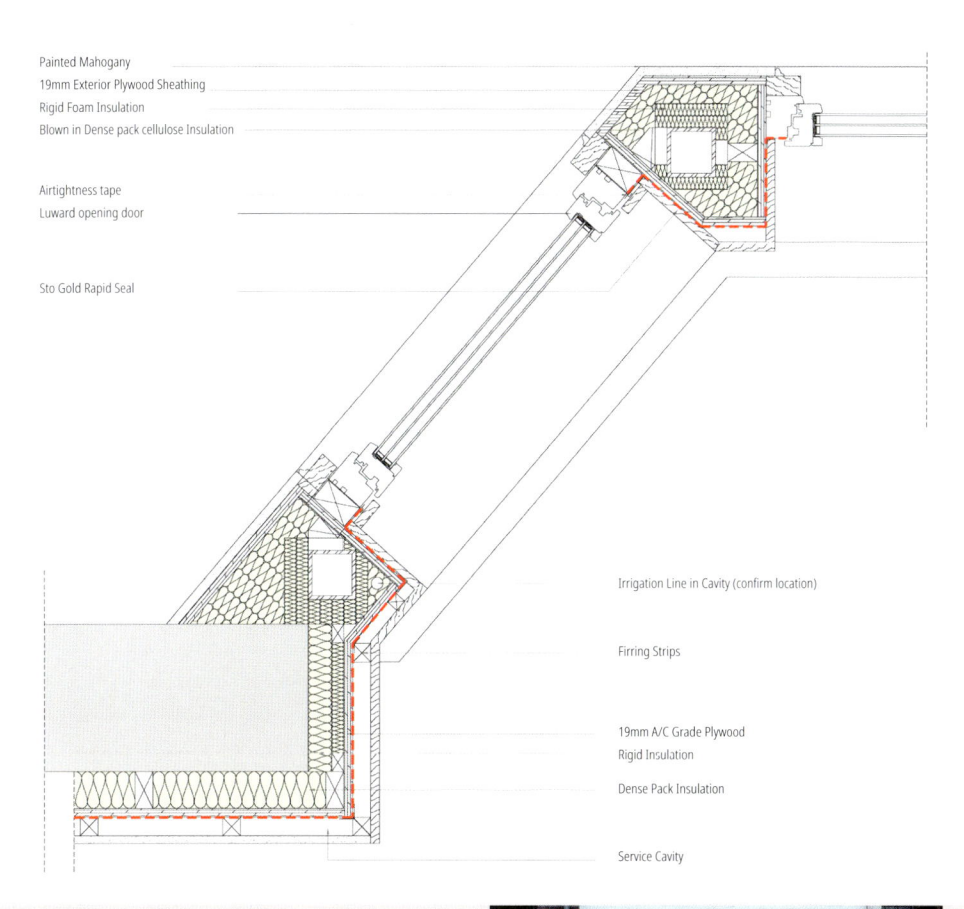

Sto Gold Rapid Seal

Irrigation Line in Cavity (confirm location)

Firring Strips

19mm A/C Grade Plywood
Rigid Insulation
Dense Pack Insulation

Service Cavity

Fig 6.42: Detailing of rear bay window

They were also unfamiliar with a house providing continuous exhaust for bathrooms, and would normally expect a 100–150 cfm fan on a user-activated switch. Although Passivhaus requirements were within the NYC code, the design team received several objections that were not relevant because the authorities were unfamiliar with Passivhaus.

Another major design challenge related to the approvals process was getting through the LPC. The LPC requires any visible facade to hold true to very particular aesthetic elements, depending on when the building was built. One hallmark of residential townhouses is a painted wood double-hung (sash) window. Simulated double-hung windows with passive-level airtightness are not yet widely available or accepted in the US. Indeed, a simulated wood double-hung window had never been approved at LPC. Therefore, Baxt Ingui worked very closely with a European window company, PH consultant and the LPC to modify the sash frame and check rail details to meet Landmark's standards. This project was Baxt

Fig 6.43: Rear bay window (full height)[47]

Residential Case Studies

Fig 6.44: Proposed floor plans

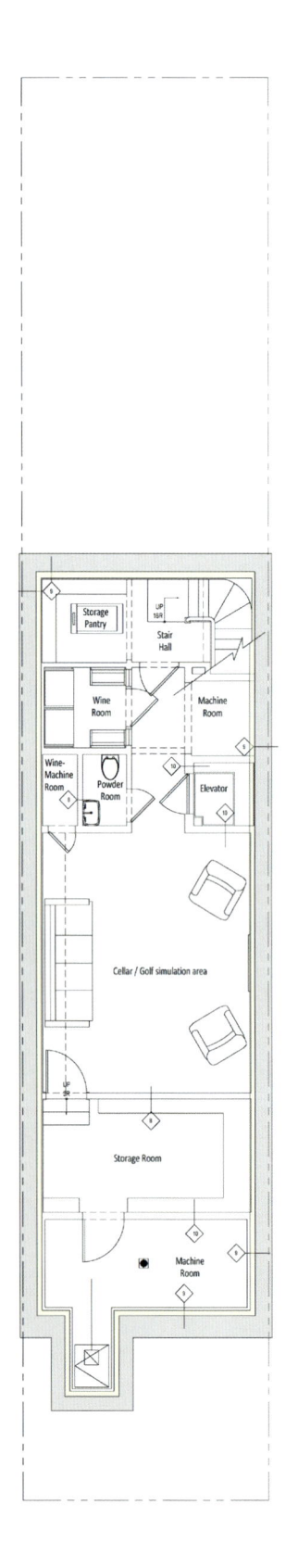

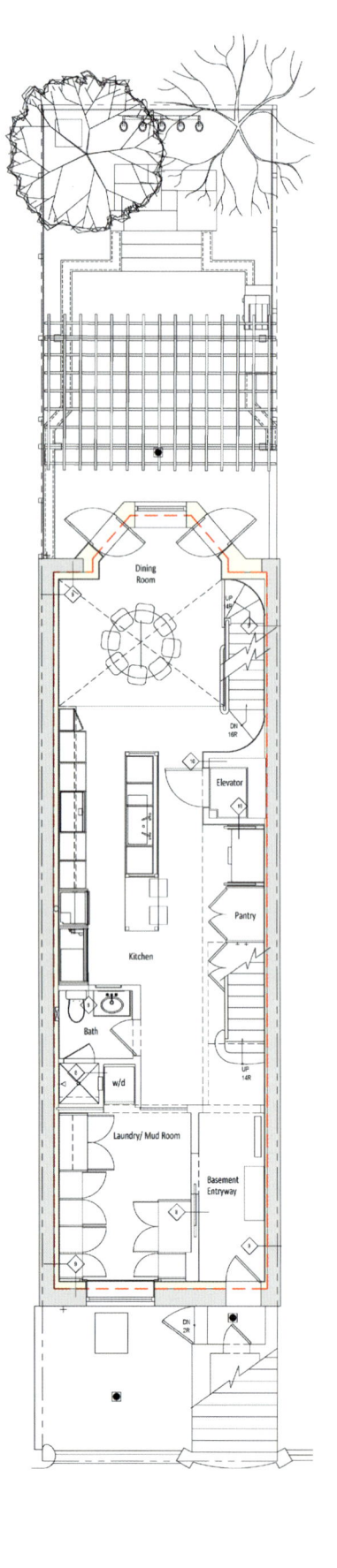

106 **EnerPHit:** A Step-by-Step Guide to Low Energy Retrofit

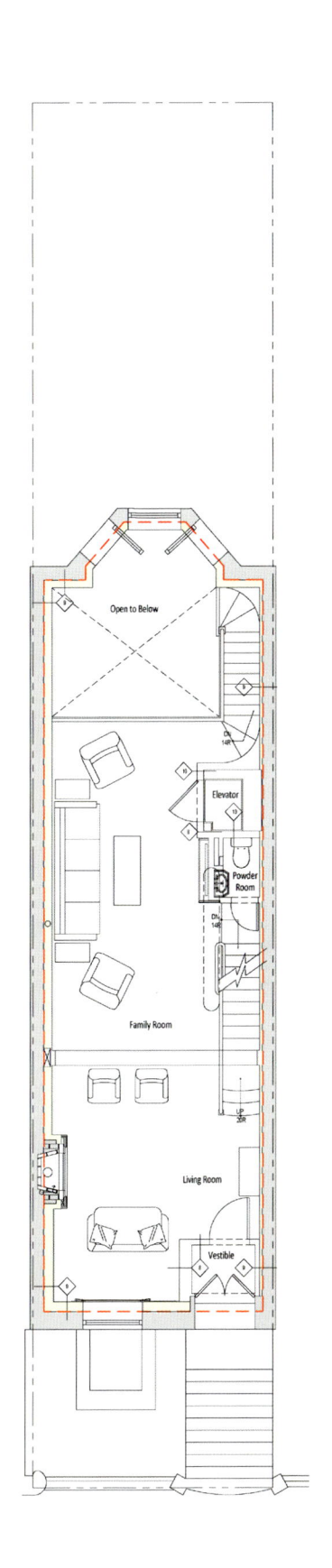

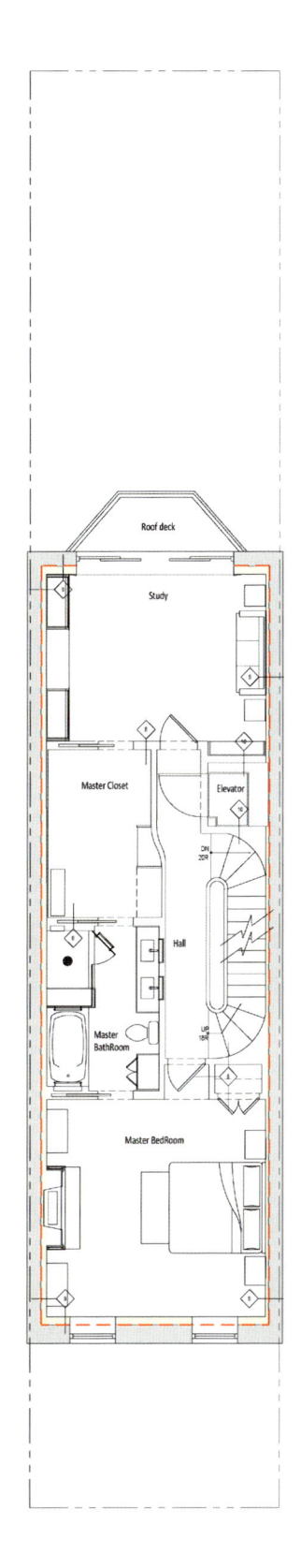

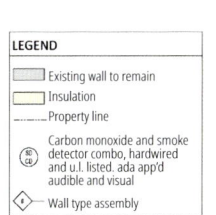

Residential Case Studies

Ingui's third Passivhaus project to get approved by LPC, but they were still required to present the windows at a public hearing in front of the Landmark review board and the community board for approval.

Given the constraints of the Landmark requirements, the existing exterior facades and being a mid-terrace townhouse, all insulation and air sealing had to be done from the interior. From a construction standpoint, this house proved to be a challenge due to its overall narrow width of 17 ft (5.1 m) yet long and tall dimensions, with a finished cellar, basement, four floors of accommodation, plus the roof terrace. The scope included a lift and an additional rear staircase on the lower levels to improve circulation and flow, so every inch was planned and checked to accommodate these elements. Mapping out and installing the heating, ventilation and air-conditioning (HVAC) and energy recovery ventilation (ERV) system also proved to be a challenge, and the only way to run pipes and ductwork consistently from floor to floor was by furring out one party wall by 7 in (178 mm), leaving a finished width of about 15 ft 6 in (4.73 m).

KEY ACHIEVEMENTS

The first-floor wood-framed bay on the rear facade became a focal point of the design. The new layout proposed continuing it down to ground and creating a double-height space out of the bay and adjacent dining room (see Fig 6.43). The bay was original but had deteriorated over the years. The architect worked closely with the contractor (Taffera Fine Building) and Passivhaus consultants (Baukraft Engineering) to ensure thermal performance and airtightness while keeping the original proportions of the bay and maintaining a slender frame.

One of the most successful aspects of the house is the rooftop deck that stretches from the front wall to the rear wall (see Fig 6.46). To the clients, this is a bonus amenity that they did not expect. A typical townhouse of this size would offer significantly less

Fig 6.45: Open-plan living[48]

108 EnerPHit: A Step-by-Step Guide to Low Energy Retrofit

useful space due to the size and number of HVAC units, as well as the level of noise pollution. The challenge of creating a continuous air seal through a new stair bulkhead, lift shaft and shared party wall was successfully overcome. The architects worked closely with the other consultants and the contractor to tweak the design slightly throughout the progress to create airtight connections that were cost-effective to build, performed well, and looked clean and proportional. Through careful coordination they were able to integrate mechanical venting into the roof deck design, blending with other amenities such as the built-in bench, outdoor kitchen and gas fireplace. The client has described the roof terrace as their 'favourite place to be … [it] truly feels like a personal escape from daily life'.

TECHNICAL STRATEGY

While the improved U-value of 0.26 W/m²K achieved for the external walls is well above the 'normal' target U-value of 0.15 W/m²K, it was compensated for by the performance of other elements and the very efficient form factor of a five-storey mid-terrace townhouse. Ventilation is provided by a Zehnder ComfoAir 550 ERV with an effective efficiency of 77% extracting from all wet rooms and providing ventilation to living rooms and bedrooms.

The design team paid careful attention to moisture and temperature control across the wall assembly. A typical row-house in NYC is built of three wythes of brick masonry. This type of wall tends to allow moisture to pass easily through its mass. Best practice is to design a wall where the inner wythe of masonry is kept 'warm' relative to winter exterior temperatures. As vapour is driven through the mass of the wall from the exterior, it heats and condenses within the wall itself and dries to the exterior – rather than driving through the mass into the interior cavity of the wall, where it will condense and cause moisture issues inside the house.

A common approach is to install steel studs against the interior masonry with mineral fibre batt or

Fig 6.46: Rooftop terrace[49]

(1) Hvac unit hung off chimney breast

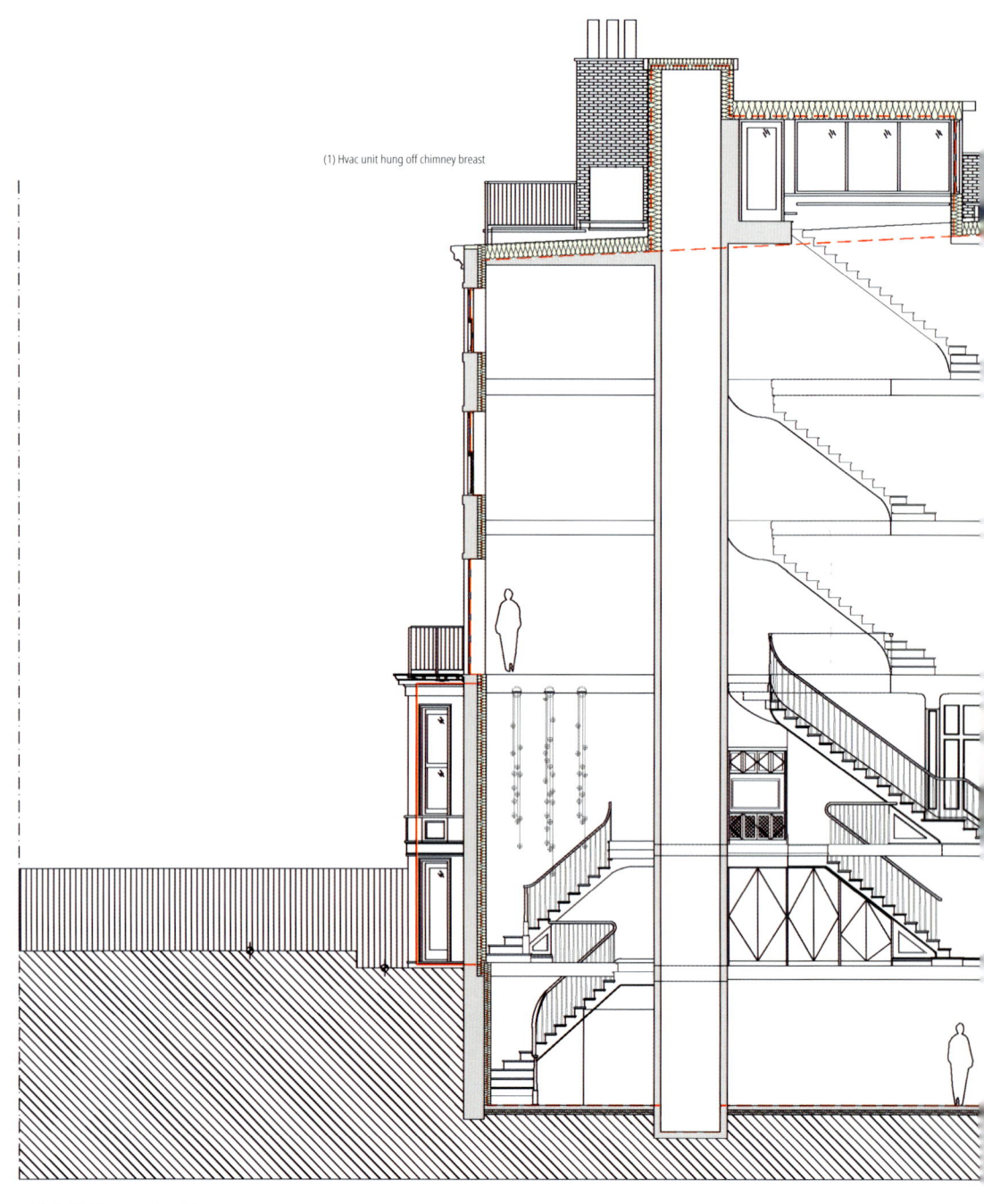

Fig 6.47: Proposed section

Bulkhead: 60'-10" (elev. = 138')

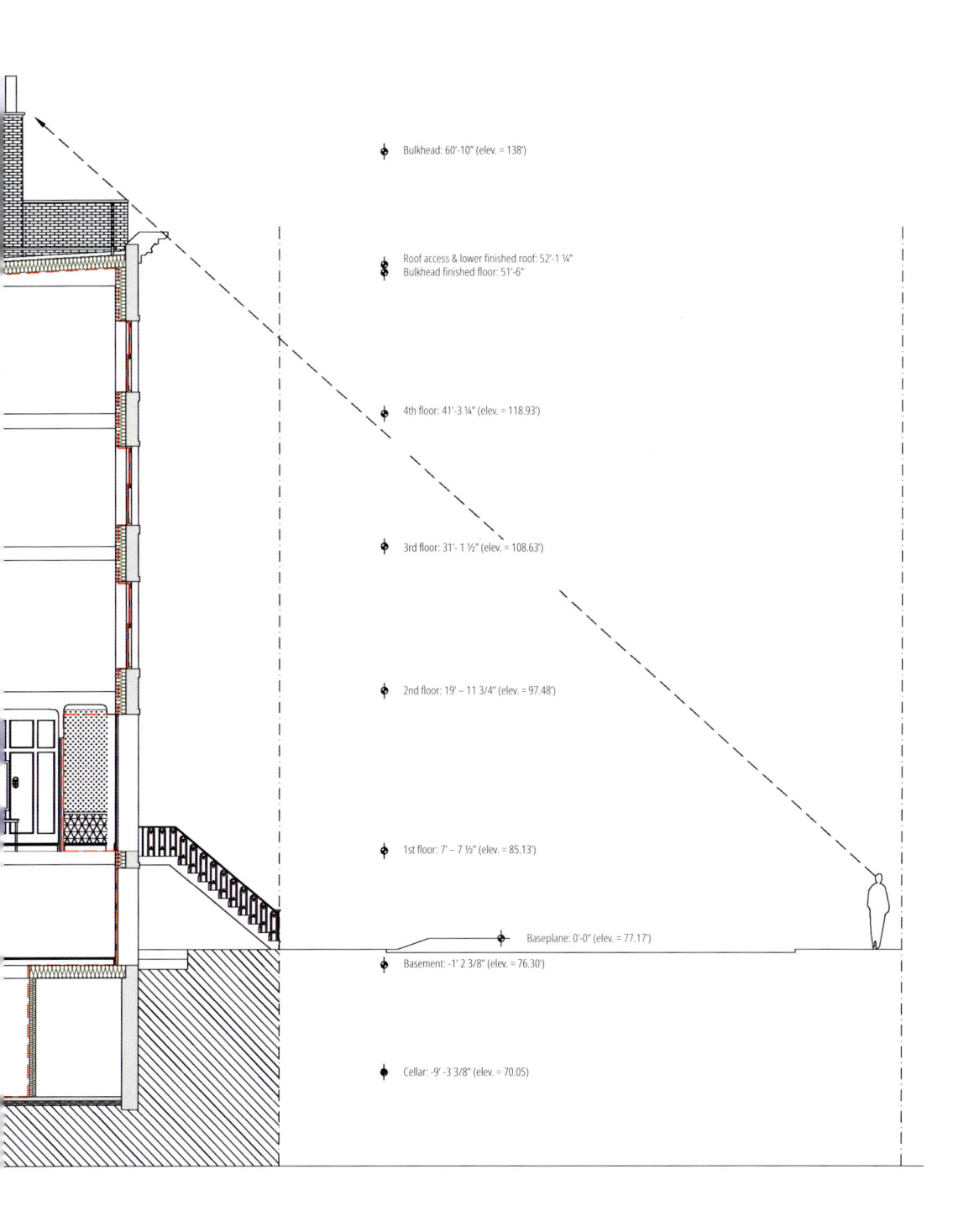

Roof access & lower finished roof: 52'-1 ¼"
Bulkhead finished floor: 51'-6"

4th floor: 41'-3 ¼" (elev. = 118.93')

3rd floor: 31'- 1 ½" (elev. = 108.63')

2nd floor: 19' – 11 3/4" (elev. = 97.48')

1st floor: 7' – 7 ½" (elev. = 85.13')

Baseplane: 0'-0" (elev. = 77.17')
Basement: -1' 2 3/8" (elev. = 76.30')

Cellar: -9' -3 3/8" (elev. = 70.05)

Residential Case Studies

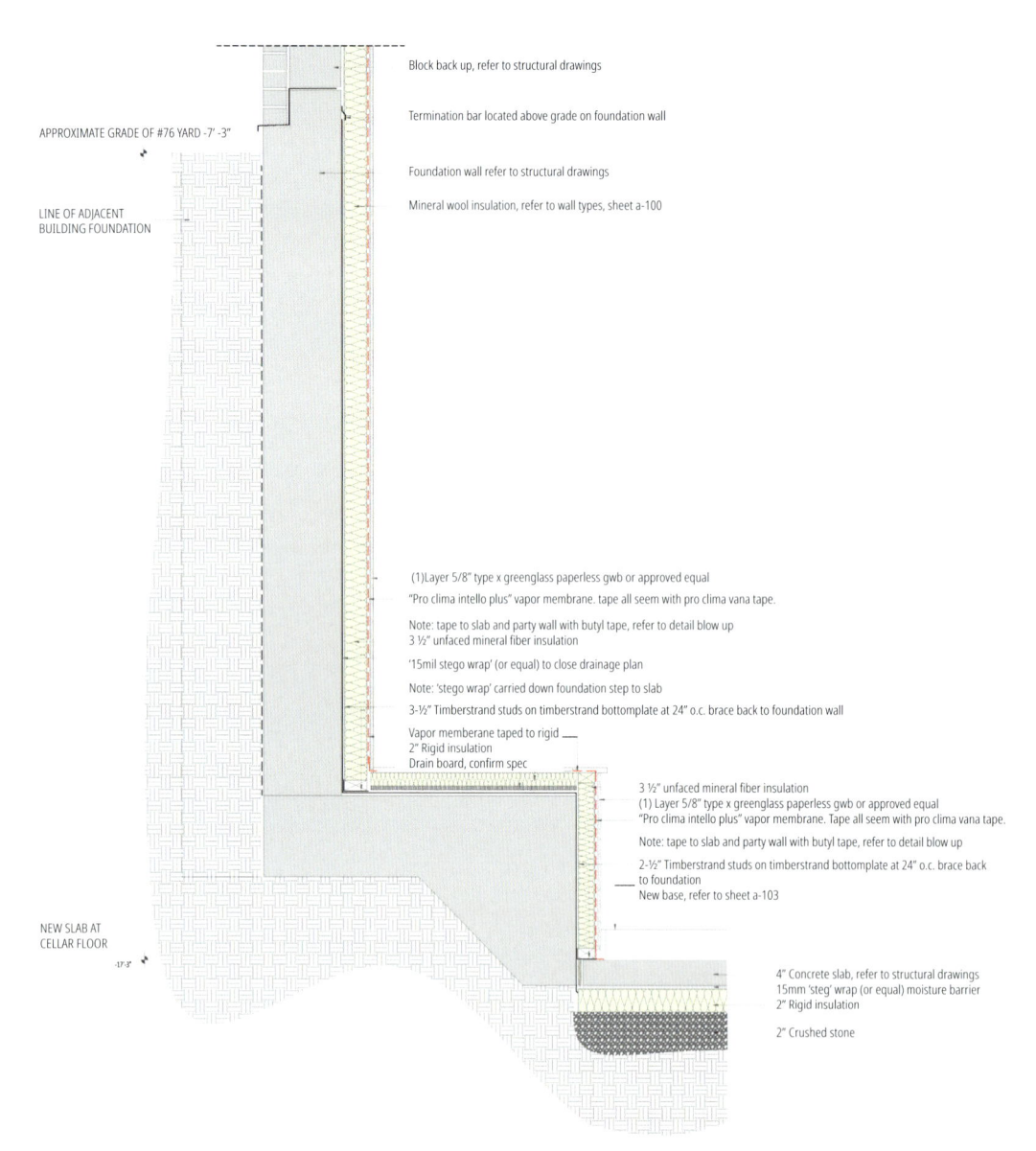

Fig 6.48: Wall junction details

spray foam insulation. Although widely utilised, this assembly creates thermal bridges that largely negate insulation values, and lacks a consistent vapour control layer. In addition, it does not sufficiently address air leakage from exterior to interior and vice versa, requiring robust mechanical systems to counteract the inherent deficiencies in the wall assembly and reach typical levels of human comfort.

Figure 6.48 shows how the wall assembly and window installation detail pays careful attention to some of these factors, using wood studs that are thermally advantageous and a blown-in cellulose insulation that can better withstand moisture. An airtight vapour-control membrane is applied to the interior face of the assembly to allow for drying in the warmer seasons but prevent indoor moisture from getting into the assembly in winter. There is also a liquid-applied air and vapour-control layer applied directly to the back of the masonry before the wall is insulated to limit inward-driven moisture from outside.

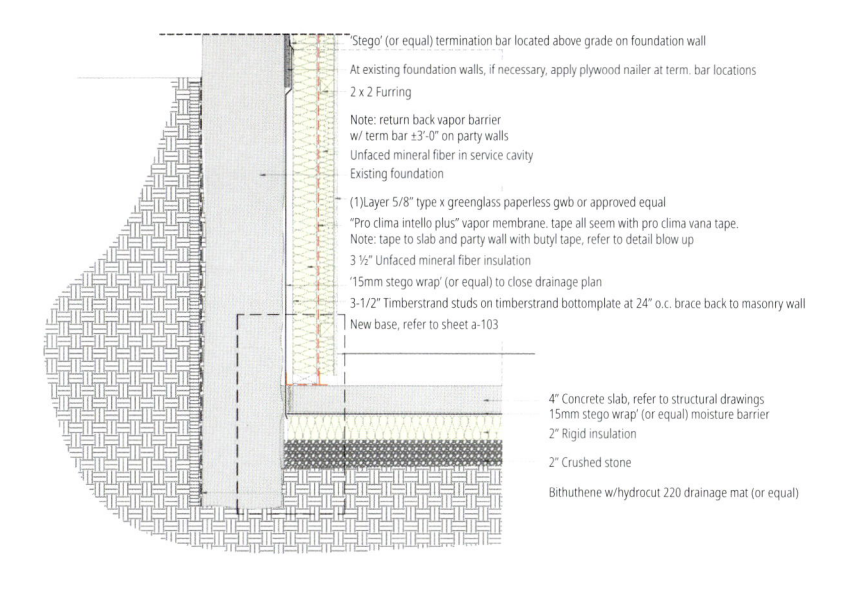

DETAIL AT EXISTING FRONT/BACK FOUNDATION WALL

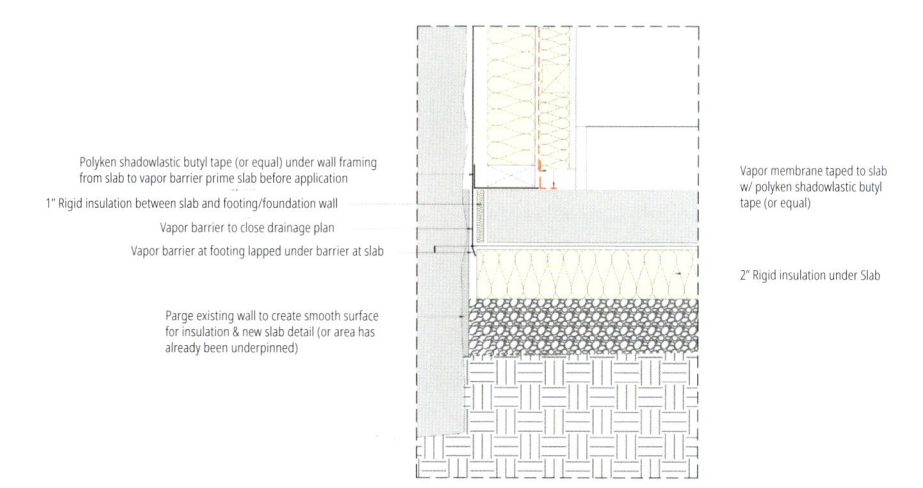

Callouts (upper detail):
- 'Stego' (or equal) termination bar located above grade on foundation wall
- At existing foundation walls, if necessary, apply plywood nailer at term. bar locations
- 2 x 2 Furring
- Note: return back vapor barrier w/ term bar ±3'-0" on party walls
- Unfaced mineral fiber in service cavity
- Existing foundation
- (1) Layer 5/8" type x greenglass paperless gwb or approved equal
- "Pro clima intello plus" vapor membrane. tape all seem with pro clima vana tape. Note: tape to slab and party wall with butyl tape, refer to detail blow up
- 3 ½" Unfaced mineral fiber insulation
- '15mm stego wrap' (or equal) to close drainage plan
- 3-1/2" Timberstrand studs on timberstrand bottomplate at 24" o.c. brace back to masonry wall
- New base, refer to sheet a-103
- 4" Concrete slab, refer to structural drawings
- 15mm stego wrap' (or equal) moisture barrier
- 2" Rigid insulation
- 2" Crushed stone
- Bithuthene w/hydrocut 220 drainage mat (or equal)

2 / A-500   SCALE: 1 1/2" = 1'-0"

Callouts (lower detail):
- Polyken shadowlastic butyl tape (or equal) under wall framing from slab to vapor barrier prime slab before application
- 1" Rigid insulation between slab and footing/foundation wall
- Vapor barrier to close drainage plan
- Vapor barrier at footing lapped under barrier at slab
- Parge existing wall to create smooth surface for insulation & new slab detail (or area has already been underpinned)
- Vapor membrane taped to slab w/ polyken shadowlastic butyl tape (or equal)
- 2" Rigid insulation under Slab

POST-COMPLETION

Current energy data is not yet available due to metering issues with NYC. However, energy use is estimated to be low. Since the project was completed the NYC Department of Buildings has made significant headway in its focus on energy components, and is now requiring much higher standards for all building assemblies. The architect notes that '... at the time that we filed this project just three years ago, we were barely required to show energy standards on our drawings, and what little notes that we included were not enforced. Since the 2016 update to the NYCECC, we have seen a major paradigm shift in thought about a wall's insulative and air-sealing value, although ... there is still a gap in understanding of the overall envelope and enforcement of new regulations' – which may compromise NYC's 80% carbon reduction by 2050 goal.

Residential Case Studies

CASE STUDY 6.6

Private Rent, Listed Building
2 Gloucester Place Mews, London, UK

Client:	Portman Estates
Architect:	Feilden+Mawson
QS:	STACE
M&E:	Leonard Design Associates
Structural Engineer:	Furnace Partnership
PH Consultant:	Sturgis Carbon Profiling
PH Certifier:	Etude
Contractor:	Richardsons of Nyewood

INTRODUCTION

This project is believed to be the first listed building in the UK to achieve the EnerPHit(i) standard and BREEAM Excellent. Similarly, it is the first property owned by the Portman Estate to do so. The building was vacant during the works, which enabled all building elements to be treated. The original building dates from the 18th century and is Grade II listed, meaning all alterations were carried out internally with no visible change to the exterior except the replacement and repositioning of the modern, unattractive garage door. As a result, the building has a TFA of only 121 m². This project was tendered from an approved client list and the cost of the works was approximately £700,000, although only a small proportion of this was for the energy-efficiency works.

Fig 6.49: View along mews to front elevation[50]

Fig 6.50: Open-plan kitchen/dining[51]

114 EnerPHit: A Step-b-Step Guide to Low Energy Retrofit

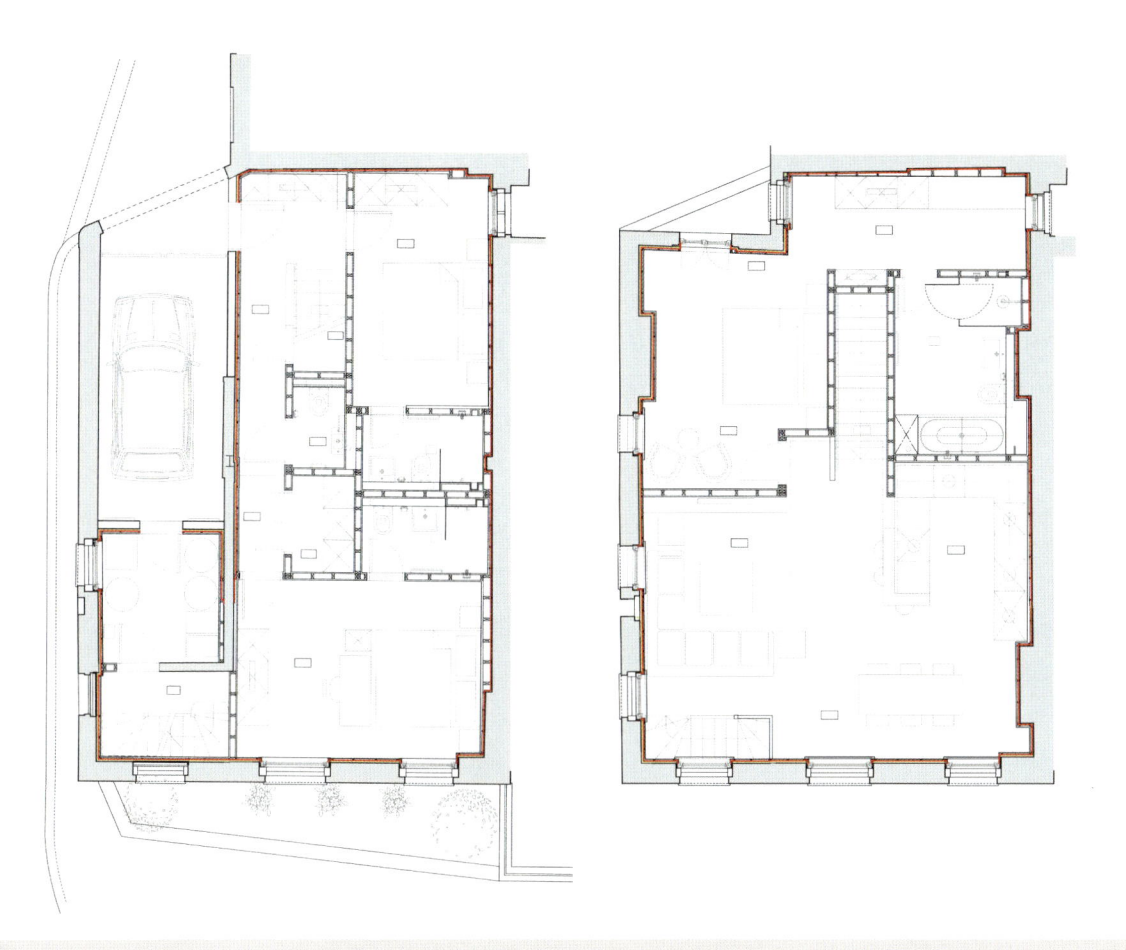

Fig 6.51: Proposed ground and first floor plans[52]

Except for the stair, most of the internal fabric was not original and could be removed. The existing cellular layout was poor, and the internal walls were removed to provide an attractive open-plan arrangement (see Fig 6.51). The existing garage was retained as an unheated space at ground floor level, and this was thermally separated from the rest of the building. This resulted in a relatively high form factor and required bespoke details to prevent thermal bridging. The existing stair was carefully removed and refurbished before being reinstalled as a secondary stair at the rear of the property.

KEY CHALLENGES

To prevent excessive loss of floor area while retaining a 'breathable' (vapour-open) wall, a high-performance aerogel insulation was used on the internal face of all external walls. In other areas a mineral wool insulation was used on the soffit and party walls. The greatest challenges to overcome included thermal bridging, with careful modelling required to prevent excessive heat loss. Due to the historic nature of the property some compromise was necessary. While the existing chimney was no longer in use (and would ordinarily be filled with a loose insulation material) it was decided to leave this empty. However, it was adequately ventilated externally and the internal face was insulated to allow any moisture to dissipate through the stack.

The building was an end-terrace property with a very large area of external exposed walls and limited options available for the insulation of those walls. This made the 'component route' the only possible route for certification, as the heating demand (37 kWh/m²/a) exceeded the EnerPHit threshold. Due to its listed nature all original windows had to remain; however, PH-certified triple-glazed

Residential Case Studies 115

Fig 6.52: Internal lining to walls[53]

Fig 6.53: Internal garage[54]

Fig 6.54: Passivhaus-certified rooflight[55]

windows were used internally. However, a PH-certified external replica door was approved by Westminster City Council and used on the scheme. The airtightness layer installation proved to be a challenge, particularly with the retention of the listed roof beams. This required a lot of detailing and meticulous attention on site. Finally, the listed staircase (which had been removed and restored) had to be reinstalled in the same location. This posed some limitations on the adjacent internal window, which ultimately required a fixed pane.

Resolving these details took longer than anticipated and the programme was extended to ensure key details were fully resolved and the airtightness target achieved. Nevertheless, long-term relationships between client, contractor and design team ensured the project was delivered on budget and without dispute. While the property was vacant and there were no specific user requirements, the building owner required the property to be simple to use.

KEY ACHIEVEMENTS

The project demonstrates that, despite the constraints imposed by a listed building, it is possible to achieve EnerPHit(i) on a traditional building where the form factor is relatively high

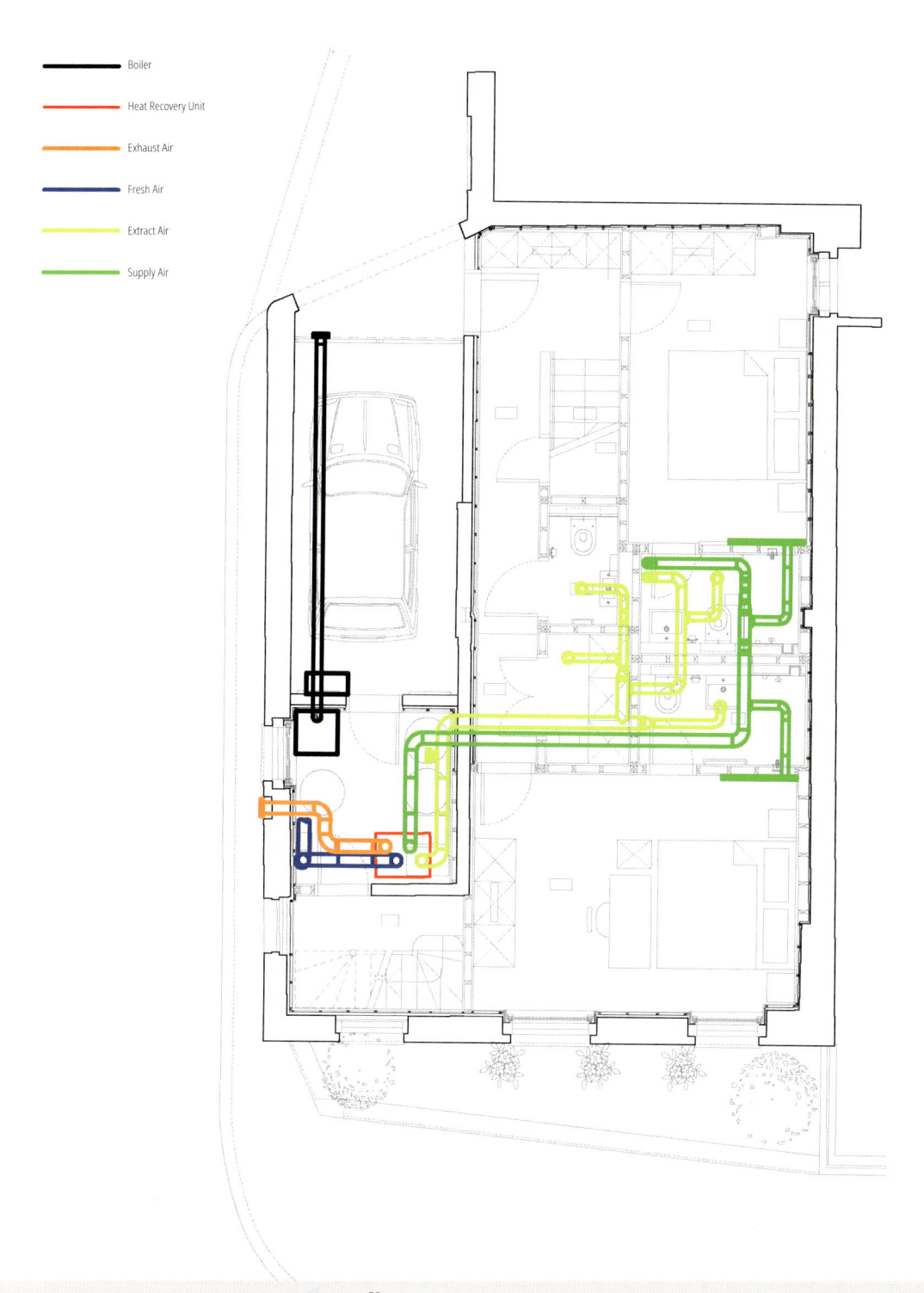

Fig 6.55: Services layout (heating and ventilation)[56]

Residential Case Studies

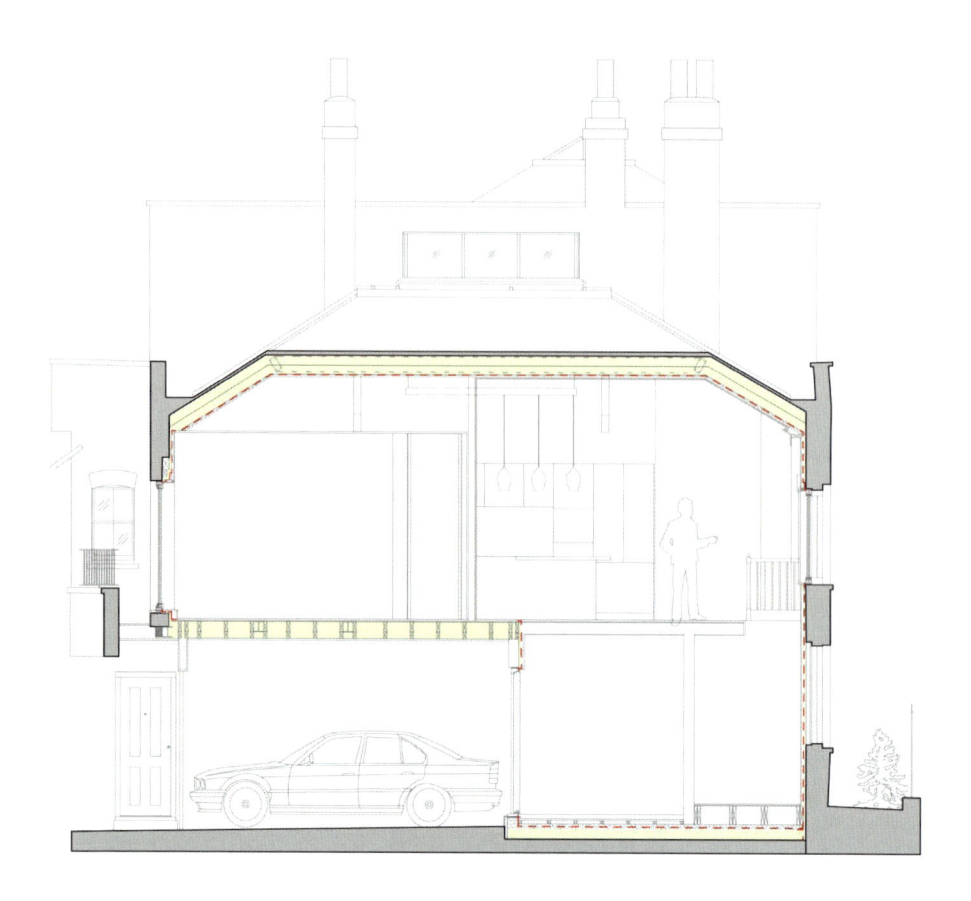

Fig 6.56: Section through garage and flat above[57]

(396 m²) and the TFA is relatively low (121 m²). The retrofit has transformed the condition and internal arrangement of the existing building, providing a high-quality, attractive residential property for rent. As a rental property the building provides flexible, easy-to-use accommodation, with the low cost of servicing (approximately £900 per year) recovered by the landlord (Portman Estates) that invested in the retrofit. Given the small and relatively complex form, the completed airtightness result of 0.7 is impressive and well within the EnerPHit threshold. Most importantly, the necessary changes were made without altering the external appearance of the building or unduly reducing the lettable (and high-value) floor area. The project represents the first of its kind in a listed building, in Central London, by a long-term land owner, and supports the Portman Estate's corporate and social responsibility towards reducing carbon emissions in the private rental sector.

TECHNICAL STRATEGY

The building was a vacant property with very few internal original features. As such, the design team obtained approval from English Heritage for the removal of all existing elements inside the property. With the exception of the staircase, which was refurbished, all other elements could be replaced. This enabled the walls to be insulated internally with 40 mm aerogel and the ground floor slab removed, with new insulated slabs installed. The roof was insulated at rafter level and a continuous airtight intelligent breathable membrane taped at all openings with materials carefully selected and detailed to avoid cold bridges.

All original brickwork and the timber structure were insulated and wrapped in an aerogel blanket, airtightness membrane, 30 mm services void and magnesium oxide board before being finished in lime plaster and specialised paint. This produces

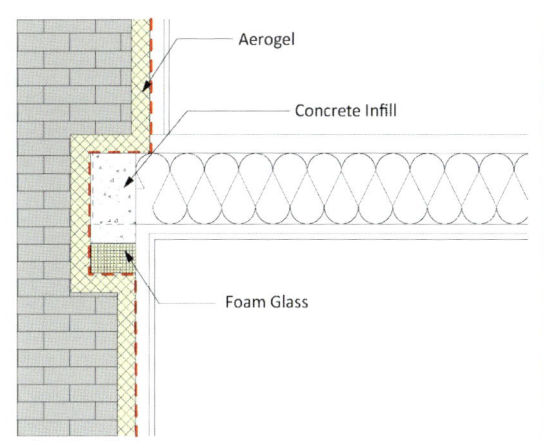

Fig 6.57a: Intermediate floor to external wall – typical padstone detail[58]

Fig 6.57b: Intermediate floor to external wall[59]

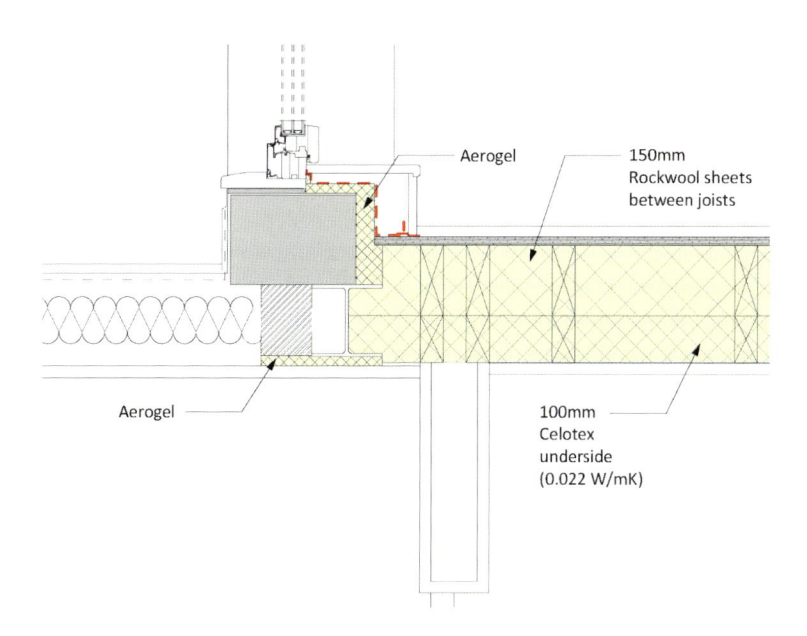

Fig 6.58: Detailing at balcony threshold over garage[60]

a breathable design that has parallels with the original construction methods employed by Georgian builders, while promoting improved indoor air quality by the inclusion of a mechanical ventilation system. The existing single-glazed windows were refurbished and retained. Triple-glazed secondary windows were installed along with Passivhaus-accredited main entrance doors and roof lanterns.

POST-COMPLETION

A simple user guide was produced on completion, with an ongoing POE monitoring of primary energy (electricity and gas), water consumption, internal/external humidity and temperature, and CO_2 levels in the property. Initial findings of the preliminary report (due to be published in 2019) suggest a positive outcome.

Residential Case Studies 119

7.0: Commercial Case Studies

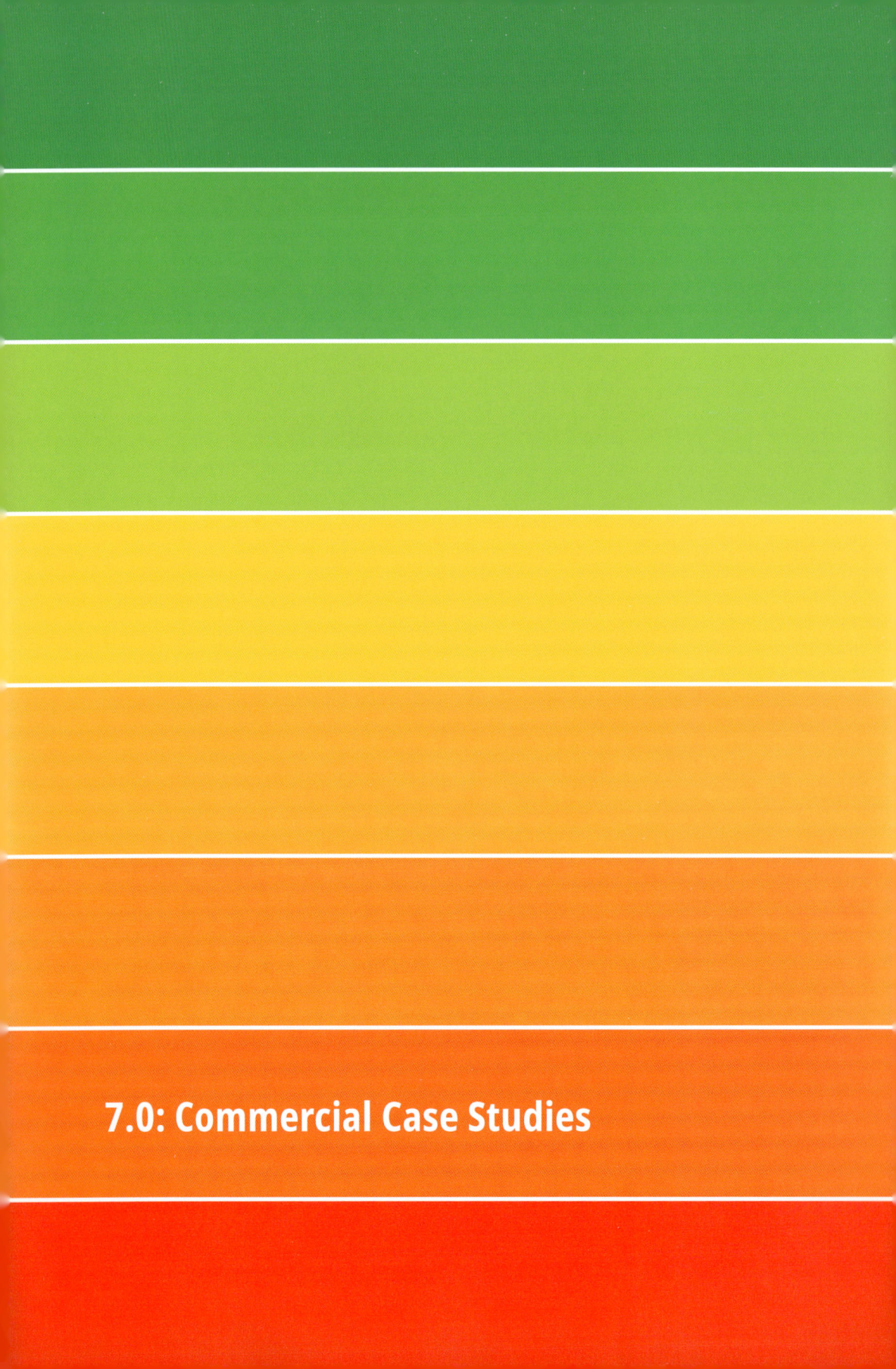

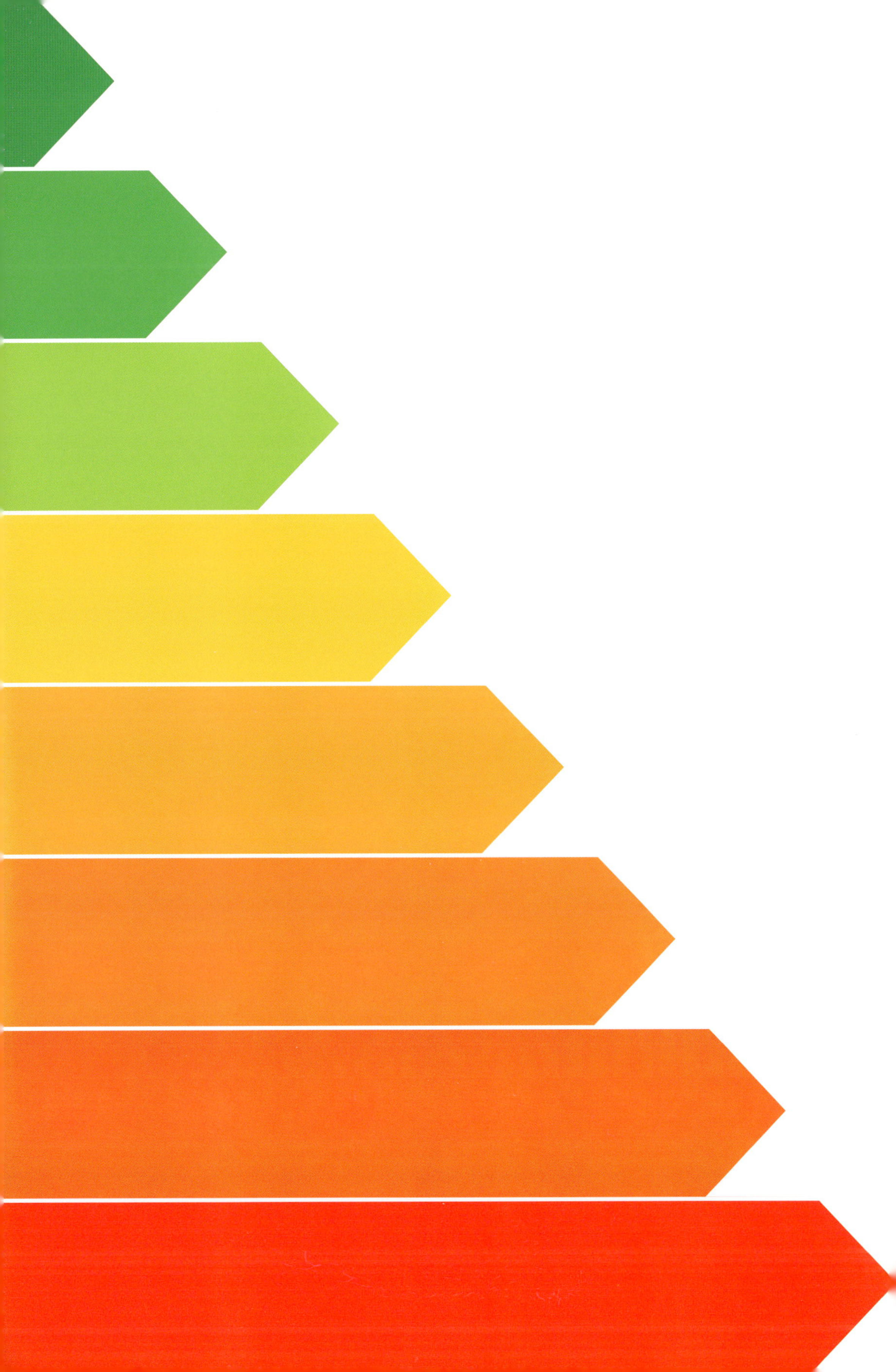

7.1: ACHIEVING ENERPHIT IN THE COMMERCIAL SECTOR

Commercial (or non-residential) buildings (including public buildings) account for 13% of UK carbon emissions,[1] with over 50% of these built before 1940. The UK has a broadly similar proportion of non-residential floorspace to other European countries (see Fig 7.1). While this is clearly a small proportion of the total building stock, it still amounts to approximately 0.75 billion m^2 in the UK alone. Non-residential uses vary, and the energy intensity of these building types also varies significantly (see Figs 7.2 and 7.3).

Unlike residential properties where unregulated energy loads are relatively consistent across property types, there are significant differences across the commercial and industrial sectors. While the energy intensity (or efficiency in kWh/m^2/a) of some sectors, such as hospitality or emergency services, is extraordinarily high, the actual consumption is relatively low due to the smaller proportion of floor area compared to offices, retail or the industrial sector. However, where high consumption is due to unregulated loads which are inherent in the use of the building (e.g. catering equipment in a restaurant or hotel) we might disregard these when considering the impact of building retrofit.

While deep retrofit can have an impact on unregulated loads (e.g. through reduced use of fans) we might restrict our consideration of the impact of deep retrofit to reduced space heating and cooling demand. In the commercial sector these account for approximately 90,000 GWh per year in England and Wales alone. The average energy intensity across all sectors is approximately 85 kWh/m^2/a, although there are wide variations across the stock, with buildings in the health and emergency sectors performing particularly poorly at over 140 kWh and 180 kWh respectively. Given the additional importance of human comfort in these building types, and long-term public ownership, we might target this sector as a priority and reduce the waste of public money.

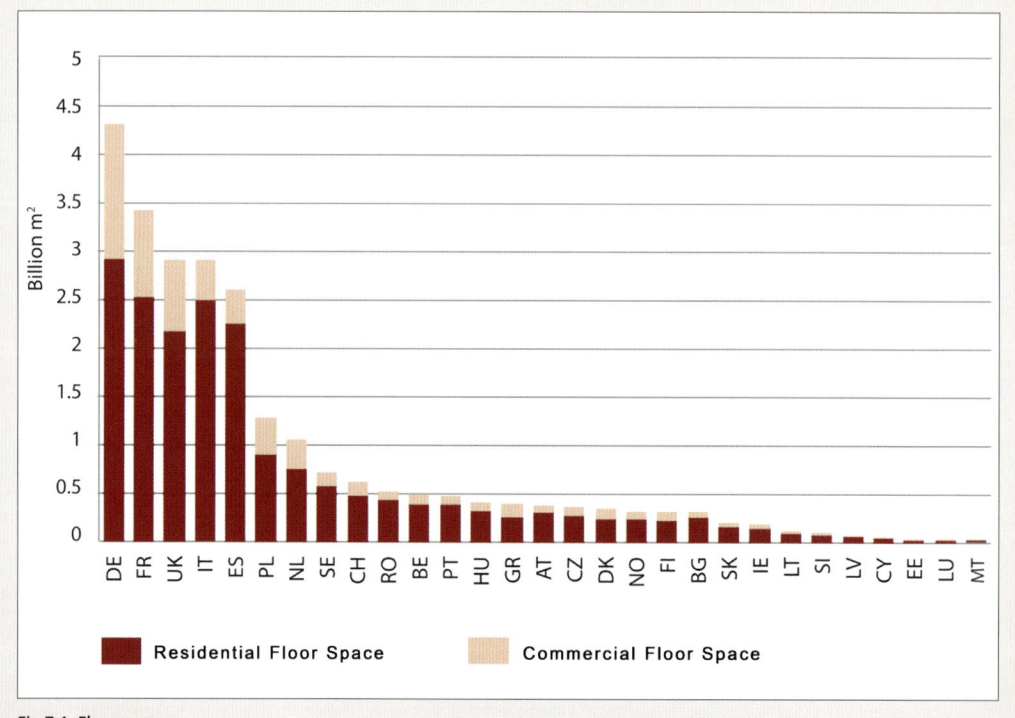

Fig 7.1: Floor space distribution by EU country[2]

122 EnerPHit: A Step-by-Step Guide to Low Energy Retrofit

Fig 7.2: Energy intensity (England and Wales) by energy end use and sector, 2014–15[3]

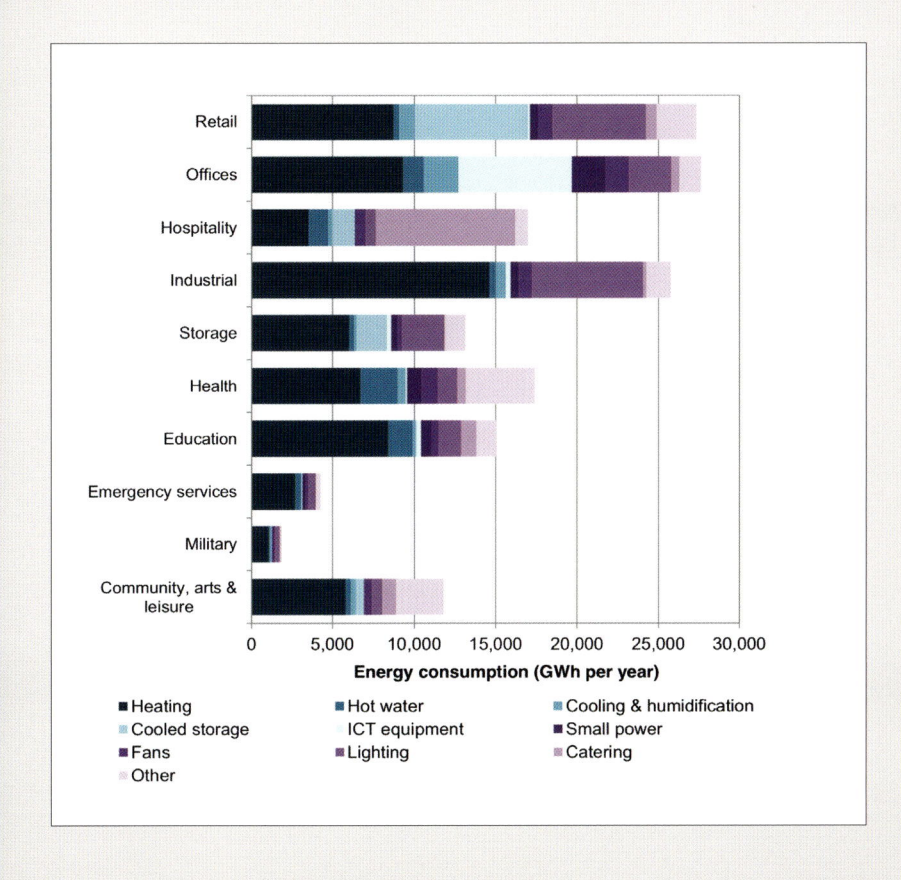

Fig 7.3: Energy consumption (England and Wales) by energy end use and sector, 2014–15[4]

Commercial Case Studies **123**

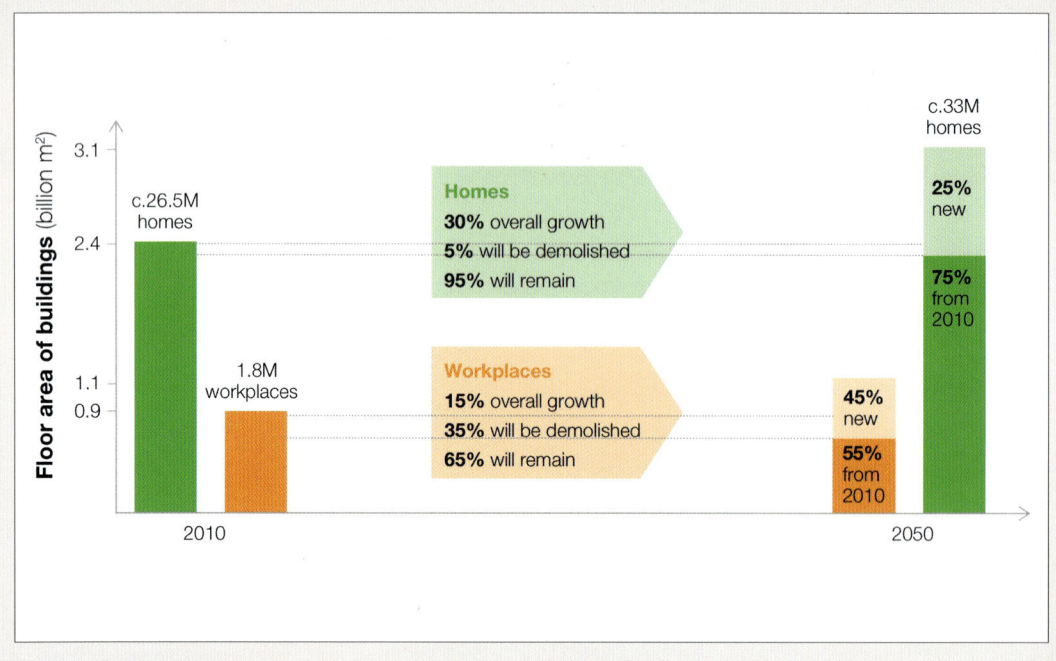

Fig 7.4: Proportion of existing buildings in the UK estimated to remain by 2050[5]

As in the domestic sector, the number of commercial buildings is predicted to increase over the next 30 years (see Fig 7.4). However, the proportion of buildings demolished is also expected to be higher, with nearly half of workplaces likely to be of new construction. 55% of the commercial buildings in use in 2050 are already built and most, if not all, of these will need to be retrofitted over the next 30 years.

Again, as with residential buildings the commercial sector has in recent years been subject to UK government policies encouraging measurement of building performance and improved energy efficiency. Since 2008 all public buildings (and large commercial buildings with public access) have been required to produce a Display Energy Certificate (DEC), which is valid for one year. All other commercial buildings have been required since 2008 to produce an Energy Performance Certificate (EPC) when sold, built or rented. This is valid for up to 10 years and applies to all non-domestic buildings over 50 m². However, a study of over 100 commercial buildings[6] found little correlation between EPC performance and actual energy consumption.

Actual energy consumption will always vary somewhat from modelled assumptions; however, the scale of the divergence is perhaps surprising. EPCs (like Part L) do not include unregulated energy use, which (unlike residential buildings) can make up a large part of commercial energy use, and therefore DECs are a much better guide to actual energy consumption. Unfortunately, there is widespread confusion about the difference between EPCs and DECs, and as the clear majority of commercial buildings are not currently required to produce a DEC this remains a major hurdle to transparency and accuracy of data.

Nevertheless, the UK government has recently introduced the Minimum Energy Efficiency Standard (MEES), effective since March 2018, which requires landlords of all properties in Band F or G (EPC) to carry out essential energy-efficiency measures before letting new tenancies. Non-compliance will be enforced by fines, although it remains to be seen whether this will be actively implemented.

As with residential buildings, the commercial sector has important barriers to retrofit which must be addressed if improvements are to be achieved. A survey of UK commercial landlords[7] identified the following barriers:

- Economic (cost and value)
- Organisational
- Lease structures/legal procedures
- Physical (building and technologies)
- Landlord/tenant relationship
- Data measurement
- Government policies

Unlike the residential sector, energy consumption in the commercial sector may only be a very small proportion of business costs and often remains low on the list of business priorities. The relationship between the landlord who undertakes the work and the tenant who will enjoy the benefit remains a challenge to be resolved. There is some evidence in the residential sector to suggest that landlords can charge more for retrofitted properties;[8] however, this is not yet widely known or reported in the commercial sector.

Fig 7.5 shows that there is still considerable potential to reduce energy consumption (and associated carbon emissions) in the commercial sector, and especially in the pre-1940 buildings which previously represented over 50% of the total. Fig 7.6 shows that many of the measures can be achieved at negative investment cost relative to energy saved.

The commercial sector is extremely diverse in terms of scale and energy use, with at least 10 different categories of building user and multiple sub-categories, each with its own specific building issues and constraints. Even where the building owner and user are part of the same organisation, there may be operational reasons why deep retrofit is impractical. In some organisations retrofit may be limited to energy-efficient lighting or controls, although the financial and energy-saving benefits of this should not be underestimated. The cost of energy may not be a reason for retrofit in the commercial sector, but there are other human factors which may play an increasingly important role in decision making. Thermal comfort and wellbeing are increasingly recognised by employers as factors in retaining staff, and poor building performance is closely linked to thermal comfort.

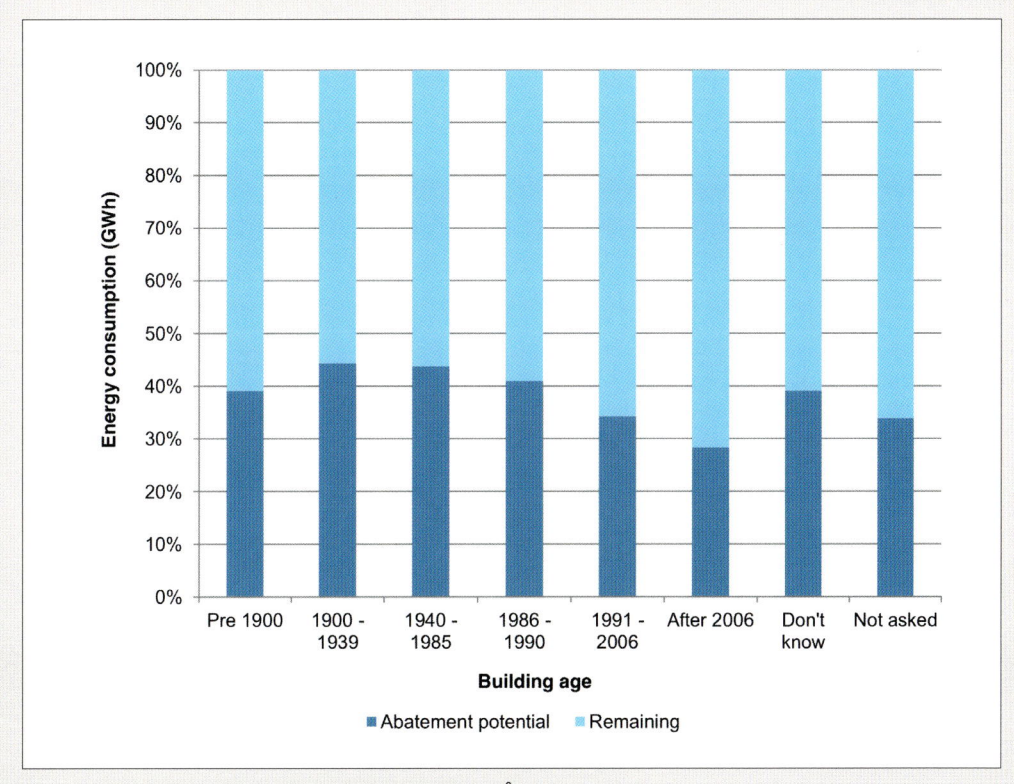

Fig 7.5: Energy abatement potential by building age, 2014–15[9]

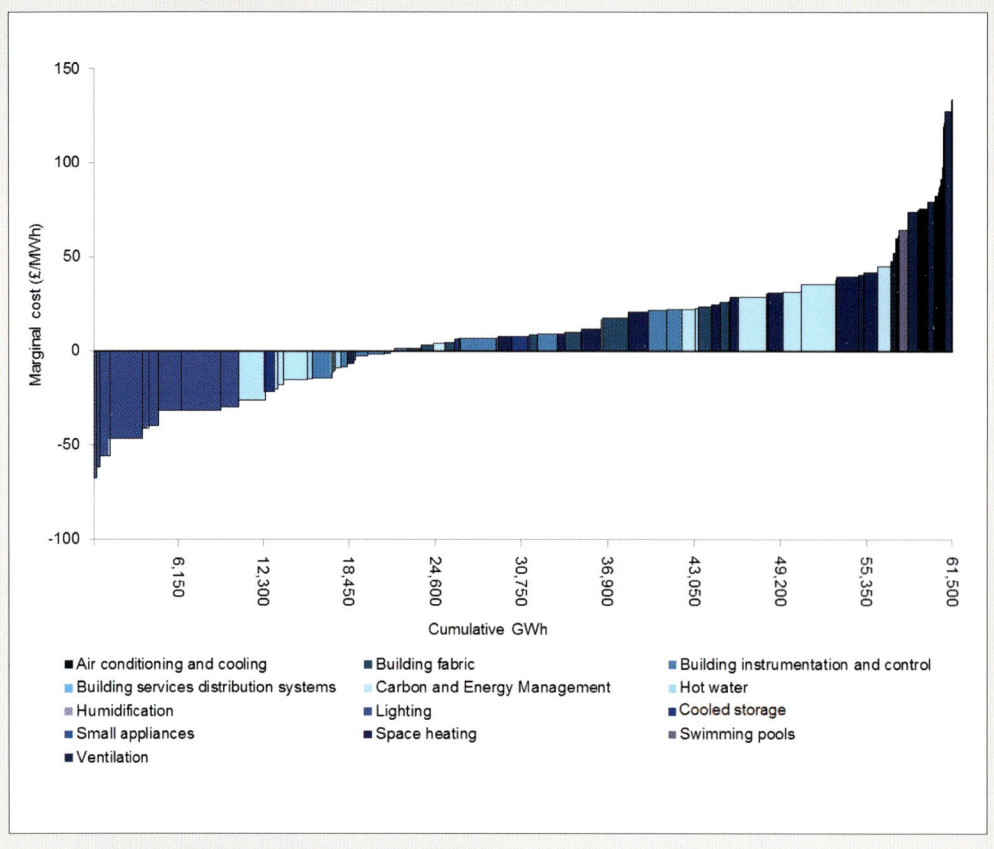

Fig 7.6: Marginal abatement cost curve for the 100 most socially cost-effective measure groups at sector level, 2014–15[10]

Unlike the residential sector, properties in the commercial sector are almost always 'managed', and investment decisions are typically planned around whether to refurbish, demolish or extend. The scale of investment is typically larger and the scope of alterations much greater, with a wider impact on the commercial operations of the business or organisation. As with residential properties, the decision to retrofit should be timed to coincide with other relevant investment decisions to avoid duplication and waste of resources.

The following case studies show how various investment drivers have been aligned to achieve deep retrofit while also delivering other benefits to the organisation. In each case the building had reached a 'tipping point', caused by a variety of factors including poor thermal comfort, poor visibility or poor amenity, which together caused the building owner to consider the long-term future of the building. In the case of University of Innsbruck, the project was driven by essential maintenance and fire safety works. This meant it did not require a commercial return but offered improved thermal comfort, increased floor area and ongoing research opportunities. In the case of the Evangelical Church at Heinsberg, the project was driven by the high running costs and poor visibility of the existing building, which coincided with an opportunity to sell off adjacent land to cross-subsidise the works. Sparkasse bank at Gross Umstadt was driven by a corporate decision to reduce its carbon emissions while addressing the thermal comfort and amenity of its staff and customers.

It would be impossible to include an EnerPHit case study of every building typology or kind of ownership. As early pioneer countries, it is perhaps unsurprising that the examples presented come from Germany and Austria.

The three examples represent the three main types of non-residential ownership: private, public and community ownership. In each case there were specific challenges which required a specific response, offering lessons that can be applied more widely. Two of the buildings have achieved EnerPHit, with one of the these following the certified component method. One of the projects was completed in phases with building users in occupation, whereas the building users were decanted in the other two examples. One of the buildings was insulated internally, while the other two were insulated externally. Two of the buildings have high internal heat gains, which have required careful consideration resulting in differing strategies but equally successful outcomes.

In all three of the case studies, the building owners have achieved massive carbon reductions (more than 80%). These case studies demonstrate what can be achieved when EnerPHit is applied at scale to commercial buildings, what challenges might be faced and how these might be overcome.

CASE STUDY 7.2

Public/Community
Evangelical Church, Heinsberg, Nordrhein-Westfalen, Germany

Client:	Evangelical Church of Heinsberg
Architect:	Rongen Architekten GmbH
M&E:	Planungsbüro Stickel
Structural Engineer:	Pulkus Egbert
PH Consultant:	Rongen Architekten GmbH
Contractor:	Various subcontracts managed by Rongen Architekten GmbH

INTRODUCTION

The church was originally built in 1953, and had remained largely unchanged since then. The building comprised a main hall with adjoining lean-to annex and a bell tower in a single thermal envelope (see Fig 7.7). The site also included a residential building used by the church minister, and a community hall which was infrequently used. The existing heating source was gas-fired heaters, and the running cost of the original building was approximately €6,500 per year, which was increasingly unsustainable. The buildings offered poor-quality accommodation which resulted in limited use by the wider community. Despite being in the historic heart of Heinsberg at the end of the central pedestrianised zone, it had limited civic presence, and the client was keen to provide facilities for wider community use. The brief was to not only reduce running costs and carbon emissions, but also to improve access and visibility without changing the character of the building.

The existing community building was therefore sold for redevelopment to fund the retrofit and redevelopment works. The work included new single-storey extensions to the existing hall, providing an improved entrance and a new community space adjacent to the church hall. A new basement area is provided adjacent to the new extension, which not only discreetly houses the new plant and toilets but also provides a delightful chapel with rooflight. To retain the character of the building, all insulation is installed internally, with the main hall thermally decoupled from the bell tower, which remains uninsulated. The TFA of the combined works totalled 2,394 m² and the project budget was approximately €1.5 million, funded by a combination of the land sale, church funds, donations and a local grant of €100,000. The project took approximately 15 months and was completed in April 2013.

Due to the complex nature of the building and the requirement to insulate internally, the building was vacant during the works and the project followed the Passivhaus component route to certification as EnerPHit(i). The space heating demand for the existing building was reduced from 183 kWh/m²/a to 8.5 kWh/m²/a. However, due to the significantly enlarged footprint and additional community uses, the completed building achieved a space heating demand of 30 kWh/m²/a.

KEY CHALLENGES

One of the key challenges was understanding the condition of the existing building and the remedial works necessary before the retrofit could begin. The existing brickwork was lined internally with a vapour-tight tar coating which had caused increased deterioration to the structure, and it was necessary to remove this and carry out essential repairs before insulation works could commence (see Fig 7.11). To avoid any risk of interstitial condensation, the team

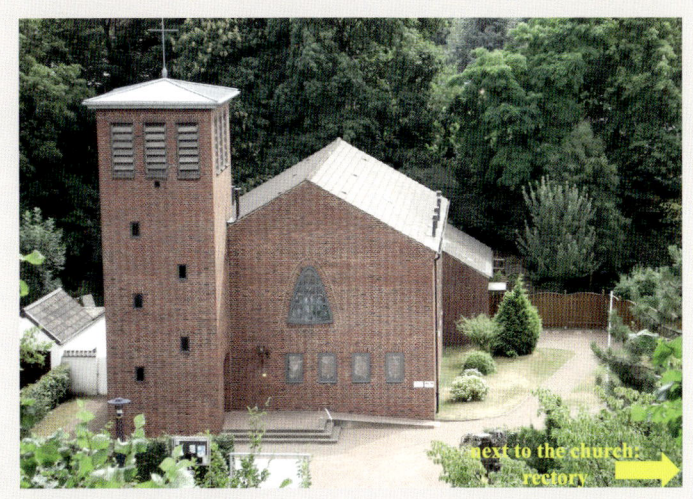

Fig 7.7: Church pre-retrofit[11]

Fig 7.8: Church post-retrofit[12]

Commercial Case Studies 129

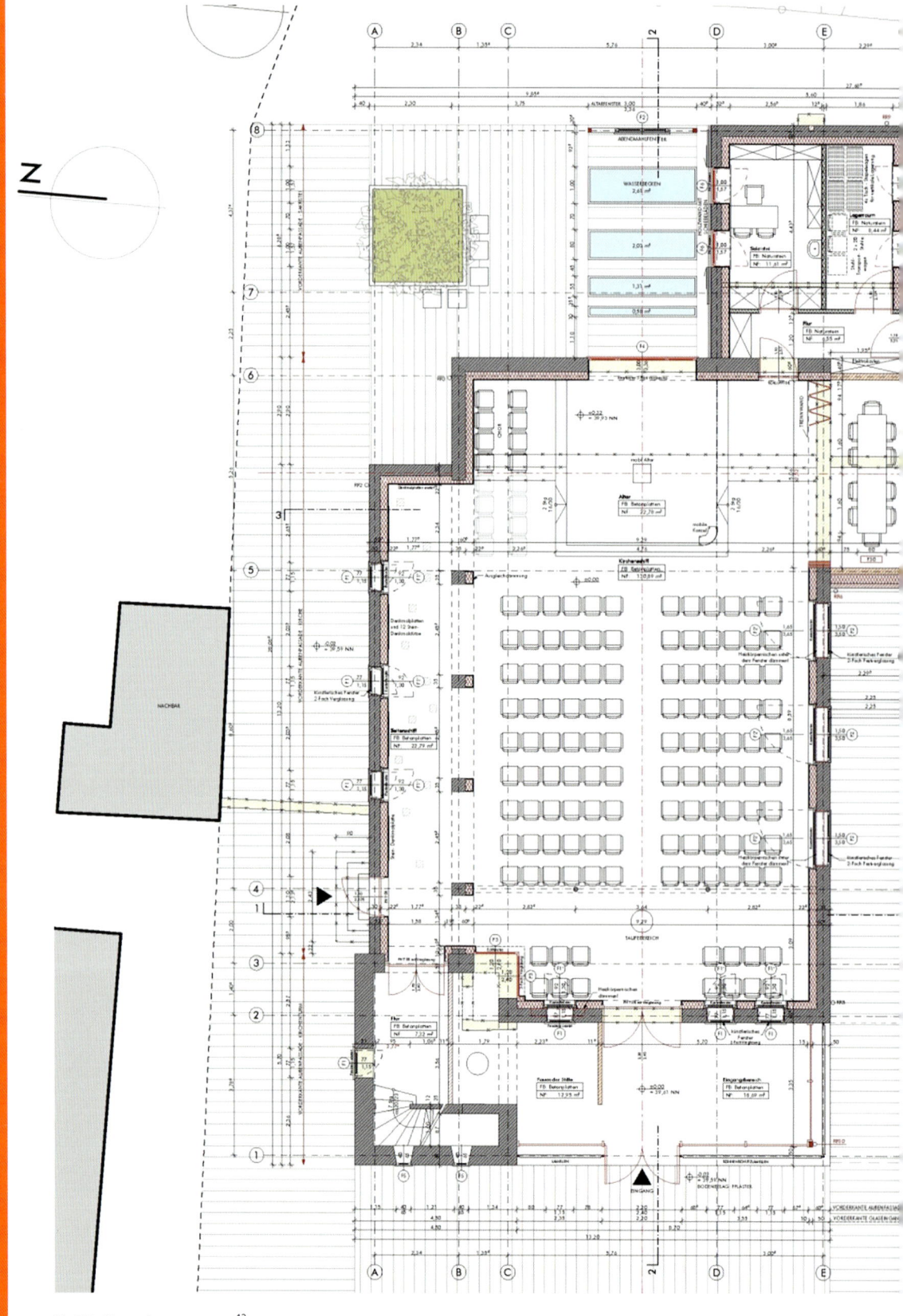

Fig 7.9: General arrangement[13]

extension

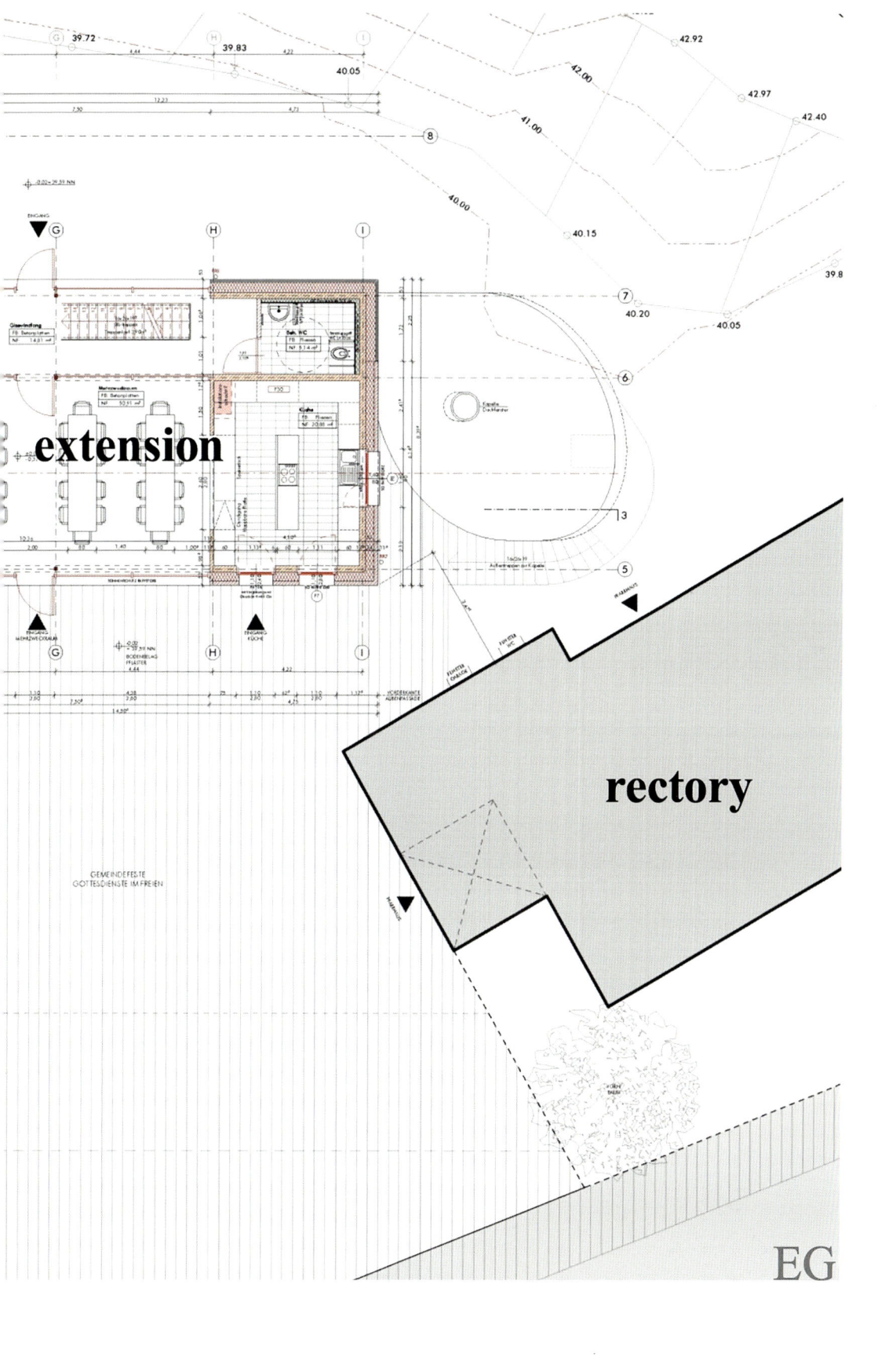

rectory

EG

Commercial Case Studies

Fig 7.10: PV array to roof[14]

Fig 7.11: Removal of diffusion-tight tar coating and repairs to brick joints (avoidance of water-repellent materials)[15]

opted for a breathable cellulose insulation, which was pumped into the void created by a new internal lining with an airtight membrane fixed to the outer face and plasterboard installed over it.

The existing single-glazed windows incorporated stained glass and were a key feature of the church, so these were generally retained, and triple-glazed secondary units were provided within the thermal envelope. The exception to this was the window at the altar, which was removed and relocated to the garden behind a new triple-glazed unit.

KEY ACHIEVEMENTS

Perhaps the most important achievement in this project has been the contribution to the wider community. Whereas the original building was only used two days per week, the refurbished building combining religious and community spaces is used seven days per week (see Fig 7.13). The new extension to the front provides a welcoming entrance, which increases the civic presence of the church and makes a positive contribution to the historic quarter. Whereas the running costs of the original building were approximately €6,500 per year, the retrofitted and extended building earns approximately €700 per year as a result of massively reduced heating bills offset by income from PV on the south-facing roof. The retrofitted church is very popular with both the congregation and the wider community in Heinsberg. It is also the first church in

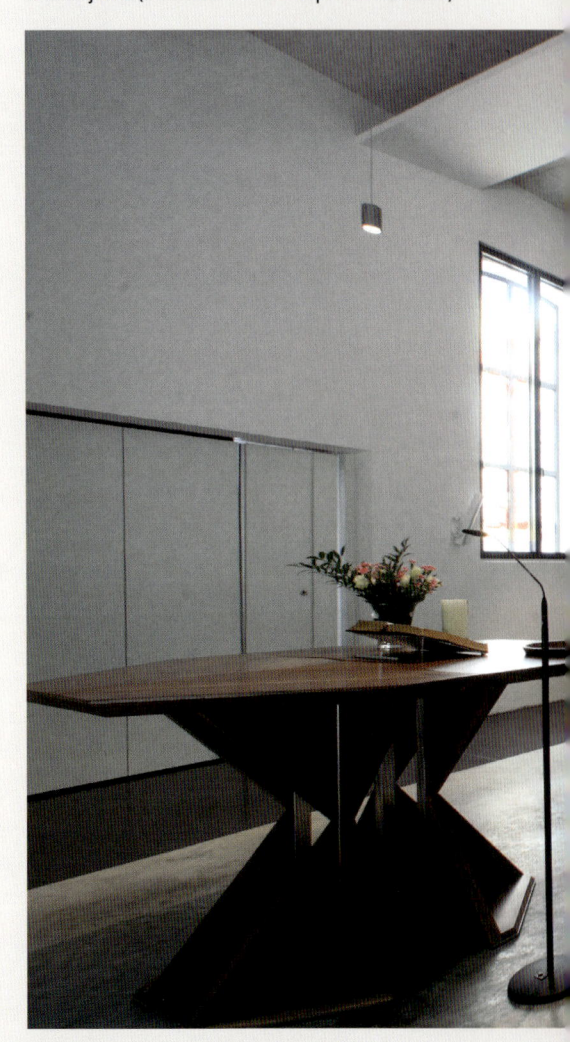

Fig 7.12: Interior of church post-retrofit[16]

132 EnerPHit: A Step-by-Step Guide to Low Energy Retrofit

the world to achieve the EnerPHit standard, and has since received many international visitors seeking to replicate this solution elsewhere.

TECHNICAL STRATEGY

EnerPHit certification was achieved using certified components throughout both the existing and new buildings, with the performance of the new building optimised to offset the lower performance of the existing building. The works included triple-glazed windows, doors, insulation, MVHR, new heating and hot water system, and all necessary airtightness measures. The windows have a U-value (glass) of

Fig 7.13: Adjacent community room in daily use[17]

Commercial Case Studies 133

0.6 W/m²K with a G-value of 50%, which reduces any risk of overheating. Pazen ENERsign doors with a U-value of 0.8 W/m²K are mostly used. The existing walls were insulated with 200 mm cellulose and achieved a U-value of 0.19 W/m²K. While slightly above the recommended U-value of 0.15 W/m²K, it is partly offset by the improved performance of the new walls, which achieved a U-value of 0.13 W/m²K using 240 mm of mineral wool. The roof of the existing church received 320 mm of mineral wool and achieved a U-value of 0.148 W/m²K, whereas the roof of the new extensions received 440 mm mineral wool, of which 240 mm was within the rafter zone, achieving a U-value of 0.079 W/m²K. Ventilation was provided by a Pichler, LG 4000 K-V System Ventech unit located in the new basement with insulated ductwork, achieving a specific efficiency of 75%. The completed airtightness test result of 0.8 ach is well within the EnerPHit threshold and the resulting

Fig 7.14: New entrance on west elevation[18]

Fig 7.15: New basement chapel under extension[19]

Fig 7.16: View to original window in garden[20]

calculated space heating demand was 30 kWh/m^2/a with a primary energy demand of 67 kWh/m^2/a.

POST-COMPLETION

Feedback from the building users has been very positive, although there has been one rather surprising outcome. Like many uninsulated and unventilated buildings of this period, the existing church had relatively high humidity levels. While this problem has been resolved by MVHR and insulation, an unlikely issue has arisen with the church organ, which now produces a different sound due to the lower humidity levels. Fortunately this can be resolved simply by occasionally spraying the organ with water droplets.

CASE STUDY 7.3

Higher Education
University of Innsbruck, Tirol, Austria

Client:	Bundesimmobiliengesellschaft (BIG), University of Innsbruck
Integrated Design (Architect, M&E, Structural Engineer):	ATP architects engineers
PH Consultant/ Building Physics:	Passivhaus Institut – Department Innsbruck and TB Rothbacher (acoustics)
Contractor:	Starmann Metallbau GmbH

INTRODUCTION

The existing building dates from 1969, when the campus was built on fields outside Innsbruck. Today the building is surrounded on three sides by new housing, with an airport to the south. Like many university buildings of this period, it is an exposed concrete frame that has experienced ongoing deterioration and has offered poor thermal comfort to its occupants. This building was one of several identical buildings on the campus, and the university

Fig 7.17: Engineering building pre-retrofit[21]

136 EnerPHit: A Step-by-Step Guide to Low Energy Retrofit

sought solutions to address the ongoing problems. ATP architects engineers subsequently won the project to retrofit the architecture and engineering buildings, and for the engineering building the decision was taken to target the EnerPHit standard. The TFA of the building is 9,649 m².

All campus buildings on the site are served by a district heating system, and while this connection was retained, 50% of the radiators in the engineering building were removed, as the estimated heating demand would be dramatically reduced by a factor of 9. At the same time internal pipework was insulated to prevent overheating risk.

KEY CHALLENGES

As a large academic building with high occupancy levels (up to 720 people) and associated internal heat gains, this building type can be prone to overheating. The existing building provided a poor thermal envelope and an unfavourable orientation. This made it prone to wide temperature swings on a seasonal and daily basis, causing overheating in the summer and excessive cold in the winter. The project team were confident that the proposed insulation and upgraded windows would reduce heat losses and provide good thermal comfort in the winter; however, there was concern that the retrofit could also reduce heat losses in the summer and

Fig 7.18: Engineering building post-retrofit[22]

Commercial Case Studies 137

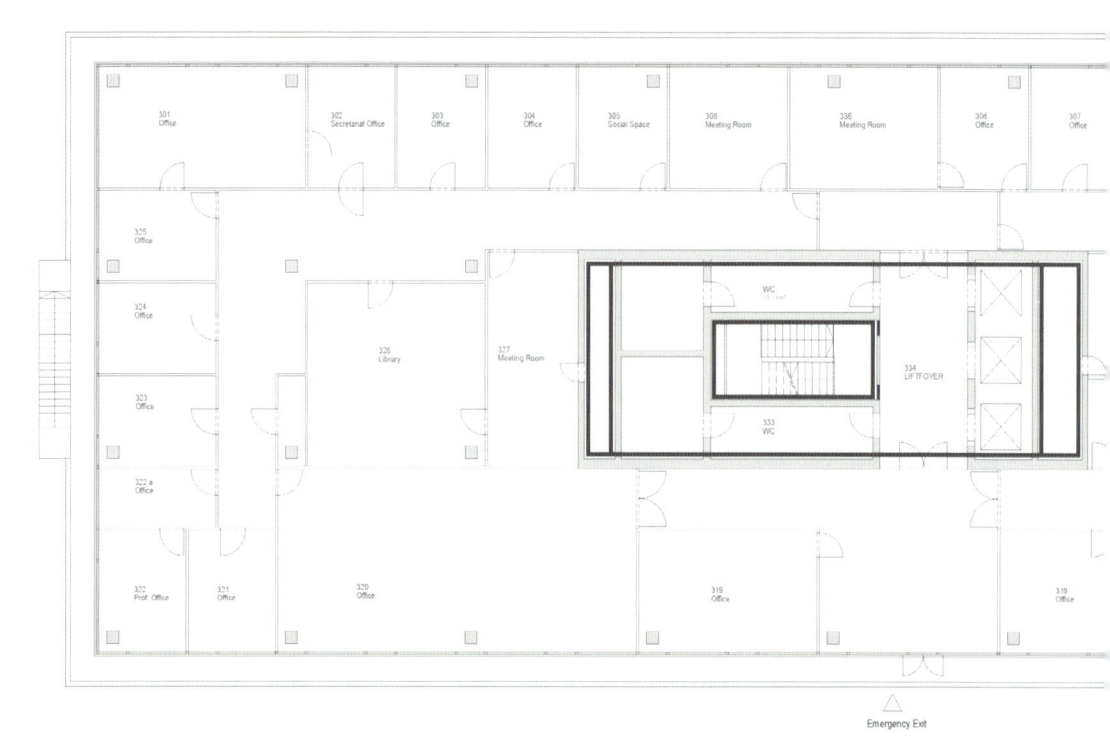

Fig 7.19: Existing typical floor plan (inset wall with 'balconies')[23]

increase overheating risk. The project team took the decision to use passive night cooling, with automated windows opening in the summer period to allow internal temperatures to reduce. Similarly, automated blinds were used to reduce overheating risk during the daytime which, coupled with low G-value glass, enables the building to achieve improved daylight levels while managing solar gains. With both the windows and the blinds, the building users can temporarily override the automatic settings, avoiding frustration. However, the building will ultimately revert to automatic settings to ensure that the shading and cooling strategy is not compromised.

Another challenge resulted from the aesthetic decision to achieve a flush detail between the cladding and windows while providing sufficient space for the automated opening mechanism and blinds. Figs 7.21 and 7.22 show that this required careful coordination in manufacture and installation, and resulted in a sub-optimal thermal bridge detail. Nevertheless, the completed windows function successfully and provide adequate shading and night cooling without causing an excessive thermal bridge.

Fig 7.20: Full-length 'balconies'[24]

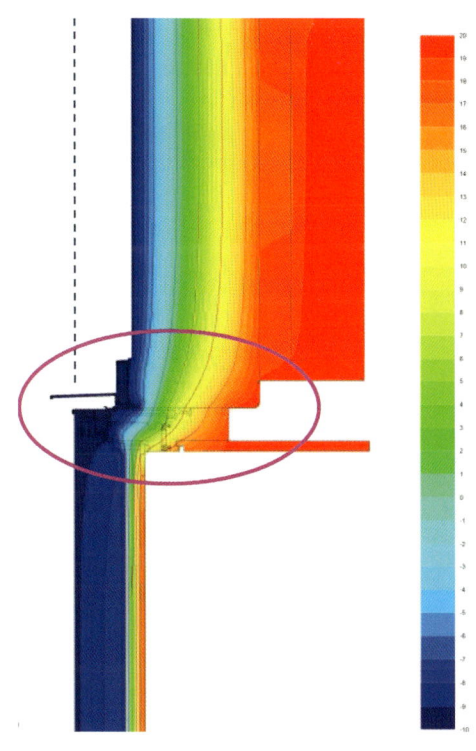

Fig 7.21: Flush detail results in less efficient thermal bridge[25]

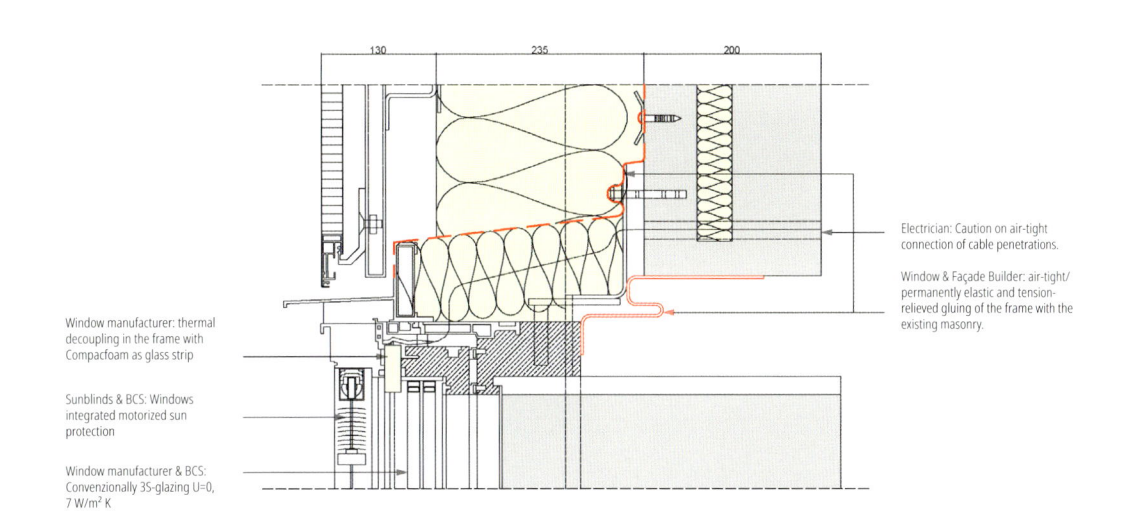

Window manufacturer: thermal decoupling in the frame with Compacfoam as glass strip

Sunblinds & BCS: Windows integrated motorized sun protection

Window manufacturer & BCS: Convenzionally 3S-glazing U=0, 7 W/m² K

Electrician: Caution on air-tight connection of cable penetrations.

Window & Façade Builder: air-tight/ permanently elastic and tension-relieved gluing of the frame with the existing masonry.

Fig 7.22: Automatic opening window head detail in flush cladding[26]

Commercial Case Studies **139**

KEY ACHIEVEMENTS

As a result of the automated night cooling strategy, the building is able to provide good thermal comfort in summer, with internal temperatures reduced as a result of the works without requiring active cooling systems (see Figs 7.23 and 7.24). This has also enabled the space heating demand to be reduced by a factor of 9 from 180 kWh/m²/a to 20 kWh/m²/a. This represents an annual carbon saving of approximately 500 tonnes per year (160 kWh/m² x TFA (9,649) x 320 g/Kg).

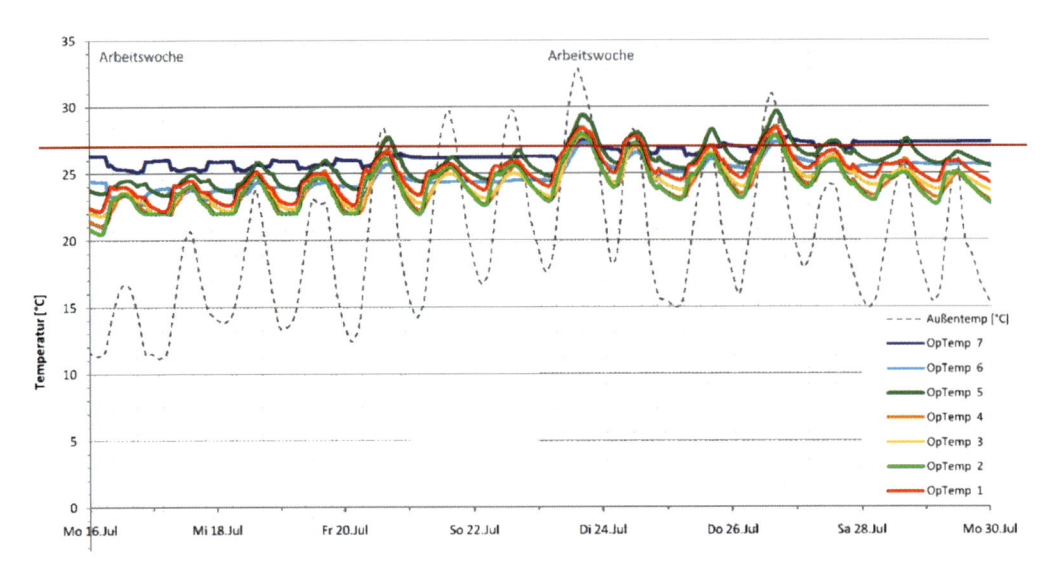

Fig 7.23: Pre-retrofit summer overheating (modelled)[27]

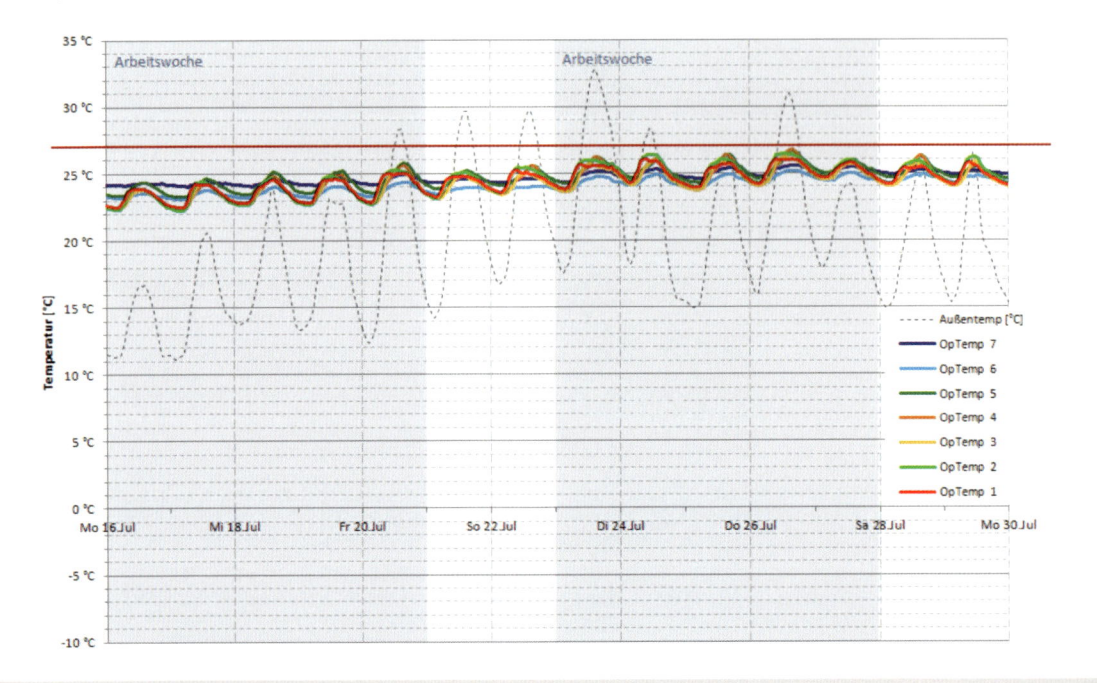

Fig 7.24: Post-retrofit summer overheating (modelled)[28]

140 EnerPHit: A Step-by-Step Guide to Low Energy Retrofit

The cellular layout of the engineering building represented a challenge to the proposed night cooling strategy, which required air movement across the building (see Figs 7.25 and 7.26). Achieving air movement between offices and the adjacent corridor without compromising acoustic separation proved a challenge which required a bespoke detail to be developed in the acoustic laboratory of Innsbruck University. The three-pane glazed transfer zone allows air to pass through while maintaining acoustic separation.

Fig 7.25: Ventilation strategy[29]

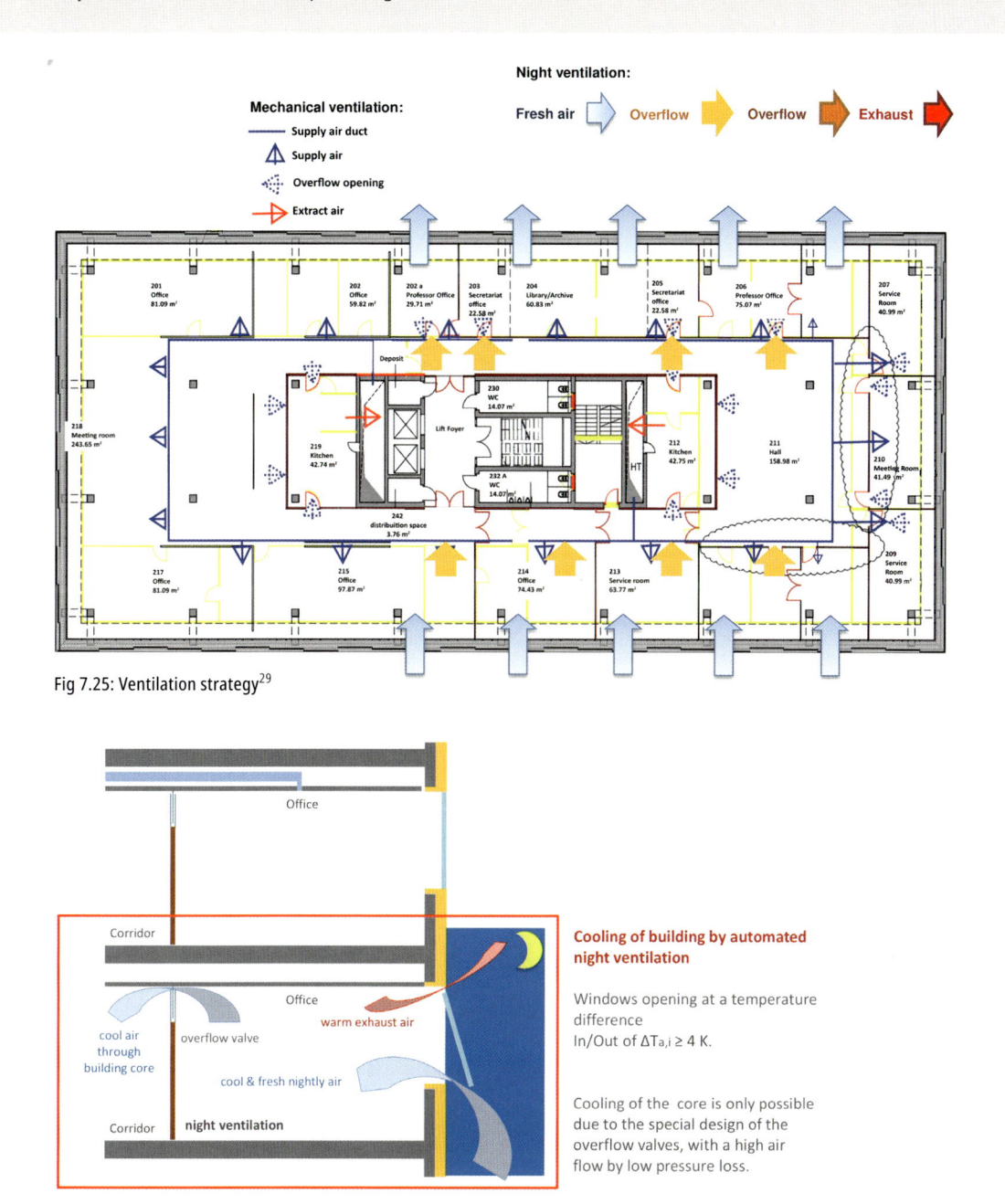

Fig 7.26: Ventilation strategy via night cooling – automatic windows open when temperature difference exceeds 4°C[30]

Cooling of building by automated night ventilation

Windows opening at a temperature difference
In/Out of $\Delta T_{a,i} \geq 4$ K.

Cooling of the core is only possible due to the special design of the overflow valves, with a high air flow by low pressure loss.

Commercial Case Studies 141

Fig 7.27: Post-retrofit office space with automated blinds and opening windows[31]

TECHNICAL STRATEGY

The new external envelope is located at the outer edge of the existing floor plate and the balconies are therefore enclosed, resulting in a slightly increased floor area. The new envelope includes 240 mm mineral wool insulation, which results in a U-value of 0.12 W/m²K. The existing basement, which is outside the thermal envelope, remains uninsulated; however, external wall insulation is provided around the perimeter at ground level to reduce thermal bridge heat losses. The roof is insulated with 240 mm XPS insulation laid to falls, achieving a U-value of 0.14 W/m²K. The glazing units are made up of four panes of glass with a triple-glazed unit and integrated blind protected behind a single-glazed screen, which may be removed for maintenance purposes. The overall U-value of the glass is 0.57 W/m²K although this is primarily achieved by the triple-glazing and is offset by the thermally broken aluminium frame,

142 EnerPHit: A Step-by-Step Guide to Low Energy Retrofit

Fig 7.28: Passive ventilation and increased daylight via door head detail with acoustic separation[32]

POST-COMPLETION

As a university building, one of the key objectives was to learn and disseminate the results from the project, and if necessary to carry out minor adjustments to optimise the building. As with the previous case study, building users report low humidity levels, especially in winter, and one of the learnings from this project may be to include humidity as well as heat recovery in any future project. Aside from the normal commissioning process, this has not been necessary as both thermal comfort and energy consumption are in line with expectations.

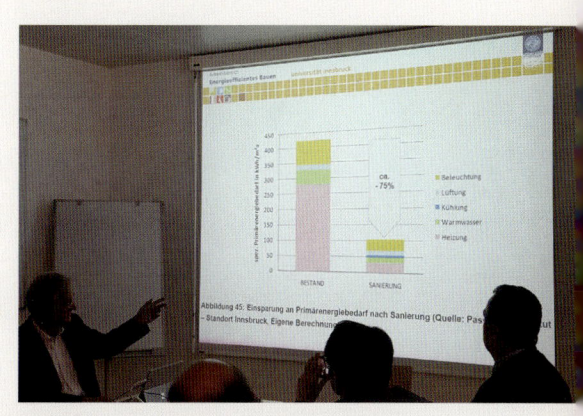

which achieved a U-value of 1.4 W/m²K. At ground floor level automatic doors are used with access via a thermal lobby, reducing heat loss. The building achieved an airtightness test result of 0.6 ach, which is well below the EnerPHit threshold. As noted above, the building employed a night cooling strategy in the summer, with automatic opening windows and cascade ventilation from offices into corridor areas. During daytime in the summer and throughout the heating season mechanical ventilation is provided via a ducted system, with all equipment located in the plant room on the roof.

Fig 7.29: Dissemination of results by Prof. Feist[33]

Commercial Case Studies 143

CASE STUDY 7.4

Offices
Sparkasse Bank, Gross Umstadt, Hesse, Germany

Client: Sparkasse Bank

Architects: schmidtploecker planungsgesellschaft mbH, GreenTech, Werner Sobek Frankfurt

M&E: Ingenieurplanung Söllner

Structural Engineer: Werner Sobek Frankfurt

PH Consultants: GreenTech, Werner Sobek Frankfurt

Contractor: Various subcontracts managed by Werner Sobek

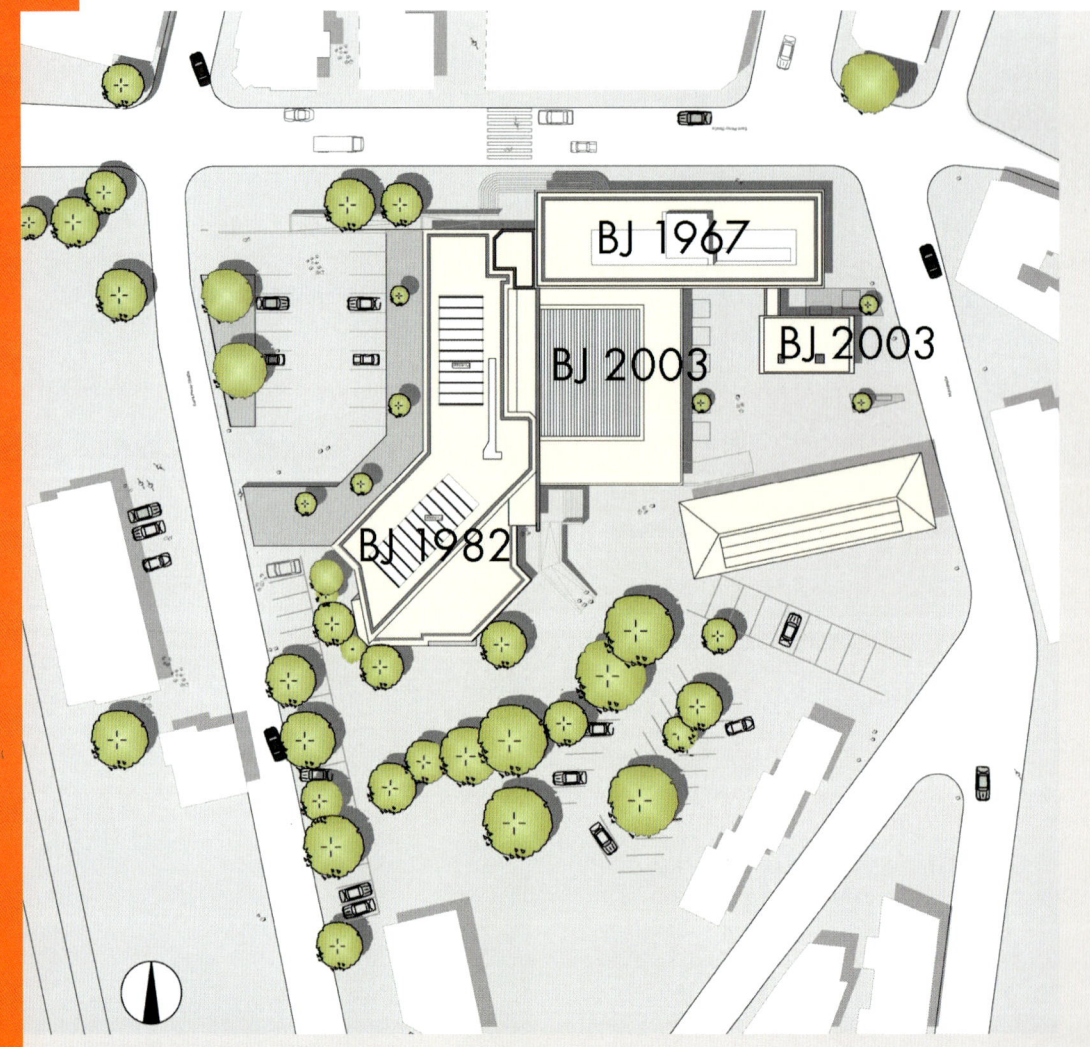

Fig 7.30: Age of existing buildings[34]

144 EnerPHit: A Step-by-Step Guide to Low Energy Retrofit

INTRODUCTION

This building is a large commercial bank and regional headquarters with public areas at ground floor level and offices above comprising a total TFA of 5981 m². The original building was constructed in three distinct periods (see Fig 7.30), with the oldest part dating from the 1960s and a large wing added in the early 1980s. Finally, a single-storey atrium and a small freestanding building were added in 2003. The atrium formed a physical connection between the earlier buildings and provided a public entrance and reception area to the bank. These incremental additions have resulted in the bank having a somewhat disjointed appearance. The client was keen to remodel the envelope of the building and the MEP to create a modern unified aesthetic, and to consider opportunities to reduce carbon emissions in line with wider corporate social responsibility objectives. The client had also undertaken a six-month pre-retrofit audit of building performance and identified significant issues to be addressed, including poor thermal comfort and poor air quality. The latter was a direct result of the limited ventilation and cooling, which was restricted to only 30% of the total floor area.

The project team proposed to wrap the building with stone cladding and reconfigure the window arrangement with triple-glazed units (see Fig 7.37).

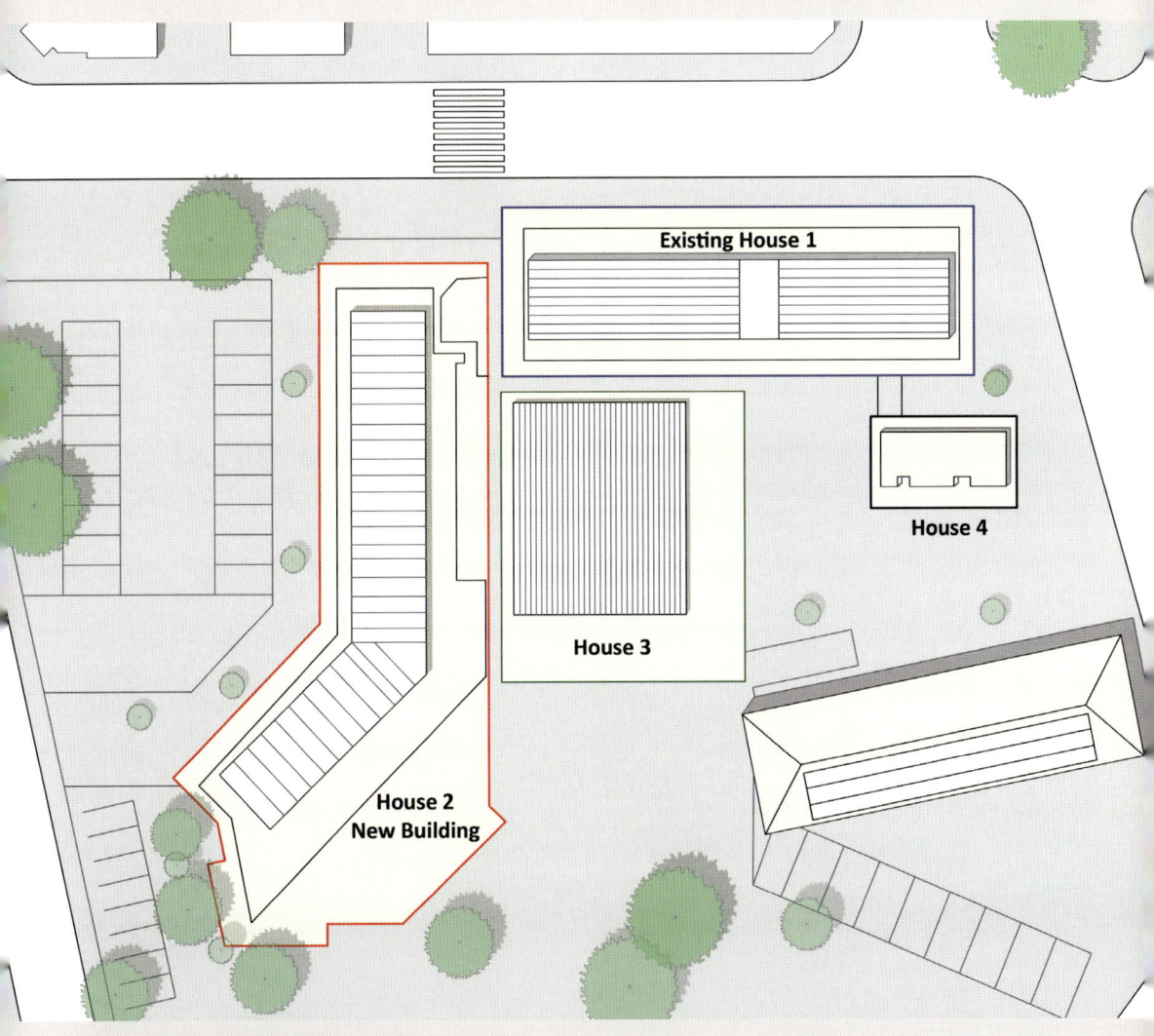

Fig 7.31: Four-phase strategy for retrofit[35]

Commercial Case Studies

Fig 7.32: Building pre-retrofit[36]

Fig 7.33: Building post-retrofit[37]

146　**EnerPHit:** A Step-by-Step Guide to Low Energy Retrofit

In doing so they introduced 240 mm mineral wool insulation to all elevations, increased the thickness of roof insulation and upgraded existing services with a new ventilation system serving all occupied areas. To reduce carbon emissions, the team opted to install a new woodchip-fired boiler to provide both heating and cooling. However, the building remained in use during the works, and therefore it was necessary to split the project over four phases, resulting in an extended programme of approximately two years, completed in 2016 at a total cost of approximately €8.5 million.

KEY CHALLENGES

Key challenges included the junction with the ground floor, which varied significantly across the existing buildings. In some areas it was not possible to insulate below adjacent ground levels, therefore where this was possible additional excavation was carried out to ensure the average depth remained acceptable. Another challenge was an existing ventilation duct, which could not be adequately insulated. A cold air pathway remains in the completed building; however, this is adjacent to a communal staircase and does not unduly affect thermal comfort or overall heat loss. Other compromises included the retention of the existing 1960s lifts, which although extremely robust and reliable are much more energy-intensive than equivalent modern units. Similarly, the project team decided to retain the double-glazed curtain walling system installed in the early 2000s and accept reduced performance and compensate elsewhere, rather than replace this with a triple-glazed system.

One of the most challenging aspects of the new design was the requirement to remove the lobby at the main entrance and provide a heat curtain in lieu. This was required by the client to improve public access and visibility, but it had a significant impact on heat loss and energy consumption. Using modelled data, the impact of the compromises could be offset by the significant thermal improvements elsewhere, and with an airtightness result of 0.9 ach the project team were reasonably confident that EnerPHit could be achieved. However, the impact of increased user

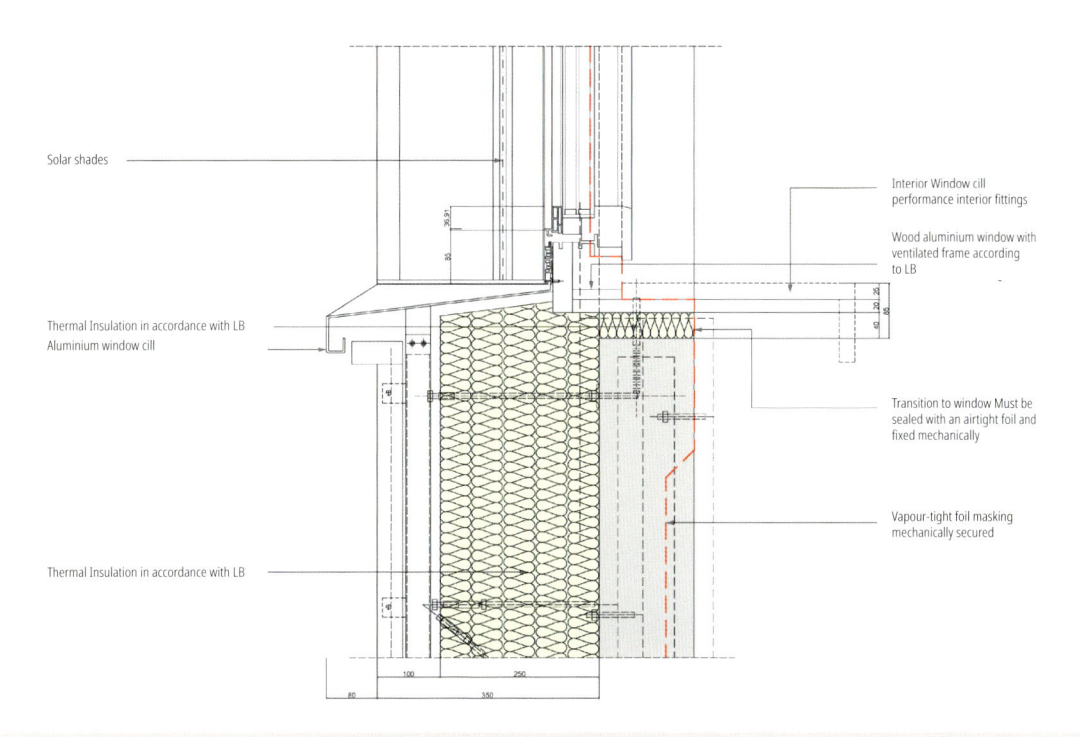

Fig 7.34: Window sill and airtightness layer detail[38]

Fig 7.35: External wall insulation and stone cladding[39]

Fig 7.36: Double-height entrance lobby[40]

demand should be considered in any retrofit. In this case the significant increase in both ventilation and cooling demand has resulted in actual performance levels above the EnerPHit threshold, with a 'realistic' PHPP suggesting a demand of 27 kWh/m², slightly higher than EnerPHit. As a result, the building is not certified as EnerPHit – but it is also clear that with modest alterations this could be achieved later if the client required it.

The introduction of woodchip boilers for both heating and cooling has resulted in a massive reduction in carbon emissions – but this also brings challenges. During the summer cooling period the system continues to burn fuel, but instead produces coolth rather than warmth. However, the process of combustion continues to release heat, which is obviously not required in the summer. As the plant room is in the existing basement this heat cannot be adequately removed and therefore these areas tend to overheat.

KEY ACHIEVEMENTS

This building remained operational throughout the works, with public access and staff accommodation phased to minimise disruption. Given the scale of the project and the comprehensive nature of the works to both the envelope and services, this was a major achievement. Although the building is not currently certified to the EnerPHit standard, it has achieved the DGNB Gold standard (German Sustainability Benchmark), which measures a series of performance criteria against sustainability factors including ecological quality, economic quality, sociocultural and functional quality, technical quality, process quality and site evaluation.

As a result of the introduction of woodchip boilers and extensive use of PV on the roof, the building has achieved a 93% reduction in carbon emissions and 33% reduction in electricity consumption, resulting in a primary energy demand of 62 kWh/m²/a, which is well below the EnerPHit threshold of 120 kWh/m²/a. Despite the varying construction types, arrangement and age of the existing buildings, the airtightness target was achieved in a single test with a result of 0.9 ach.

Perhaps one of the most important achievements has been the significant improvement in thermal comfort, with mechanical ventilation now provided to all areas and internal temperatures remaining above 20°C with a lower seasonal range. Improved performance has also resulted in raised expectations

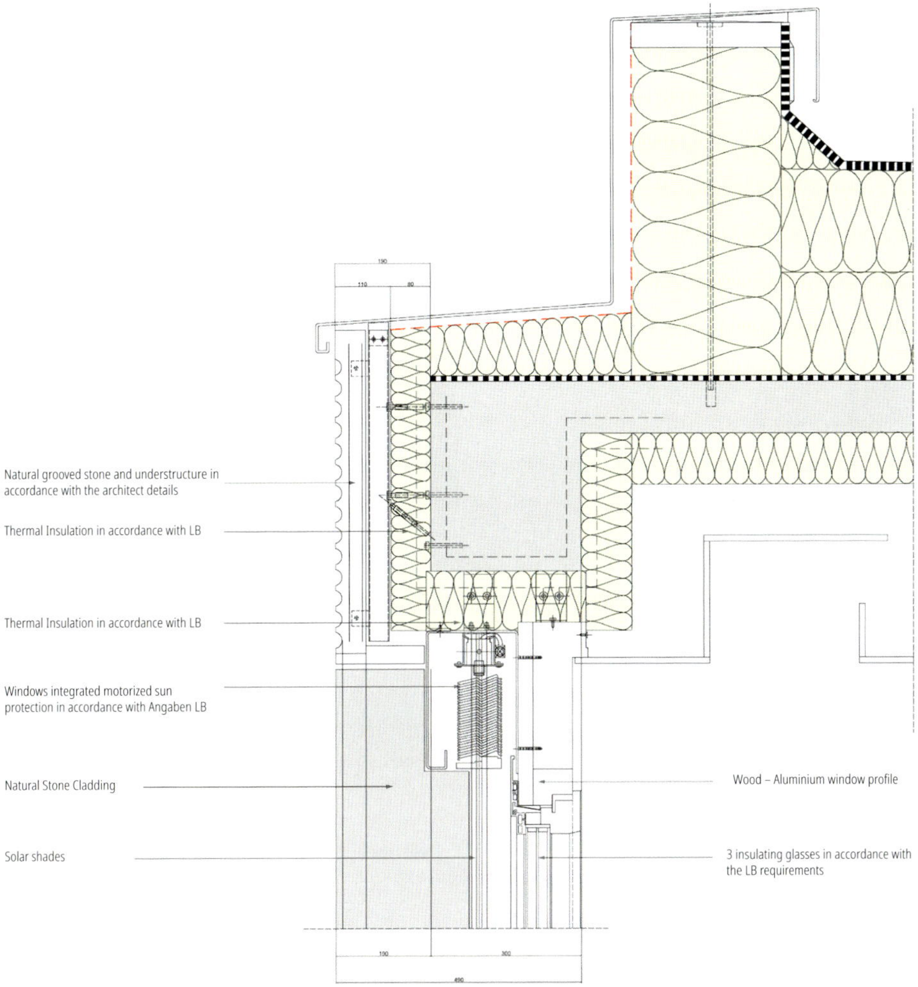
Natural grooved stone and understructure in accordance with the architect details
Thermal Insulation in accordance with LB
Thermal Insulation in accordance with LB
Windows integrated motorized sun protection in accordance with Angaben LB
Natural Stone Cladding
Solar shades
Wood – Aluminium window profile
3 insulating glasses in accordance with the LB requirements

Fig 7.37: Eaves and window head detail[41]

for higher internal temperatures in the winter (23°C) and air-conditioning in the summer, which may only be resolved through building management.

TECHNICAL STRATEGY

The main intervention was the replacement of the existing building envelope with new stone cladding and mineral wool insulation. A standard rainscreen cladding system of this type would have resulted in multiple thermal bridges and excessive heat loss due to the metal fixings typically used. To resolve this problem, the design team worked with the manufacturer to develop a new type of fixing with an angled suspension strap to the cladding frame (see Fig 7.38), which reduced the size of the frame profiles by a factor of five.

Given the multiple existing building types, the decision was taken to install the airtightness layer on the inside of the thermal envelope. While this solution can be easier to install, it does require the building owner to be aware of the risk of puncturing the layer at a future date, and a services void is often provided inside this layer, allowing both routing of cables and wall fixings to be made without risk of puncture. This additional layer was provided at Sparkasse Bank and most of the services installations and cables are situated inside this layer.

One of the challenges common to many retrofit

Fig 7.38: Angled strap through insulation reducing thermal bridge[42]

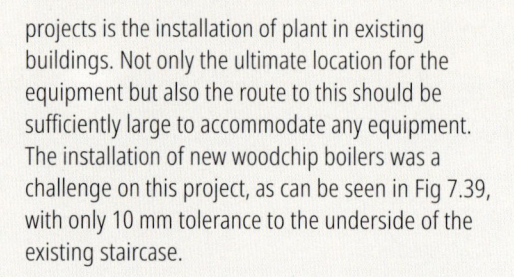

Fig 7.39: Installing large plant in existing building[43]

projects is the installation of plant in existing buildings. Not only the ultimate location for the equipment but also the route to this should be sufficiently large to accommodate any equipment. The installation of new woodchip boilers was a challenge on this project, as can be seen in Fig 7.39, with only 10 mm tolerance to the underside of the existing staircase.

This project was delivered by multiple specialist trades managed by the consultant team and without a single main contractor. While this procurement route (construction management) is unusual in the UK it is common in Germany on smaller, complex projects. This route allows the client and project team to retain very close scrutiny of the selection and performance of each trade, resulting in improved quality. It requires increased input from the consultant team and can bring additional risk of increased cost and delay. The project was completed on time and within budget, and this route may be worth considering for future retrofit projects.

One of the most interesting findings from the project has been the investigation into the assumed leak over the entrance lobby. This part of the building was completed in 2003 and had a chilled beam system installed in the concrete roof deck to provide increased coolth. The building users had reported water droplets falling into the hall since completion, and it was assumed that the roofing membrane had failed. Water tests had proved inconclusive, and there was no evidence of any failure in the membrane. The consultant team opened the roof and carried out WUFI analysis, which showed that due to a faulty and perforated vapour barrier the internal moisture was condensing on the cold side of the insulation, and droplets were falling on to building occupants below. By installing a new vapour barrier any future condensation was prevented and the mystery was solved. At the same time, the insulation on the roof was increased to Passivhaus standard.

POST-COMPLETION

The client undertook a six-month pre-retrofit study of building issues to inform the brief. On completion the client has also carried out a two-year POE to understand actual performance and overall building user satisfaction. This demonstrated that the building was providing thermal stability in both winter and summer periods. Fig 7.40 shows that internal temperatures remained relatively stable despite the heatwave of 2015.

The POE also identified a massive reduction in carbon emissions, with a 33% reduction in electricity consumption. Perhaps surprisingly it also demonstrated that there was no overall reduction in energy consumption. The project team had accepted the reduced performance of a number of existing building elements, e.g. lifts and curtain walling, and that the energy consumption was higher than expected. However, this was compounded by additional factors, including:

- Increased ventilation and cooling demand to include 100% of TFA
- Increased volume and enlarged windows on the top floor leading to increased heat loss in winter/gain in summer
- Window blinds required to reduce glare have also reduced passive heat gain in winter
- Removal of entrance lobby and inclusion of heat curtain has increased energy demand and heat losses in winter

Despite exceeding the EnerPHit threshold the retrofit of this building is a good example of the retrofit challenges that are faced in large, complex building types with multiple users. It has nevertheless achieved massive reductions in carbon emissions and dramatically improved thermal comfort for the building users.

Current German energy ordinance targets[45] require overall energy reduction rather than carbon reductions; however, as demonstrated in the retrofit of Sparkasse Bank, this may not adequately capture improvement. While retrofit projects will typically result in improved human comfort, the client may not achieve the energy or carbon savings predicted, as the user was not previously heating or cooling the building adequately (Jevons paradox). While this paradox applies to both energy and carbon, international emissions targets (COP 23) are measured in carbon rather than energy, and the performance of Sparkasse Bank has prompted a debate in Germany on the future measurement of building performance.[46]

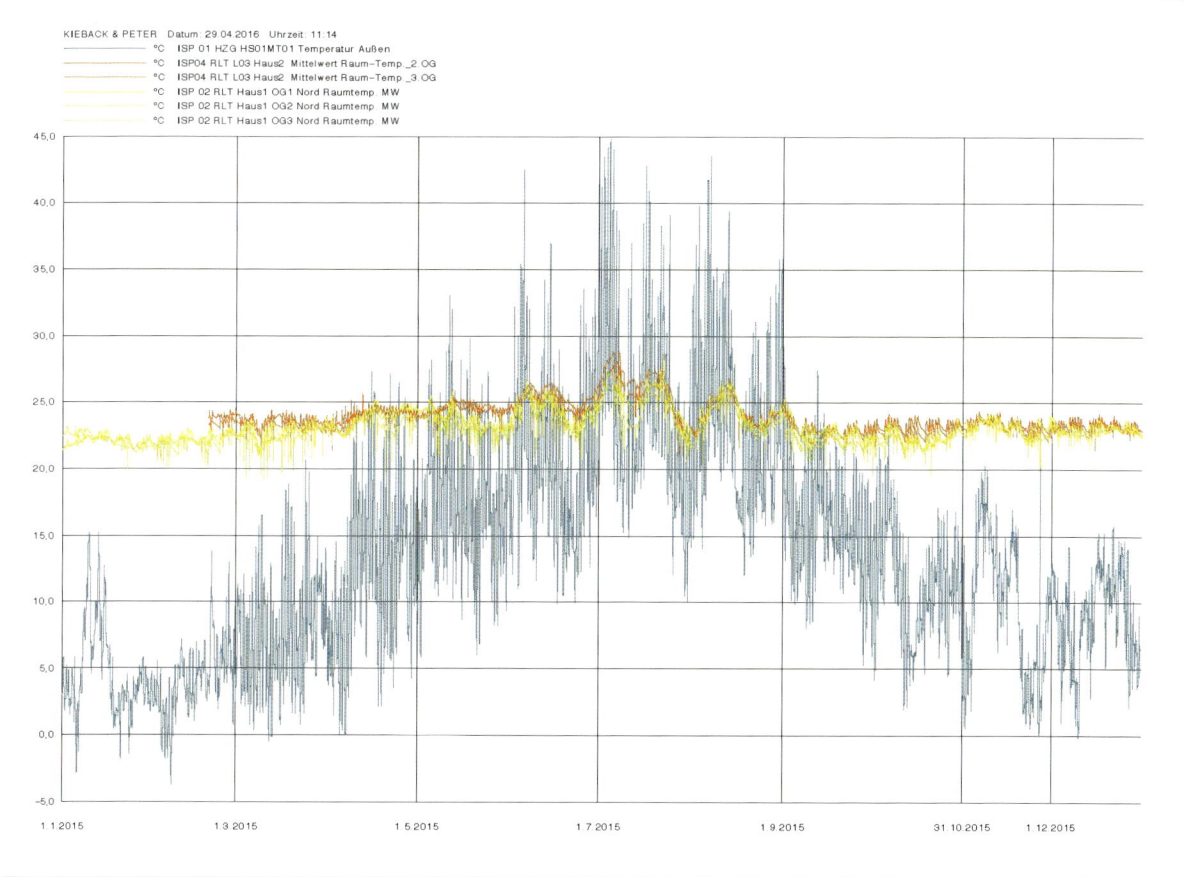

Fig 7.40: Interior temperatures (January to December 2015) showing slow reaction time to external temperature change[44]

8.0: Delivering EnerPHit

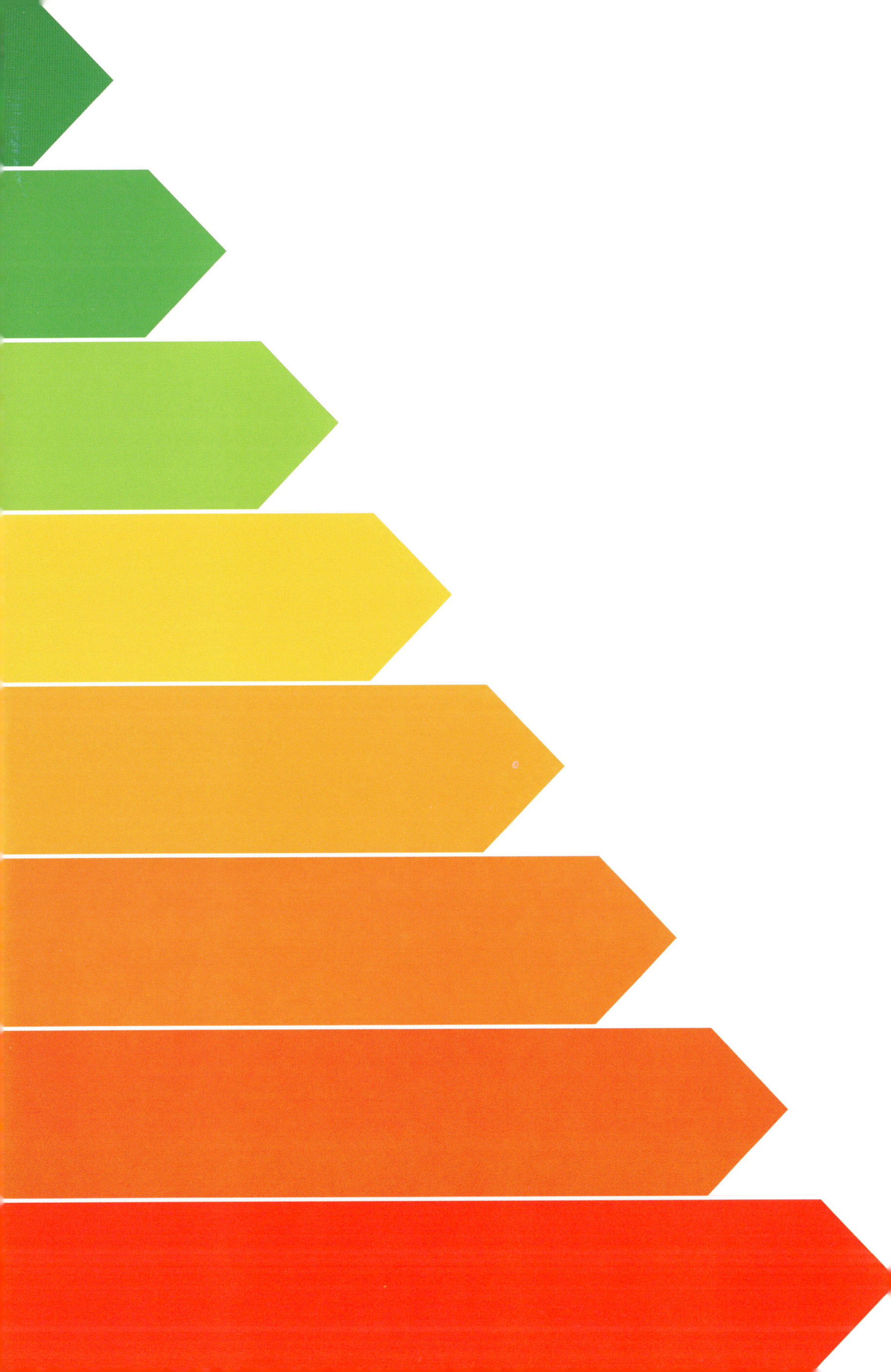

8.1: HOW TO APPROACH ENERPHIT

Construction projects in the UK typically follow the RIBA Plan of Work (2013) covering all stages of the life cycle of a building from RIBA Stage 0 (Strategic Definition) to Stage 7 (In Use). To maximise the benefit and minimise the cost of pursuing Passivhaus or EnerPHit, it is crucial to consider the option as early as possible in the design process (RIBA Stages 0 or 1). While it is possible to pursue these standards at a later stage, it is also very likely that key design decisions will already have been made which lock in lower performance and will cost more to resolve. This might include orientation of the building, internal layout, glazing ratio, location of services, wall thickness, and so on.

The case studies show how deep retrofit to the EnerPHit standard can be applied to virtually any building type. The full spectrum of building types that have achieved EnerPHit can be seen on the International Passivhaus Database.[1] The range of energy performance across existing building types varies enormously, and it is important to establish both the existing performance and condition of any building type before undertaking deep retrofit. For a building owner considering deep retrofit the energy balance between losses and gains must be understood. This must be specific to the building and location to both reduce excessive losses and prevent excessive gains, which in turn might result in overheating. Having established the baseline position of the building in kWh/m^2/a, the building owner can then understand the long-term cost of maintaining the building in its existing state and compare a range of retrofit options.

Alternatively, the building owner may be considering retrofit due to other planned works such as extension or facade replacement. Building regulations in England and Wales require the building owner (non-domestic) to undertake consequential improvements where alterations to more than 25% of the building envelope are proposed. While these improvements may only require performance to be improved to Part L2B (currently approximately 80 kWh/m^2/a), some building owners may decide to go beyond this threshold for particular elements in order to prevent lock-in of mediocre improvement. Others may wish to consider deep retrofit as a means of providing a holistic solution and avoiding the increased risk of potentially damaging unintended consequences. Others still may be frustrated by the poor thermal comfort offered by their existing building, and wish to dramatically improve their internal environment either for themselves or other building users.

Whatever the reason for deep retrofit, having decided to pursue this strategy it is important to ensure that the right skills are available to suit the project. The PHI maintains a database of several thousand qualified Passivhaus designers and consultants,[2] and any client wishing to target Passivhaus or EnerPHit compliance should ensure that their designers are suitably qualified. To maintain quality control, certification is independently managed by the PHI, with delegated authority to several independent organisations accredited by the PHI. The Passivhaus designer/consultant should refer to the certification guide[3] and seek early engagement with the certifier to understand any potential complexity or barriers to certification.

Having considered options for certification, the team can then begin to model a number of options to optimise the design solution. PHPP v9 (perhaps using a plug-in such as designPH) offers the designer the tools necessary to understand the relative performance and cost of each option and thus advise the building owner. Having decided which option to pursue, the building owner may then decide whether to achieve this target in a single step or whether they would prefer to implement it over a longer period, as described in the ERP. Having established the target measures, outline cost and programme, the building owner or their design team should then prepare a detailed set of drawings and information based on the measures identified in the PHPP. These tender documents should describe in sufficient detail the measures necessary to achieve EnerPHit and confirm responsibility for compliance and independent certification.

8.2: THE PRACTICAL CHALLENGES OF ENERPHIT

There are numerous barriers to deep retrofit, and it is therefore important to take a holistic approach to retrofit and recognise that each building presents a unique set of challenges. However, there are also standard requirements which all projects must address if they are to deliver deep retrofit over the short or long term. There are five key aspects which need to be addressed in any Passivhaus or EnerPHit scheme:

- **Achieving airtightness**
- **Providing a continuous thermal envelope**
- **Providing mechanical ventilation with heat recovery (MVHR)**
- **Avoiding thermal bridging**
- **Optimising solar gain**

Achieving airtightness

Any project targeting EnerPHit must deliver excellent levels of airtightness. To achieve this, the designer must confirm the airtightness barrier around the whole envelope of the building. At the outset of the project it is essential to identify in plan and section the location and method of achieving airtightness across each element of the building, and crucially at all junctions and penetrations (see example in Fig 8.1). To understand existing performance a pre-retrofit airtightness test is also recommended, as it can be a useful method of identifying problematic areas to address in the retrofit.

On larger buildings the airtightness strategy and the means of effective testing both during construction and at completion can be more complex, and advice should be sought from an experienced airtightness consultant. During construction it is particularly

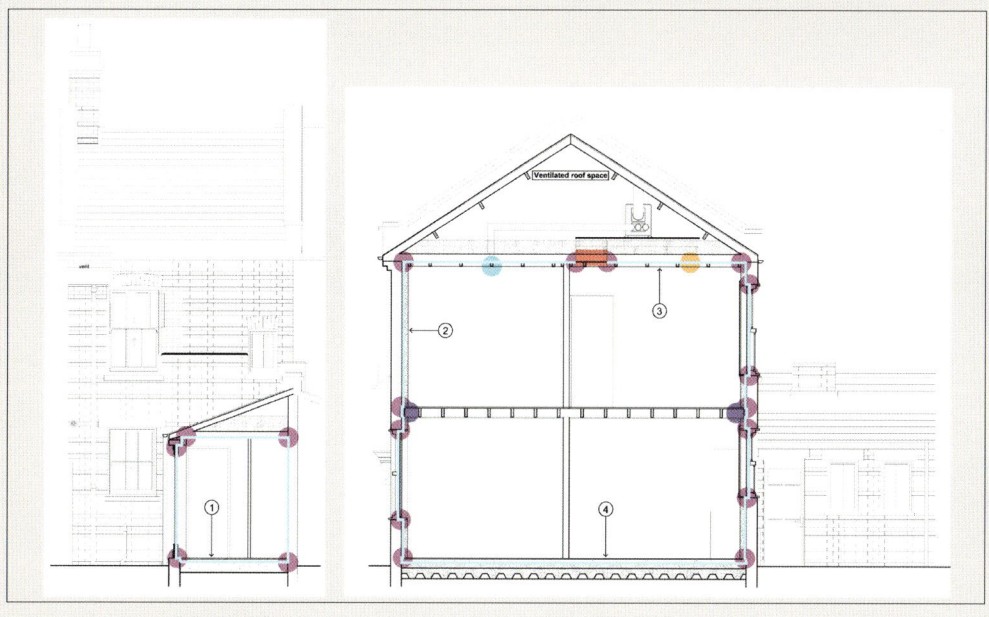

Fig 8.1: Planning for airtightness[4]

NOTES:

① Rear Floor: Existing Floor stripped back and overlaid with Spacetherm – C. Existing slab. Seal all joints, junctions and penetrations in chipboard and perimeter abutment to external.

② Walls: Lay Intello plus membrane over ply face. Seal all joints, junctions and penetrations

③ Existing ceiling stripped back and replaced with 18mm OSB board. Penetrations, junctions and gaps to be taped and sealed.

④ Main Floor: Existing Floor stripped back and replaced with ECO-SLAB insulated EPS formwork – overlaid with Proband 880 1600g Polythene DPM & EPS insulation board and sealed with 75mm Sand & Cement screed.

- Tescon Profil/No. 1 tape
- Rolflex grommets to seal all duct penetrations
- Apply expanding foam to a depth of 50mm to all exposed brickwork
- Orcon F adhesive
- Air tight envelope
- 600x600mm Wellhofer air tight insulated loft hatch.

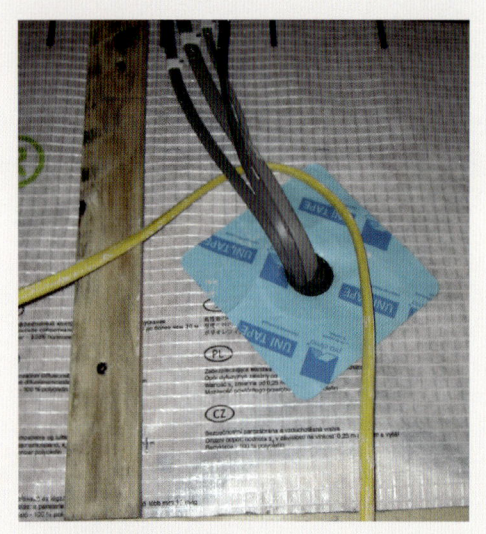

Fig 8.2: Maintaining airtightness at service penetrations[5]

Fig 8.3: Improving the thermal performance of external walls[6]

important that all tradespeople are aware of the airtightness barrier and understand the need to prevent this being damaged. The contractor should appoint an 'airtightness champion' (often the site manager) to ensure all subcontractors are aware of this risk via toolbox talks, and the contractor (or consultant) should carry out interim tests at key stages, i.e. first fix of services. For example, it is essential that any services installed by the electrician and plumber passing through the airtight barrier are sealed with the use of certified grommets and tapes (see Fig 8.2). All other penetrations through the envelope – i.e. windows, doors and loft hatches – must be appropriately taped to the adjacent airtight barrier, and the component itself should also be certified for airtightness.

Providing a continuous thermal envelope

The thermal envelope of a building typically comprises the following:

- External walls
- Ground floor
- Roof
- Windows and doors

Each building element must provide high levels of thermal performance, and it is essential that where these meet, the junctions must be thermally continuous to avoid thermal bridging. The treatment of each element must be considered as part of a holistic solution to improve the thermal performance of the building.

External walls

The thermal performance of existing solid-wall properties in the UK is typically very poor. These make up a significant proportion of the total stock and must be tackled. At a building level, external walls (especially in detached properties) are often the single biggest source of heat loss, and this must be addressed in any deep retrofit. The U-value of a typical solid wall in the UK is estimated to be 2.1 W/m^{2}K (RdSAP), while the U-value of external walls in a newbuild property is typically 0.18 W/m^{2}K. It can be assumed that the external walls in a Passivhaus or EnerPHit building will need to achieve not less than 0.15 W/m^{2}K compared to 0.3 W/m^{2}K in a standard UK retrofit. Understanding the implications and limitations of this at the outset of any project is crucial. Many older solid-wall properties will require internal insulation to avoid changing the appearance of the property. However, achieving a U-value of 0.15 W/m^{2}K on a solid-wall property would typically require more than 200 mm of insulation depending on the lambda value of the insulation used. On the external face of the building this may be acceptable, subject to detailing at junctions, e.g. party walls, eaves and windows. However, on the internal face of the wall this would result in a significant loss of floor area, and the building owner may wish to consider high-performance insulation alternatives

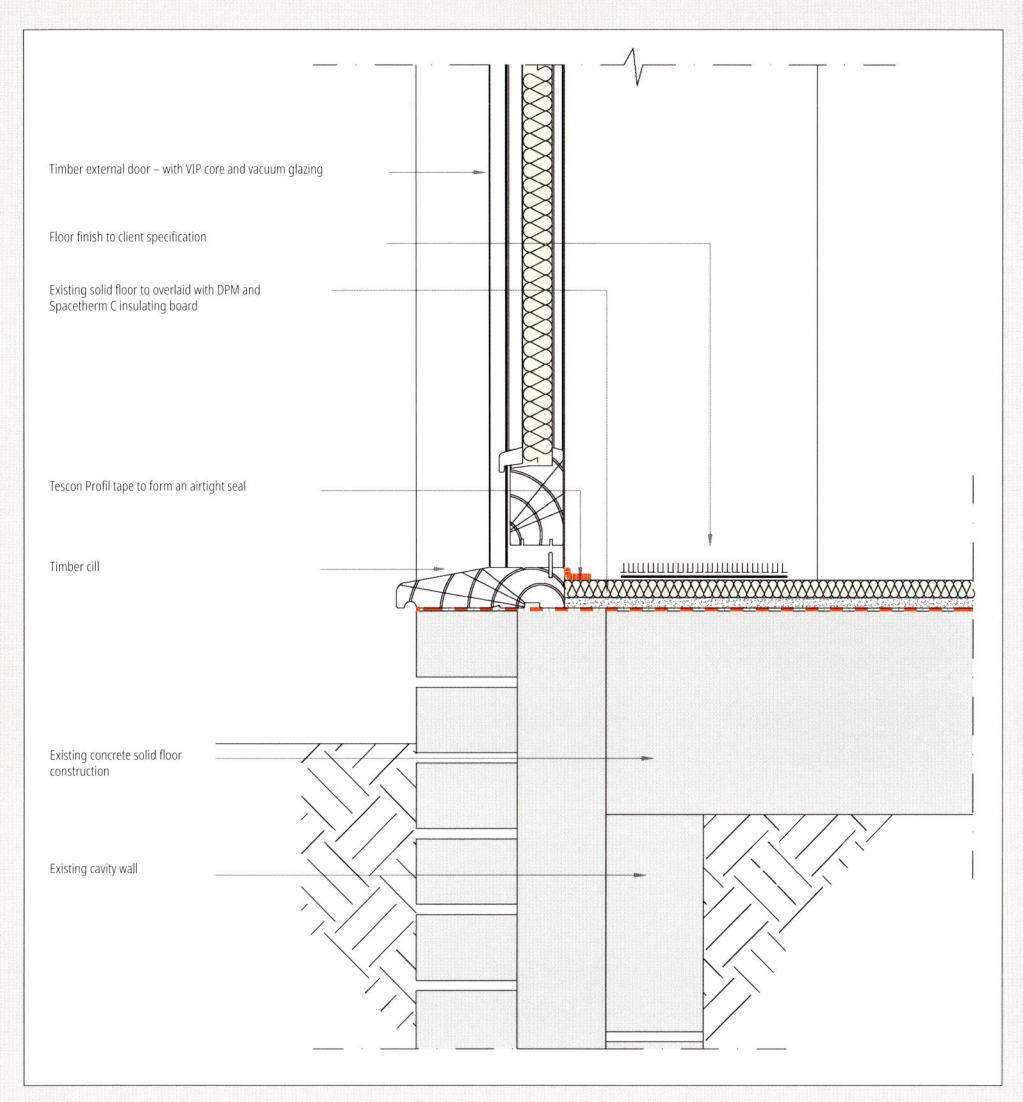

Fig 8.4a: Laying a new timber floor with bonded insulation over an existing concrete slab[7]

Fig 8.4b: Laying a new timber floor with bonded insulation over an existing concrete slab[8]

Delivering EnerPHit 157

Timber external door with VIP core and vacuum glazing

40mm Pavaboard Load bearing Insulation laid onto floor joists. All joints, junctions and edges to be sealed as per manufacturers recommandations

6mm WBP ply to be laid over insulation boards. Joints & junctions to be sealed with airtightness tape.

3mm protective hardboard

Seal door frame to ply board to form an airtight seal

Timber packer to suit floor level

Existing external render made good

75mm cellulose insulation fitted between joists

Existing SW timber floor joists

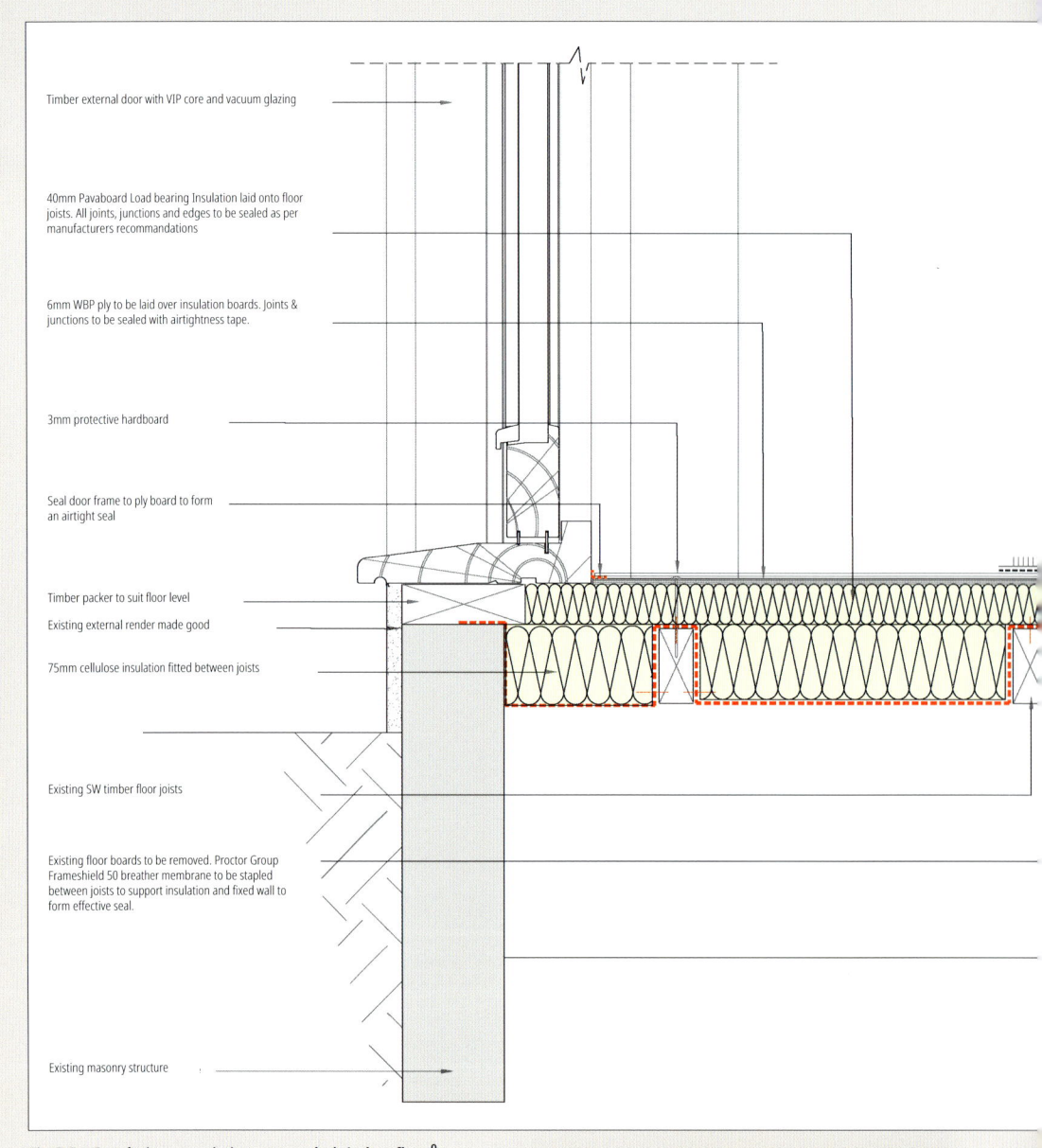

Existing floor boards to be removed. Proctor Group Frameshield 50 breather membrane to be stapled between joists to support insulation and fixed wall to form effective seal.

Existing masonry structure

Fig 8.5a: Insulating an existing suspended timber floor[9]

Fig 8.5b: Insulating an existing suspended timber floor[10]

158   **EnerPHit:** A Step-by-Step Guide to Low Energy Retrofit

this element to achieve EnerPHit. Nevertheless, even here insulation to the adjacent external walls must be extended down to create a thermal 'skirt' around the base of the building. For most low-rise building types, it will be necessary to insulate the ground floor. For buildings with a solid concrete floor this can be achieved by laying a new timber floor with bonded insulation over the top, as shown in Fig 8.4. This will typically result in changes to the finished floor level and will have a direct impact on almost every building element including doors, staircases, kitchens and sanitary ware. As a result, the retrofit of solid ground floors is typically only tackled in vacant properties where significant investment is already required, perhaps due to existing defects.

For buildings with suspended timber floors it may be possible to insulate the floor without raising the floor level. As shown in Fig 8.5a, insulation can be installed in between and over existing floor joists. However, it is essential to maintain ventilation to the floor void beneath to avoid the risk of condensation. Until recently it has been necessary to remove both the floor finish and all existing fixtures and fittings to insulate this area, but innovations in the means of access may in future reduce the cost and upheaval currently associated with insulating suspended timber floors, provided that sub-floor ventilation is not compromised.

Roof

The roof is often regarded as the easiest target to insulate, with relatively quick return on investment. This is due to the high proportion of heat loss from an uninsulated roof, and the often limited access to both flat and pitched roofs. In pitched roofs the building owner can decide whether to insulate at ceiling level (creating a 'cold roof') or rafter level (creating a 'warm roof'). While the latter option is typically more expensive, it gives the opportunity to create an additional room in the roof, and many properties have been retrofitted in this way. However, when tackling deep retrofit it is essential to maintain thermal continuity with the walls at both the eaves and gables to prevent excessive heat loss and concentrated thermal bridging. This should be coordinated with the airtightness strategy to ensure there are no weak points at the junction of the roof and walls, as shown in Fig 8.6, or indeed the loft

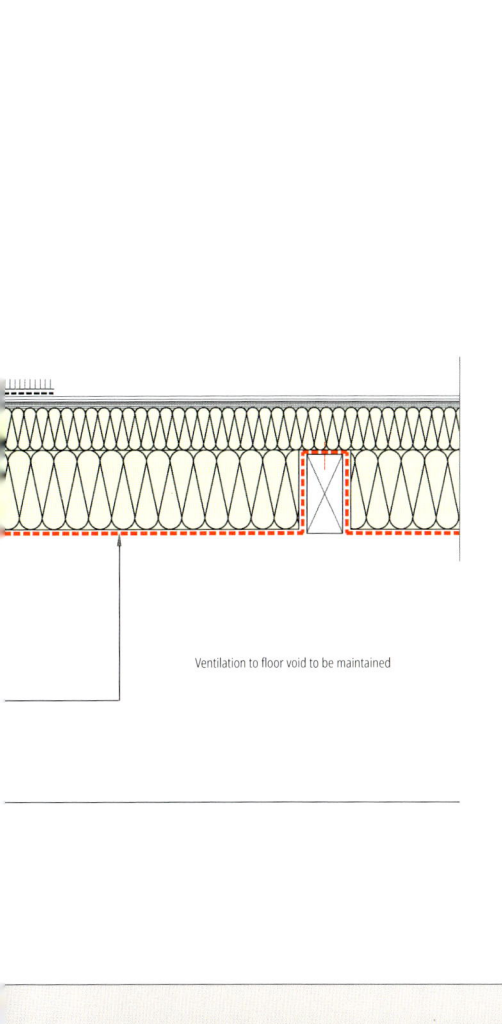

Ventilation to floor void to be maintained

such as aerogel (see Fig 8.3) which offer the same performance at a fraction of the thickness. All options should be modelled in PHPP, and where internal wall insulation is proposed this should also be modelled in WUFI to avoid any risk of interstitial condensation.

Ground floor

The ground floor is often the most challenging aspect of any deep retrofit. Where this represents only a small proportion of the building envelope (e.g. in a tower block) it may not be necessary to insulate

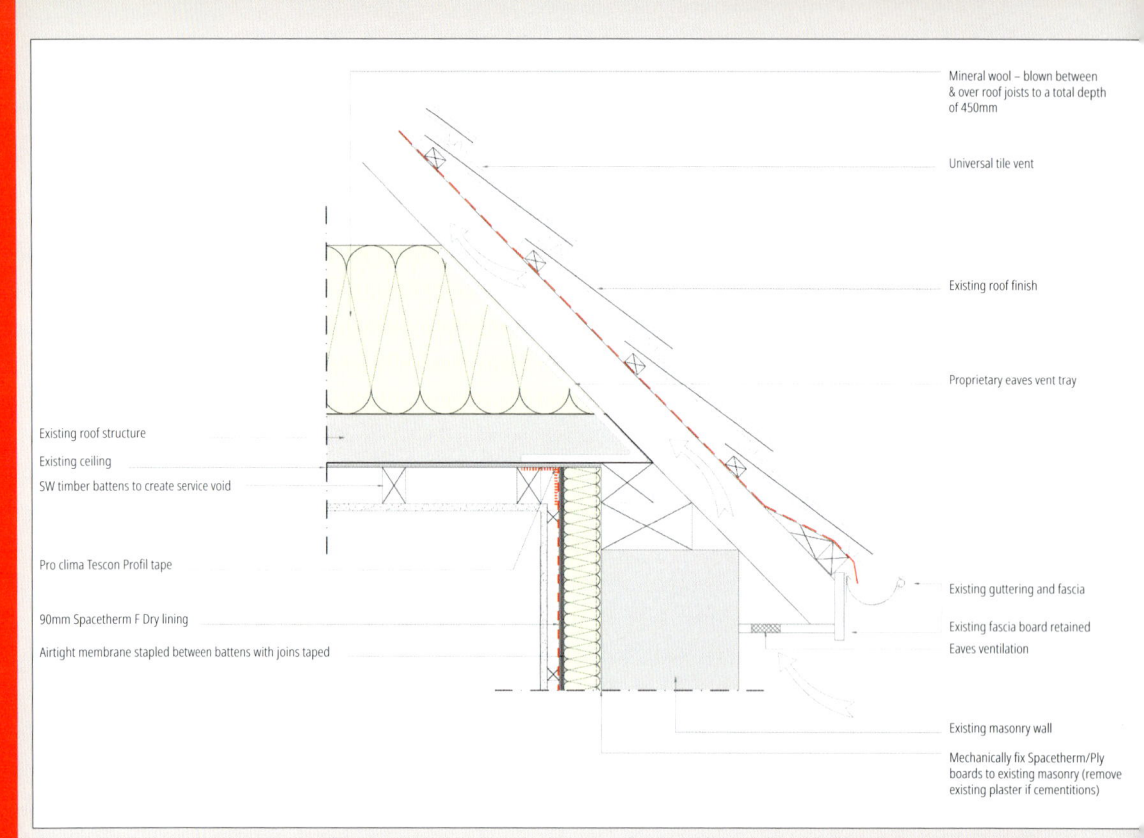

Fig 8.6: Thermal continuity at the roof (eaves)[11]

hatch as in Fig 8.7. Even when phased works are proposed it can be prudent to carry out works to the roof and walls at the same time.

Windows and doors
Windows and doors should be replaced with components which are either PH certified or satisfy PH criteria of 0.85 W/m²K (installed) to ensure compliance. As described above, these components must be fully taped and sealed to the adjacent envelope to avoid a breach in the airtight layer. They should also be installed within the thermal envelope to avoid thermal bridging. In retrofit projects this typically means that windows and doors must be brought forward. Alternatively, where the designer requires a recessed 'punched' window aesthetic, the external reveals must be insulated up to the frame, preventing or reducing thermal bridging.

Providing mechanical ventilation with heat recovery (MHVR)
Passivhaus and EnerPHit-certified buildings require MVHR. While MVHR is increasingly common in the UK for newbuild residential properties, the minimum performance criteria of PH-certified MVHR units is significantly higher than UK standards. The designer should therefore use PH-certified components or otherwise ensure the minimum performance criteria are met. Furthermore, the efficiency of the unit is strongly determined by the proximity of the unit to the facade, and the type of ductwork used. Incoming ducts will need to be heavily insulated, which may have spatial implications (see Fig 8.8). The designer is therefore recommended to consult with the manufacturer at the earliest opportunity to ensure the location is optimised and the right unit is specified. The designer also needs to consider whether a communal system is appropriate to the building type (as in case study 6.2) as this will typically result in an ongoing management charge. Where individual units are proposed the designer can select from a range of units which serve the whole building (sized to suit location) with extract from wet rooms and supply to habitable rooms. Alternatively, where ventilation is required from a single room, a wall-mounted decentralised unit can be installed as a discreet alternative to a whole-house unit (see Fig 8.11).

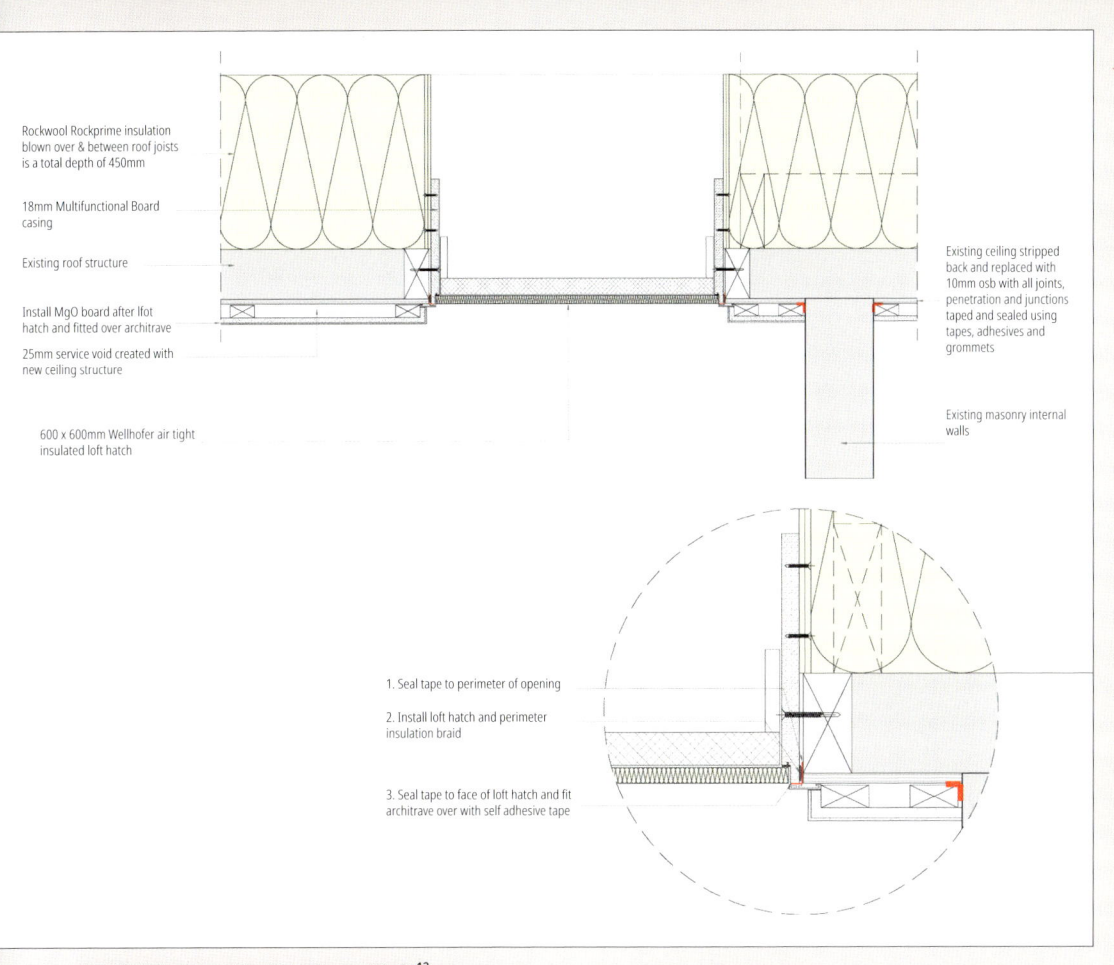

Fig 8.7: Thermal continuity at the roof (loft)[12]

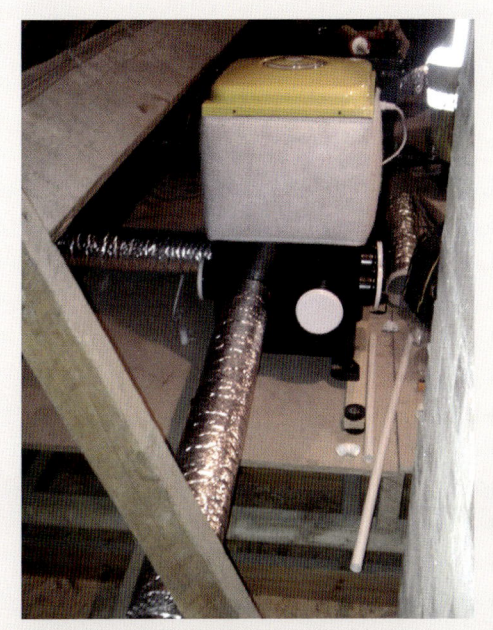

Fig 8.8: Loft-mounted MVHR[13]

Fig 8.9: MVHR within a flat[14]

Delivering EnerPHit **161**

Fig 8.10: Routing of ductwork in the ceiling void[15]

Fig 8.11: Decentralised MVHR (single room)[16]

In existing buildings, the installation of MVHR can be particularly challenging where ceiling heights are relatively low (2.4 m or less), and the coordination of ductwork is particularly important. Acoustic attenuation must be provided between habitable rooms to avoid sound transfer, and where ducts cross over, a lower ceiling will be required. In a residential property this is typically located in the hallway, which also acts as the air-balancing zone between extract areas (wet rooms) and supply areas (habitable rooms). This is usually achieved by undercutting doors, although other innovative solutions are available.

Avoiding thermal bridging

Each junction in the building envelope is a potential thermal bridge. In uninsulated properties the whole envelope might be regarded as a thermal bridge, with heat loss occurring across the entire building. Over the last 50 years measures have gradually been introduced into national legislation to reduce heat loss. Unfortunately, there was very little understanding of the importance of thermal bridging, and these measures were limited to elemental improvement, such as target U-values for walls, floors, windows and roofs. For example, while cavity wall insulation became common this did not address the substantial heat losses occurring through junctions such as lintels, jambs and other structures which penetrated the envelope. This can result in localised cold spots – which, coupled with high humidity and poor ventilation, can cause mould growth.

Even in 2019, UK building regulations do not adequately account for heat losses through thermal bridges. Psi values are not typically calculated, and even where these are used generic data is applied via SAP based on internal values, rather than the more onerous external values calculated by PHPP. Meanwhile the Passivhaus methodology (PHPP) requires any thermal bridge greater than 0.01 W/m^{2}K to be calculated, as above this threshold the detail will contribute to the overall heat loss of the building. In new buildings it can be relatively easy to avoid thermal bridging through careful design. In existing buildings there may be complex geometries or existing junctions which may be difficult to resolve, although even here there is an opportunity to address thermal bridging while improving the overall form factor, as described in case study 6.2.

Optimising solar gain

PHPP uses highly specific weather files to ensure the accuracy of the model in a specific location. It also enables the designer to consider both altitude and local factors which may affect the solar shading of the building, e.g. deciduous trees, adjacent buildings or indeed mountains. Having optimised the thermal envelope in the model and assumed appropriate levels of airtightness the designer can quickly determine the optimal level, location and

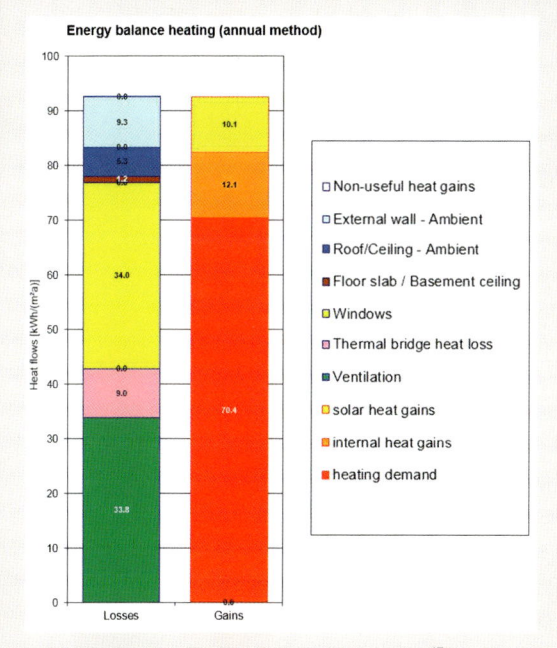

Fig 8.12a: Annual energy balance (pre-retrofit)[17]

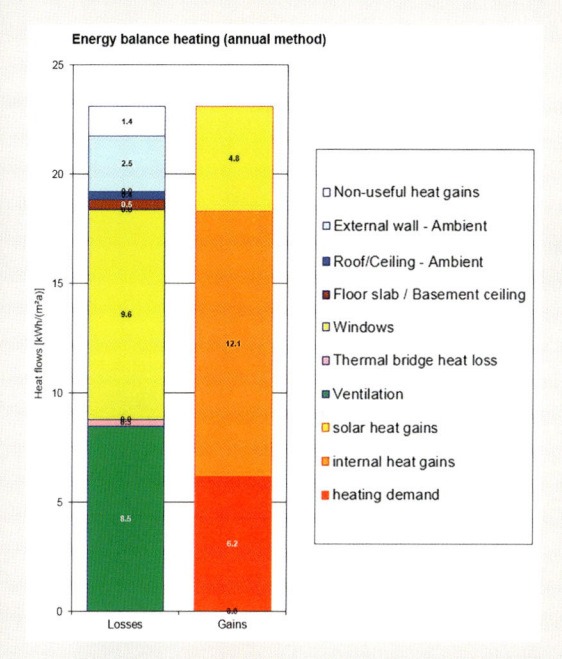

Fig 8.12b: Annual energy balance (post-retrofit) *note scale difference[18]

specification of glazing to ensure sufficient solar gain in the winter but prevent excessive gains in the summer. In northern European latitudes the optimal arrangement would typically result in larger windows on the southern elevation to benefit from solar gain in the winter, with brise-soleils offering protection in the summer. The glazing specification can also be optimised to prevent solar gain, depending on the orientation. For example, east- and west-facing windows can be more difficult to protect via fixed shading, and it may be appropriate to alter the G-value of the glass instead. The designPH plug-in offers a relatively quick and dynamic tool for the modelling of solar shading, and the impact of this can be easily seen in the monthly energy balance, as shown in Figs 8.12a and b. Again, tabs within PHPP enable the designer to model the size and specification of glazing to provide optimal solar gain on each facade in the winter without excessive gain in the summer.

8.3: HOW TO DELIVER ENERPHIT

Delivering EnerPHit requires attention to detail. This is not only in setting the scope and preparing design documentation, but also in managing and monitoring the construction process. Until Passivhaus becomes the norm, this means much greater engagement with the construction process than many designers are familiar with. However, it also enables the designer to understand the energy demand and supply in sufficient detail to constructively challenge the M&E contractor or consultant. As with BIM, this can give the designer the tools necessary to more effectively lead the team and provide accurate guidance to their client.

In seeking to achieve any task the destination is often a good place to start. By understanding what will be required to achieve EnerPHit certification, the designer can prepare the client and the design team to deliver the necessary information. As described in the building certification guide, EnerPHit is an evidence-based standard which uses PHPP and incorporates measured data (e.g. airtightness test results) and site photographs with construction drawings. Ensuring PHPP is kept up to date is therefore crucial, as this will be the primary evidence

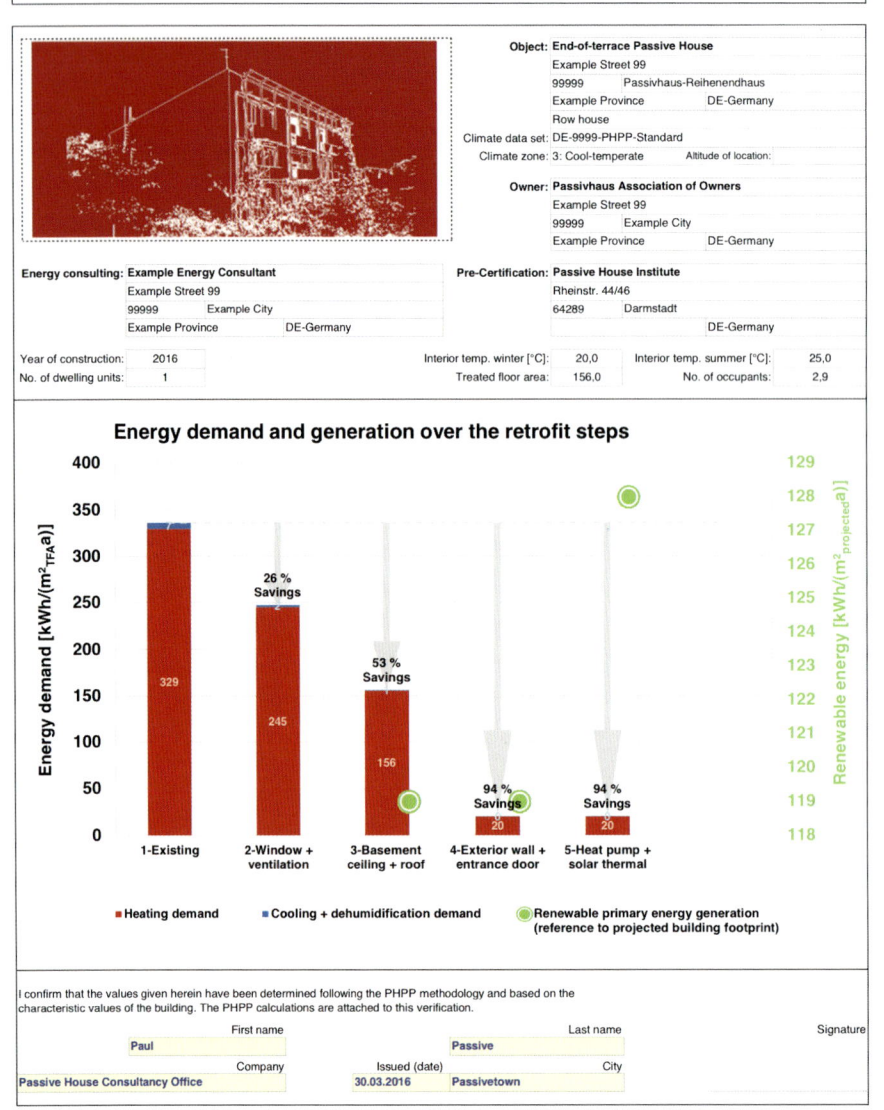

Fig 8.13: Start with a plan[19]

Diagram PHPP 2015 (Version 9)

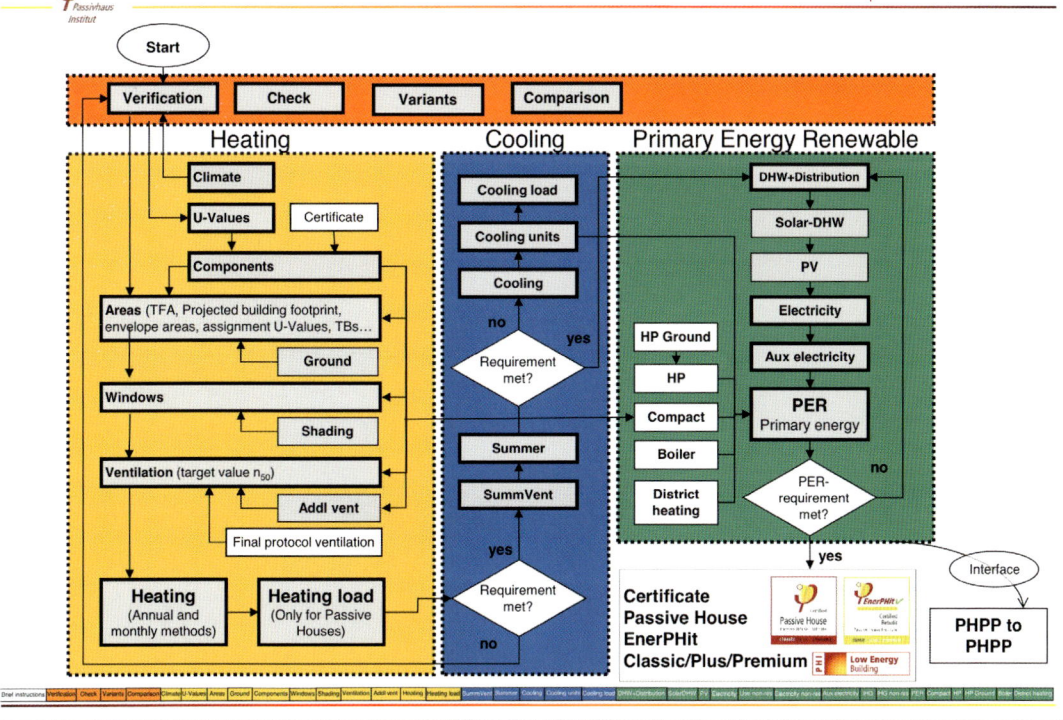

Fig 8.14: The structure and interrelated tabs of PHPP[20]

supplied to the certifier. However, supplementary information is also required to demonstrate compliance. Unlike many other compliance tools, such as SBEM or SAP, PHPP incorporates measured data of the completed building and is therefore a much more reliable tool in predicting actual use.

For many architects and designers PHPP can appear a daunting tool, comprising numerous interlinked tabs on an Excel spreadsheet. Fortunately, the 'Instructions' tab provides a helpful overview of the purpose and description of each worksheet. The 'Verification' tab shows the performance of the design against Passivhaus or EnerPHit standards and the specific criteria of each – space heating demand, PER, etc. PHPP is essentially a flow diagram (see Fig 8.14) with three main sections covering heating, cooling and PER. These feed into the high-level verification tabs where alternatives can also be modelled. Unlike many other energy modelling or compliance tools, it is not a 'black box' with hidden algorithms. By following the links in PHPP the designer can see exactly how the calculations are derived, which ultimately aids understanding and refinement.

A designer unfamiliar with PHPP might also fear that it requires far too much data on a building which may be at an early stage of concept development. The development of any design is an iterative process, and it is typically a response to the site and brief with numerous factors affecting design development, from commercial viability to planning and other statutory regulations. The architect would typically develop a sketch proposal based on the client brief and budget and shaped by the factors outlined above. Energy considerations have traditionally been left until much later in the design process, and have often been delegated to the M&E consultant tasked with ensuring compliance using SAP or SBEM.

Fortunately, there are now plug-ins for PHPP such as designPH (see Fig 8.15) that allow the designer

Delivering EnerPHit

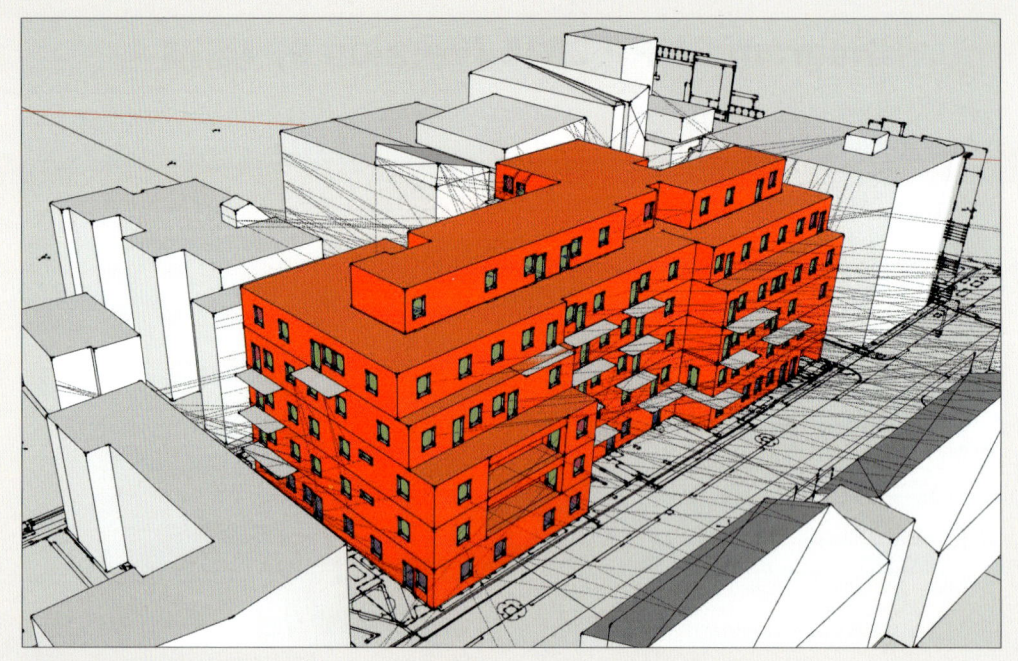

Fig 8.15: Modelling within designPH[21]

Fig 8.16: Impact of retrofit in designPH[22]

166 EnerPHit: A Step-by-Step Guide to Low Energy Retrofit

to create a very simple 3D model (as they might normally at RIBA Stage 1) using SketchUp or Revit, for example, and dynamically view the impact of design changes to the orientation, window sizes, shading, etc. While this is perhaps aimed at newbuild schemes considering the Passivhaus standard, it can also be applied to retrofit schemes targeting the EnerPHit standard. One of the new features allows the designer to review the areas of significant heat loss, which can be particularly useful on retrofit projects (see Fig 8.16). One of the most time-consuming aspects of PHPP has traditionally been the calculation of the TFA on the 'Areas' tab, as this differs from other more conventional methods of measurement such as gross internal floor area. The development of plug-ins has largely automated this process, although the user can still alter this in PHPP.

8.4: SUMMARY

EnerPHit is a standard with a very clear methodology that offers reliable outputs but requires active engagement by the client and design team as early as possible in the design process. It can be applied to virtually any building type and has fixed performance criteria that reflects geographic location and is based on universal metrics of energy use, i.e. $kWh/m^2/a$. It can also be modelled using future climate files and is suitable for demonstrating the impact of climate change on building performance in a given location. Although designers are recommended to use certified products, this is not mandatory provided that suitable alternatives can demonstrate acceptable performance. While building owners are strongly advised to appoint a Passivhaus designer/consultant, this is also not mandatory provided that the lead consultant can demonstrate to the certifier that all necessary performance criteria have been met using the PHPP model. The PHPP model is an inexpensive tool compared to other energy modelling software, and the Excel format means it does not require extensive user training, although users are strongly advised to read relevant guidance.[23] As with any certification process there is a considerable amount of evidence required to demonstrate performance; however, this has also been streamlined in recent years with a new online platform available. The Passivhaus methodology is focused on building-specific performance with regard to operational energy and does not consider other aspects of sustainability, such as water consumption or embodied carbon. The rigorous methodology which it requires and the reliable performance in use of many thousands of buildings around the world offer the building owner and designer a powerful tool for understanding and improving building performance.

POSTSCRIPT

Europe, including Britain, is a highly urbanised continent, with many hundreds of cities and towns. For this reason, we are facing a serious energy problem in the built environment. Around 50% of all emissions come from the buildings we already have, including the 'embodied energy' that goes into producing bricks, steel, concrete, and glass – the most energy-intensive of building materials.[1] In spite of significant efforts to raise the standards of energy efficiency for new buildings, far too little has been done either to reduce the embodied energy in new buildings, or retrofit the existing stock of around 200 million European homes, over 25 million of them in the UK.

Even if we run an efficient programme to demolish our 'worst' housing, the overall cost of doing this would far exceed the cost of retrofit, while creating a chronic shortage of affordable housing. But in addition to these problems, fully 85% of our existing homes will still be standing in 50 years' time. Even with a large building programme, fitting millions of new homes into a crowded country and a crowded continent is extremely difficult. In a highly built-up country like England, building 200,000 new homes a year will still mean that at least 75% of all homes in 2050 are those already built today. Besides, we are the most densely populated country in Europe, level with the Netherlands, so building outside our existing urban footprint raises major environmental issues. This only underlines the need to drastically reduce the energy use in our existing buildings by at least 50% if we are to seriously tackle our contribution to greenhouse gases and accelerating climate change.

The Dutch government has evolved an imaginative approach to retrofit, where whole streets and blocks are made energy-efficient in one go, to significantly reduce both costs and energy use. This idea is now being trialled in England. The German retrofit programme initiated in the 1970s, called Zukunfthaus or 'Future Home', showed that it was possible to reduce energy use in homes by up to 80% using tried-and-tested methods. They called it the 'tea cosy' approach. The ambitious programme of energy saving has spread to schools and other public buildings across Germany. Freiburg in southern Germany boasts the first high-rise block to be retrofitted to virtually zero-energy, or Passivhaus, standard. It is called the Hochhaus.

In London, three 23-storey council tower blocks on the Edward Woods Estate in the London Borough of Hammersmith and Fulham were over-clad in 2014 with non-combustible, spun-rock cladding. These conspicuous towers have solar panels from top to bottom of their south-facing facades, in order to power the communal services in the high-rise blocks, helping to reduce tenants' bills. They mirror Grenfell Tower, only a short walk way, which was inadequately clad in flammable cladding, and where 72 residents lost their lives.

In Portsmouth, three lower high-rise council blocks, 13 storeys high, have been retrofitted to match the exacting German standard of Passivhaus. The Portsmouth example is clearly written up in this book, and offers an invaluable guide to the way three challenging, concrete high-rise blocks, housing low-income families with children, can be retrofitted with striking success while saving tenants and the council money. These examples show that it is possible to get retrofit right within the constraints of tight budgets. Retrofit happens if, and only if, existing buildings are valued and prioritised, and more importantly only if tenants are properly consulted and buy into the project.

Anyone involved in housing and urban planning would be foolish to sit on the sidelines while these problems only grow more urgent. But in order to win the argument with landlords, owners and government, it is crucial to grasp the upside of retrofitting. It is expensive and complicated when carried out with existing tenants in place. One of the key benefits of retrofitting existing homes is that the whole building is treated to an overhaul. Outstanding repairs are picked up and dealt with, fuel poverty is significantly reduced, and renewable energy makes an ever bigger contribution as the volume of energy used decreases. If, as in Edward Woods and the Hochhaus, solar PV is added then the energy savings become a double gain.

James Traynor's exhaustive study of the energy standards that are possible in retrofitting existing homes offers many lessons. The detailed case studies demonstrate the extraordinary value of both delivering and documenting live projects to address maybe the greatest challenges facing the developed world – how we live and how we consume energy. The varied case studies in the book, including Energiesprong from the Netherlands and Wilmcote House from Portsmouth, show how it is possible to save existing buildings, cut energy use by at least 50%, and make our already built environment work. It would be wrong to imagine that we can tear down homes built of brick, concrete and steel in order to build more energy-efficient homes without running up an even bigger carbon debt, and without destroying our planet. For these reasons, and in order to enhance community stability, we need to stop destroying existing homes and building new ones at high environmental cost. We can save and reuse more and more of our less popular, less insulated, less valuable homes if we follow the principles outlined in this fascinating study. Existing low-cost homes are more accessible to people on lower incomes, so retrofit becomes a triple win – save energy, save homes and save communities.

The message of Greta Thunberg, now joined by hundreds of thousands of young people across Europe, is that we, who are responsible for so much damage to our environment, have to do our homework just like them in order to protect their future. The advice in this eye-opening book will help us to do just that – save the planet, while solving our most critical housing problem and preserving and upgrading our supply of low-cost homes.

Anne Power
Professor of Social Policy
Head of LSE Housing and Communities
London School of Economics

IMAGE CREDITS

CHAPTER 1
Page 7 UK Government (top and bottom)
Page 9 UK Government (top and bottom)

CHAPTER 2
Page 21 ECD Architects
Page 23 ECD Architects
Page 25 Passivhaus Trust

CHAPTER 3
Page 35 Better Building Partnership
Page 36 Building Research Establishment (BRE)
Page 38 STBA
Page 39 ECD Architects
Page 40 ECD Architects
Page 41 Smartwin windows (top); ECD Architects (bottom)
Page 43 ECD Architects (top); Passivhaus Trust (bottom)

CHAPTER 4
Page 47 UK Government
Page 48 Passivhaus Institute
Page 49 Passivhaus Institute
Page 50 Mariana Moreira, MosArt Ltd., Wicklow, Ireland, 2018 (top); Passivhaus Institute (bottom)
Page 51 Passivhaus Institute
Page 52 Passivhaus Institute
Page 53 MosArt Ltd, Wicklow, Ireland, 2018
Page 54 MosArt Ltd, Wicklow, Ireland, 2018 (top and bottom)
Page 55 MosArt Ltd, Wicklow, Ireland, 2018 (left and right)
Page 56 James Traynor
Page 57 MosArt Ltd, Wicklow, Ireland, 2018
Page 58 MosArt Ltd, Wicklow, Ireland, 2018 (all)
Page 59 MosArt Ltd, Wicklow, Ireland, 2018 (top and bottom)
Page 61 James Traynor

CHAPTER 5
Page 65 UK Government (top and middle); Energy Research Partnership (bottom)
Page 67 CBxchange
Page 68 Passivhaus Trust/ AECOM, January 2015 (top and bottom)
Page 69 ECD Architects (top); Building Performance Institute Europe, October 2011 (bottom)
Page 71 University of Southampton
Page 72 University of Southampton (top and bottom)
Page 77 Wuppertal Institut (top and bottom)

CHAPTER 6
Page 80 UK Government
Page 81 UK Government (top, centre bottom and bottom); Energy Research Partnership, October 2016 (centre top)
Page 82 Building Performance Institute Europe, October 2011
Page 83 UK Government (top and bottom)
Page 84 UK Government (top and bottom)
Page 85 UK Government
Page 86 University of Southampton
Page 87 University of Southampton (top); Portsmouth City Council (bottom)
Page 88 ECD Architects
Page 89 University of Southampton (top); ECD Architects (bottom)
Page 90 ECD Architects
Page 91 ECD Architects
Page 92 ECD Architects
Page 93 ECD Architects
Page 94 Dun Laoghaire Rathdown Council (left and right)
Page 95 ECD Architects (top and bottom)
Page 96 ECD Architects (top), MosArt Ltd, Wicklow, Ireland, 2018 (centre left and right)
Page 97 Donal Murphy Photography
Page 98 Donal Murphy Photography
Page 99 ECD Architects
Page 100 Ervins Krauklis (left and right)
Page 101 ECD Architects (top); Ervins Krauklis (bottom)
Page 102 Ervins Krauklis (left and right)
Page 103 Ervins Krauklis, Riga Technical University (all)
Page 104 Peter Pierce Photography
Page 105 ECD Architects (top); Peter Pierce Photography (bottom)
Page 106 ECD Architects
Page 108 Peter Pierce Photography
Page 109 Peter Pierce Photography
Page 110 ECD Architects
Page 112 ECD Architects
Page 114 Fielden + Mawson, Architects (left and right)
Page 115 ECD Architects
Page 116 Fielden + Mawson, Architects (left, right and bottom)
Page 117 ECD Architects
Page 118 ECD Architects
Page 119 ECD Architects (top left and bottom); Fielden + Mawson, Architects (top right)

CHAPTER 7
Page 122 Building Performance Institute Europe, October 2011
Page 123 UK Government (top and bottom)
Page 124 Energy Research Partnership, October 2016
Page 125 UK Government
Page 126 UK Government
Page 129 Rongen Architects (top and bottom)
Page 130 Rongen Architects
Page 132 Rongen Architects (top left, top right and bottom)
Page 133 ECD Architects
Page 134 Rongen Architects (left and right)
Page 135 ECD Architects
Page 136 Passivhaus Institute, Innsbruck
Page 137 Thomas Jantscher, Photographer
Page 138 ECD Architects (top), ATP Architekten (bottom)
Page 139 Passivhaus Institute, Inssbruck (top and bottom)
Page 140 Passivhaus Institute, Inssbruck (top and bottom)
Page 141 Passivhaus Institute, Inssbruck (top and bottom)
Page 142 Thomas Jantscher, Photographer
Page 143 ECD Architects (top and bottom)
Page 144 Stefan Oehler
Page 145 Stefan Oehler
Page 146 Stefan Oehler (top); Dirk Altenkirche, Photographer (bottom)
Page 147 ECD Architects
Page 148 Stefan Oehler (left); ECD Architects (right)
Page 149 ECD Architects
Page 150 Stefan Oehler (left and right)
Page 151 Stefan Oehler

CHAPTER 8
Page 155 ECD Architects
Page 156 ECD Architects (left and right)
Page 157 ECD Architects (top and bottom)
Page 158 ECD Architects (top and bottom)
Page 160 ECD Architects
Page 161 ECD Architects (top, bottom left and bottom right)
Page 162 ECD Architects (left); Zehnder Ventilation Systems (right)
Page 163 ECD Architects (top and bottom)
Page 164 Passivhaus Institute
Page 165 Passivhaus Institute
Page 166 ECD Architects (top and bottom)

BIBLIOGRAPHY

BOOKS

Baeli, M., *Residential Retrofit: 20 Case Studies*, RIBA Publishing, 2013

Gething, B. & Puckett K., *Design for Climate Change*, RIBA Publishing, 2013

Gonzalo, R. & Vallentin, R., *Passive House Design*, Detail Green Books, 2016

Lewis, S., *PHPP Illustrated (Second Edition)*, RIBA Publishing, 2017

Oehler, S., *Emissionsfreie Gebaude*, Springer Vieweg, 2017

Pelsmakers, S., *The Environmental Design Pocketbook (Second Edition)*, RIBA Publishing, 2015

Prasad, S., *Retrofit for Purpose*, RIBA Publishing, 2014

REPORTS

Association of Environment Conscious Building (AECB), 'Projecting Energy Use and CO2 Emissions from Low Energy Buildings', *A Comparison of the Passivhaus Planning Package (PHPP) and SAP*, <www.aecb.net>, 2008, (accessed 27th February 2019)

Association of Environment Conscious Building (AECB), 'AECB Carbonlite Programme', *Volume Four: Step One Design Guidance*, <www.aecb.net>, 2007, (accessed 27 February 2019)

Association of Environment Conscious Building (AECB), 'AECB Carbonlite Programme', *Volume Five: Steps Two And Three Design Guidance*, <www.aecb.net>, 2007, (accessed 27 February 2019)

Better Buildings Partnership (BBP), 'Mitigating risks through the procurement and interpretation of Energy Performance Certificates', *Minimum Energy Efficiency Standards and Heritage Properties*, <www.betterbuildingspartnership.co.uk>, 2018, (accessed 5 March 2019)

Better Buildings Partnership (BBP), 'Are EPCs a true indicator of energy efficiency?', *A Tale of Two Buildings*, <www.betterbuildingspartnership.co.uk>, 2012, (accessed 5 March 2019)

Building Performance Institute Europe (BPIE), 'A country-by-country review of the energy performance of buildings', *Europe's Buildings under the Microscope*, <www.bpie.eu>, 2011, (accessed 5 March 2019)

Building Performance Institute Europe (BPIE), '10 Principles to Deliver Real Benefits for Europe's Citizens', *Smart Buildings in a Decarbonised Energy System*, <www.bpie.eu>, 2016, (accessed 5 March 2019)

Building Research Establishment, 'RdSAP Manual Version 8.0', *Energy Performance Certificates for Existing Dwellings*, <www.bre.co.uk>, 2012, (accessed 5 March 2019)

Building Research Establishment, 'The Government's Standard Assessment Procedure for Energy Rating of Dwellings', *SAP 2012*, <www.bre.co.uk>, 2012, (accessed 5 March 2019)

Building Research Establishment, 'The Government's Standard Assessment Procedure for Energy Rating of Dwellings', *SAP 2016*, <www.bre.co.uk>, 2012, (accessed 5 March 2019)

Building Research Establishment, 'An Aid to Understanding the Key Principles of the Passivhaus Standard', Passivhaus Primer: Introduction, <www.passivhaus.org.uk>, (accessed 5 March 2019)

Building Research Establishment, 'So you've been asked to build a Passivhaus?', *Passivhaus Primer: Contractor's Guide*, <www.passivhaus.org.uk>, (accessed 5 March 2019)

Building Research Establishment, 'A guide for the design team and local authorities', *Passivhaus Primer: Designer's Guide*, <www.passivhaus.org.uk>, (accessed 5 March 2019)

Building Research Establishment, 'Report on the failure rate and remediation costs for external and cavity wall insulation', *Wales Low and Zero Carbon Hub*, <www.bre.co.uk>, 2015, (accessed 5 March 2019)

Building Research Establishment, 'Consequences for Consideration to Maximise SWI Benefits: A Route-Map for Change', *Solid Wall Heat Losses and the Potential for Energy Saving*, <www.bre.co.uk>, 2016, (accessed 5 March 2019)

Building Research Establishment, 'Reducing carbon emissions from the UK housing stock', <www.bre.co.uk>, 2005, (accessed 5 March 2019)

Energy Saving Trust, 'Response to the Public Consultation on the Energy Performance of Buildings Directive', <www.energysavingtrust.org.uk>, 2015, (accessed 5 March 2019)

German Sustainable Building Council (DGNB), 'Building Emissions Act, Valid Until 2050 (GEG 2050)', *The Contents of a Future German Building Energy Law in Just Three Pages – Proposal*, <dgnb.de>, 2018, (accessed 5 March 2019)

Innovate UK, 'Reducing Energy Use in Existing Homes. A Guide to Making Retrofit Work', *Retrofit for the Future*, <retrofit.innovateuk.org>, 2014, (accessed 5 March 2019)

Innovate UK, 'The Retrofit for the Future Projects: Data Analysis Report', *Retrofit Revealed*, <retrofit.innovateuk.org>, 2013, (accessed 5 March 2019)

Innovate UK, *Retrofit Revealed*, <retrofit.innovateuk.org>, 2013, (accessed 5 March 2019)

Innovate UK, 'For the Technology Strategy Board Final Report', *Retrofit for the Future: Data Analysis Report*, <retrofit.innovateuk.org>, 2014, (accessed 5 March 2019)

National Energy Foundation (NEF)/ Energy Efficiency Partnership for Buildings (EEPB), 'An Industry Review of the Barriers to Whole House Energy Efficiency Retrofit and the Creation of an Industry Action Plan. Summary Report', *Breaking Barriers*, <nef.org.uk> 2014, (accessed 5 March 2019)

Passivhaus Institute, 'Building Certification Guide', *Passivhaus Institute*, <passiv.de>, 2018 (accessed 5 March 2019)

BIBLIOGRAPHY

Passivhaus Institute, 'Criteria for the Passive House, EnerPHit and PHI Low Energy Building Standard', *Passivhaus Institute,* <passiv.de>, 2016 (accessed 5 March 2019)

Passivhaus Institute, 'Implementing Deep Energy Step-by-Step Retrofits', *EuroPHit: Increasing the European Potential*, <europhit.eu>, 2016 (accessed 5 March 2019)

Passivhaus Institute, 'Step-by-Step Retrofits with Passivhaus Components', *Passivhaus Institute*, <passiv.de>, 2016 (accessed 5 March 2019)

Passivhaus Institute, 'Passive House Regions with Renewable Energies', *PassREg. Final Report*, <passivhaustrust.org.uk>, 2014, (accessed 5 March 2019)

Passivhaus Institute, 'Defining the Nearly Zero Energy Building', *PassREg Municipalities Lead the Way*, <europa.eu>, (accessed 5 March 2019)

Passivhaus Trust, 'Good Practice Guide to Insulation', *Passivhaus Trust*, <passivhaustrust.org.uk>, 2017, (accessed 5 March 2019)

Passivhaus Trust, 'Claiming the Passivhaus Standard: Technical Briefing Document', *Passivhaus Trust*, <passivhaustrust.org.uk>, 2015, (accessed 5 March 2019)

Passivhaus Trust, 'Passivhaus Quality Assurance: Large and Complex Buildings', *Passivhaus Trust*, <passivhaustrust.org.uk>, 2015, (accessed 5 March 2019)

Passivhaus Trust, 'Designing for Summer Comfort in the UK', *Passivhaus Trust*, <passivhaustrust.org.uk>, 2016, (accessed 5 March 2019)

Passivhaus Trust, 'The Performance of Passivhaus in New Construction: Post Occupancy Evaluation of Certified Passivhaus Dwellings in the UK: Early Results', *Passivhaus Trust*, <passivhaustrust.org.uk>, 2017, (accessed 5 March 2019)

Passivhaus Trust, 'How to Develop User Guidance for a Passivhaus Building. Technical Briefing Document', *Passivhaus Trust*, <passivhaustrust.org.uk>, 2013, (accessed 5 March 2019)

Passivhaus Trust, 'Passivhaus Capital Cost Research Project', *Passivhaus Trust*, <passivhaustrust.org.uk>, 2015, (accessed 5 March 2019)

Royal Institute of British Architects (RIBA), '01 Climate Change Briefing', *Climate Change Toolkit*, <gci.org.uk>, 2010, (accessed 5 March 2019)

Royal Institute of British Architects (RIBA), 'Climate Change Toolkit. 02 Carbon Literacy Briefing', *Climate Change Toolkit*, <gci.org.uk>, 2010, (accessed 5 March 2019)

Royal Institute of British Architects (RIBA), 'Climate Change Toolkit. 03 Principles of Low Carbon Design and Refurbishment', *Climate Change Toolkit*, <gci.org.uk>, 2010, (accessed 5 March 2019)

Royal Institute of British Architects (RIBA), 'Climate Change Toolkit. 05 Low Carbon Design Tools', *Climate Change Toolkit*, <gci.org.uk>, 2010, (accessed 5 March 2019)

Royal Institute of Chartered Surveyors (RICS), 'Good Practice Measures for Offices. Version 1.2', *SKA Rating*, <pefc.co.uk>, 2013, (accessed 5 March 2019)

Royal Institute of Chartered Surveyors (RICS), 'Good Practice Measures for Higher Education Version 1.0', *SKA Rating*, <pefc.co.uk>, 2012, (accessed 5 March 2019)

Royal Institute of Chartered Surveyors (RICS), 'SKA Rating. Good Practice Measures for Retail. Version 1.0', *SKA Rating*, <pefc.co.uk>, 2016, (accessed 5 March 2019)

The Scottish Government, 'A Comparison of Space Heating Energy Demand Using SAP, SBEM, and PHPP Methodologies', *Benchmarking Scottish Energy Standards: Passive House and CarbonLite Standards*, <gov.scot>, 2009, (accessed 5 March 2019)

Sustainable Traditional Buildings Alliance (STBA), 'A Report on Existing Research and Guidance with Recommendations', *Responsible Retrofit of Traditional Buildings*, <sdfoundation.org.uk>, 2012, (accessed 5 March 2019)

Sustainable Traditional Buildings Alliance (STBA), 'Moisture risk assessment and guidance', <sdfoundation.org.uk>, 2014, (accessed 5 March 2019)

Sustainable Traditional Buildings Alliance (STBA), 'A Short Paper on Internal Wall Insulation', *STBA Internal Wall Insulation (IWI) Paper*, Neil May, <sdfoundation.org.uk>, 2012, (accessed 5 March 2019)

Sustainable Traditional Buildings Alliance (STBA), 'Planning Responsible Retrofit of Traditional Buildings', *STBA*, Neil May, <sdfoundation.org.uk>, 2015, (accessed 5 March 2019)

Sustainable Traditional Buildings Alliance (STBA), 'A Scoping Study Prepared for Historic England & The National Trust', *EPCs and the Whole House Approach*, <historicengland.org.uk>, 2018, (accessed 5 March 2019)

UK Green Building Council (UKGBC), 'Task Group Report', *Regeneration and Retrofit,* <ukgbc.org>, 2017, (accessed 5 March 2019)

UK Green Building Council (UKGBC), 'Task Group Report', *Retrofit Incentives,* <ukgbc.org>, 2013, (accessed 5 March 2019)

US Green Building Council (USGBC), 'LEED® for New Construction & Major Renovations (US Green Building Council) Version 2.2', <usgbc.org>, 2005, (accessed 5 March 2019)

US Green Building Council (USGBC), 'LEED® Rating System Selection Guidance (US Green Building Council) Version 4', <usgbc.org>, 2001, (accessed 5 March 2019)

UK GOVERNMENT PUBLICATIONS

Houses of Parliament: Parliamentary Office of Science & Technology, Postnote (Number 523, May 2016)

BIBLIOGRAPHY

Department of Communities and Local Government (DCLG)/Ministry of Housing, Communities & Local Government (MHCLG), Dame Judith Hackitt, 'Building a Safer Future – Independent Review of Building Regulations and Fire Safety: Final Report' MHCLG, May 2018

Department of Communities and Local Government (DCLG)/Ministry of Housing, Communities & Local Government (MHCLG), 'English Housing Survey, Headline Report, 2015–16', DCLG (Department of Communities and Local Government)

Department of Communities and Local Government (DCLG)/Ministry of Housing, Communities & Local Government (MHCLG), 'Energy Performance of Buildings Certificates Statistical Release: Q3 2017: England and Wales', DCLG, January 2018

Department of Communities and Local Government (DCLG)/Ministry of Housing, Communities & Local Government (MHCLG), 'Approved Document L1A Conservation of Fuel and Power in New Dwellings', DCLG, 2013 edition incorporating 2016 amendments

Department of Communities and Local Government (DCLG)/Ministry of Housing, Communities & Local Government (MHCLG), 'Approved Document L1B Conservation of Fuel and Power in Existing Dwellings', DCLG, 2010 edition incorporating 2016 amendments

Department of Communities and Local Government (DCLG)/Ministry of Housing, Communities & Local Government (MHCLG), 'Approved Document L2A Conservation of Fuel and Power in New Buildings other than Dwellings', DCLG, 2013 edition incorporating 2016 amendments

Department of Communities and Local Government (DCLG)/Ministry of Housing, Communities & Local Government (MHCLG), 'Approved Document L2B Conservation of Fuel and Power in Existing Buildings other than Dwellings', DCLG, 2010 edition incorporating 2016 amendments

Department of Energy & Climate Change (DECC), Energy Efficiency Statistical Summary 2015, January 2015

Department of Energy & Climate Change (DECC), 'UK Housing Energy Factfile 2013' Prepared by Cambridge Architectural Research; Eclipse Research Consultants & Cambridge Energy for DECC, 2013

National Audit Office (NAO), 'Department of Energy & Climate Change: Green Deal and Energy Company Obligation', April 2016

OFGEM, *Energy Companies Obligation – Final Report,* September 2015

Office for National Statistics, 'Construction Statistics: Number 18,' 2017 edition

Department for Business Energy & Industrial Strategy (BEIS) and DCLG, Dr Peter Bonfield: 'Each Home Counts an Independent Review of Consumer Advice, Protection, Standards and Enforcement for Energy Efficiency and Renewable Energy', December 2016

Department for Business Energy & Industrial Strategy (BEIS) and DCLG, *Building Energy Efficiency Survey, 2014–15: Overarching Report,* November 2016

OTHERS

Energy Research Partnership, 'Heating Buildings: Reducing Energy Demand and Greenhouse Gas Emissions', October 2016

Ecofys, 'Towards Nearly Zero-Energy Buildings: Definition of Common Principles under the EPBD: Final Report', 2013

ARUP, 'Towards the Delivery of a National Residential Energy Efficiency Programme: Creating the Right Conditions to Halve the Energy Consumed in All UK Homes Within 25 Years', May 2016

Prince of Wales Corporate Leaders Group, 'Renovation Roadmap: Making Europe's Homes Fit for the 21st Century', University of Cambridge, Institute for Sustainability Leadership, 2018

Gentoo, 'Retrofit Reality', 2011

Changeworks, 'Modelled and Actual Energy Usage Comparison Results', March 2017

Labour Party Green Paper, 'Housing for the Many', April 2018

Better Buildings Partnership, 'Issues Considered in Developing the LER: A Contribution to the Development of a Landlord's Energy Rating', April 2013

Sustainable Energy Ireland (SEI), 'Retrofitted Passive Homes: Guidelines for Upgrading Existing Dwellings in Ireland to the Passivhaus Standard', 2009

Energiesprong UK, 'Performance Requirements: Part L UK vs Energiesprong vs Passivhaus', 2017

Thema, J. & Rasch, J., 'Calculating and Operationalising the Multiple Benefits of Energy Efficiency in Europe (COMBI): Final Quantification Report', Wuppertal Institut, May 2018

ARTICLES

de Selincourt, K., 'Disastrous Preston Retrofit Scheme Remains Unresolved', *Passive House Plus,* issue 24, 2018

Dixon, T., 'Scaling Up Commercial Property Retrofitting: Challenges and Solutions', *Estates Gazette*, University of Reading, issue 1405, 2014

CONFERENCE/ACADEMIC PAPERS

Atkinson, J., 'Evaluating Retrofitted External Wall Insulation', Cardiff Metropolitan University, 2015

Bastian, Z., 'The EnerPHit Retrofit Plan', International Passive House Conference, 2017

Buisman, F.K., 'Historic 1870 2-Whyte Brick House to EnerPHit Standard in Upstate New York', International Passive House Conference, 2016

BIBLIOGRAPHY

Calderon, E.P., 'First EnerPHit Experience in Spanish historical heritage', International Passive House Conference, 2017

Calderon, E.P., 'Pilot Office Building from the National Government of Spain meets Passive House and BREEAM', International Passive House Conference, 2018

Dequaire, X., 'Passivhaus as a Low-Energy Building Standard: Contribution to a Typology' *Energy Efficiency*, Oslo and Akershus University College of Applied Sciences, 2012

Fasouli, M., 'EnerPHit on London's Heritage Properties: Adams Row Case Study', International Passive House Conference, 2017

Fasouli, M., 'First Privately Rented EnerPHit homes in London, Whole Life Carbon Story', International Passive House Conference, 2016

Freundorfer, F., 'Cross-Trade Retrofit Systems: An EnerPHit Innovation', International Passive House Conference, 2016

Grant, N. & Grylis, C., 'Passivhaus for the Many Not the Few', International Passive House Conference, 2018

Ince, R., 'Examining Domestic Retrofit Systems and Governance in Haringey, London: Final Report', Durham University, 2016

Ingui, M., 'Better Design and Community through Passive House', International Passive House Conference, 2017

Ingui, M., 'Game Changing Realities', International Passive House Conference, 2018

Ingui, M., 'Masonry Retrofits: Repeatable Results in a Collaborative Environment', International Passive House Conference, 2016

Johnston, D. & Siddall, M., 'The Building Fabric Thermal Performance of Passivhaus Dwellings: Does it Do What it Says on the Tin?', *Passive House Development and High Energy Efficiency Sustainable Buildings*, ed. A Pitts, Sustainability, 2016

MacLean, J., 'Methodology to Assess Cost Optimality for Retrofitting Existing Scottish Housing Stock to Meet EnerPHit Energy Efficiency Standards' (A thesis submitted in partial fulfilment for the requirement of degree in Master of Science in Renewable Energy Systems and the Environment), Department of Mechanical and Aerospace Engineering, University of Strathclyde, 2015

McCormack, A. & Moreira, M., 'Step-by-Step EnerPHit Retrofit Coordinated Design and Build', International Passive House Conference, 2016

Moreira, M. & McCormack, A., 'EnerPHit for Social Apartments: Marrying Old and New', International Passive House Conference, 2016

Moreno-Vacca, S., 'Large-Scale Total Passive House Renovations in Brussels', International Passive House Conference, 2016

Nesi, F., Larcher, M., Bombasaro, A. & Iannone, I., 'La Provvidenza: Passivhaus Energy Retrofit of a Large Non-Residential Building in Italy', International Passive House Conference, 2017

Nettleton, L., Whartnaby, M., 'EnerPHit in the United States: Multi-Unit Residential and Commercial Retrofit Case Studies', International Passive House Conference, 2016

Oehler, S., 'Holistic Retrofit of the Gross-Umstadt Sparkasse', International Passive House Conference, 2016

Oehler, S., 'The Contents of a Future German Building Energy Law in Just Three Pages', DGNB, 2018

Schoberl, H. & Kronberger, A., 'Passive House Refurbishment on an Occupied Property', International Passive House Conference, 2018

Sharpe, R., Thornton, C., Nikolaou, V. & Osborne, N., 'Higher Energy Efficient Homes are Associated with Increased Risk of Doctor Diagnosed Asthma in a UK Subpopulation', *Environment International*, 2015

Steiger, J. & Vahlova, E., 'Overall Retrofit Plan for Step-by-Step Retrofits to EnerPHit Standard', International Passive House Conference, 2016

Stephen, J., 'Summer Thermal Comfort and Overheating Risk Mitigation Strategies in Social Housing' (Unpublished Doctoral Thesis, Sustainable Energy Research Group), University of Southampton

Sternova, Z., 'Deep Renovation of a Residential Building Towards the NZEB Standard', International Passive House Conference, 2017

Stone, A., Shipworth, D., Biddulph, P. & adj Oreszczyn, T., 'Key Factors Determining the Energy Rating of Existing English houses', *Building Research & Information*, vol. 42, UCL Energy Institute, 2014

Style, O., 'Step-by-Step or One Big Jump? A Multi-Storey Residential EnerPHit Project in Girona, Spain', International Passive House Conference, 2018

Teli, D., Dimitriou, T., James, P.A.B., Bahaj, A.S., Ellison, L. & Waggott, A., 'Fuel Poverty-Induced "Prebound Effect" in Achieving the Anticipated Carbon Savings from Social Housing Retrofit', University of Southampton, 2015

Traynor, J., Newmann, N. & Brown, H., 'Large Scale EnerPHit – Whole Life Costs and Lessons Learned on High Rise Retrofit', International Passive House Conference, 2016

Zakrezewski, S. 'Strategies to Retrofit Typical Existing US Housing Stock into EnerPHit and EnerPHit Plus', International Passive House Conference, 2017

REFERENCES

CHAPTER ONE

[1] D. Teli, T. Dimitriou, P.A.B. James, A.S. Bahaj, L. Ellison & A. Waggott 'Fuel Poverty-Induced "Prebound effect" in Achieving the Anticipated Carbon Savings from Social Housing Retrofit', University of Southampton, UK/Chalmers University of Technology (Gothenburg), Sweden. 10.1177/0143624415621028

[2] B. Boardman, et al., *40% House*, Environmental Change Institute, 2005

[3] Royal Institute of British Architects (RIBA), '01 Climate Change Briefing', *Climate Change Toolkit*, 2010

[4] DECC, Energy Efficiency Strategy: The Energy Efficiency Opportunity in the UK, 2012

[5] 'Heating buildings: Reducing energy demand and greenhouse gas emissions', Energy Research Partnership, October 2016,

[6] W. Wilson & C. Barton: 'Tackling the Under-Supply of Housing in England' House of Commons Library, 3 September 2018

[7] W. Wilson: 'Housing Market Renewal Pathfinders' SN/SP/5953, 30 October 2013

[8] National Audit Office, 'Green Deal and the Energy Company Obligation', 14 April 2016

[9] Dr Peter Bonfield, 'Every Home Counts', DBEIS & DCLG, December 2016

[10] Peter Rickaby, 'PAS 2030: 2017 Specification for the Installation of Energy Efficiency Measures In Buildings', *National Housing Maintenance Forum Case Study: PAS 2030*, Rickaby Thompson Associates, 2017

[11] 'Toward Near Zero Energy Buildings: Definition of Common Principles Under EPBD, Final Report', Ecofys by order of European Commission, 14 February 2013, para 6.1.7.2: Recommendations for the Design Process, p 223

[12] A. Menezes, *The Performance Gap: Carbon Bites from the CIBSE Energy Performance Group*, February 2012

[13] 'Stopping Building Failures: How a Collaborative Approach Can Improve Quality and Workmanship', Housing Forum, June 2018

[14] Dr Peter Bonfield, 'Every Home Counts', DBEIS & DCLG, December 2016

[15] Government Soft Landings, Cabinet Office, April 2013

[16] 5th Carbon Budget Analysis, 'Next Steps for UK Heat Policy', Committee on Climate Change, October 2016

[17] 5th Carbon Budget Analysis, 2016

[18] 'UK Housing Energy Factfile', DECC, 2013

[19] Building Performance Institute Europe (BPIE), *Europe's Buildings under the Microscope*, 2011

[20] Ibid

[21] L.D. Shorrock, J. Henderson & J.I. Utley, 'Reducing Carbon Emissions from the UK Housing Stock', BRE/DEFRA, 2005

[22] 'Future-Proofing Flats: Overcoming Legal Barriers to Energy Improvements in Private Flats. Workshop Report' Westminster City Council; Oxford University; Future Climate, 17 March 2015

[23] D. Weatherall, F. McCarthy & S. Bright 'Property Law as a Barrier to Energy Upgrades in Multi-Owned Properties: Insights from a Study of England and Scotland' Springer, 1 August 2017

[24] English Housing Survey, Department of Communities and Local Government, 2015

[25] Dr Peter Bonfield, 'Every Home Counts', DBEIS & DCLG, December 2016

[26] Department of Energy and Climate Change, 'Annual Fuel Poverty Statistics Report 2015', London: HM Government, 2015

[27] P.O. Fanger, 'Thermal Comfort-Analysis and Applications in Environmental Engineering', Danish Technical Press, 1970

[28] R.A. Sharpe, C.R. Thornton, V. Nikolaou & N.J. Osborne, 'Higher Energy Efficient Homes are Associated with Increased Risk of Doctor Diagnosed Asthma in a UK Subpopulation' *Environment International*, 75, 2015, pp 234–44

CHAPTER TWO

[1] Labour Party Green Paper, 'Housing for the Many', April 2018, para 5.1

[2] J. Schnieders & A. Hermelink, 'CEPHEUS Results: Measurements and Occupants' Satisfaction Provide Evidence for Passive Houses Being an Option for Sustainable Building', *Energy Policy*, vol. 34, no. 2, 2006, pp 151–71, doi:101016/jenpol200408049J

[3] S. Lewis, *PHPP Illustrated (2nd Edition)*, RIBA Publishing, 2017

[4] Note: Unregulated energy may include white goods etc. which are not normally included in other energy tools

[5] SketchUp software by Trimble

[6] Revit software by Autodesk

[7] Z. Bastian, D. Arnautu, J. Schnieders, B. Kaufmann, T. MikeSKA & S. Peper, *Building Certification Guide (2nd Edition)*, Passivhaus Institute, February 2018

[8] This author

[9] P. Touhy, *Benchmarking Scottish Energy Standards: Passive House and CarbonLite Standards: A Comparison of Space Heating Energy Demand Using SAP, SBEM and PHPP Methodologies*, ESRU for Scottish Government, 2009

[10] L. Reason & A. Clarke, *Projecting Energy Use and CO2 emissions from Low Energy Buildings. A Comparison of the Passivhaus Planning Package (PHPP) and SAP*, Association of Energy Conscious Builders (AECB), 2008

REFERENCES

[11] S. Cran-McGreehin, et al., 'Heating Buildings: Reducing Energy Demand and Greenhouse Gas Emissions', Energy Research Partnership, October 2016

[12] A. Menezes, *The Performance Gap: Carbon Bites from the CIBSE Energy Performance Group,* February 2012

[13] J. Schnieders & A. Hermelink, 'CEPHEUS Results: Measurements and Occupants' Satisfaction Provide Evidence for Passive Houses Being an Option for Sustainable Building', *Energy Policy,* vol. 34, no. 2, 2006, pp 151–71, doi:101016/jenpol200408049J

[14] R. Mitchell (University of Bath), *The Performance of Passivhaus in New Construction: Post Occupancy Evaluation of Certified Passivhaus Dwellings in the UK: Early Results,* Passivhaus Trust, July 2017

[15] Ibid

[16] M. Fujara, *PassREg Final Report,* Darmstadt, Passivhaus Institute, 2015

[17] J. Squires & A. Goater, 'Carbon Footprint of Heat Generation', Houses of Parliament Office of Science & Technology PostNote 523, May 2016

CHAPTER THREE

[1] ExeSeed Framework, Exeter City Council; Fabric First Framework, Norwich City Council

[2] H. Barrett-Duckett, L. Warren & C. McLaren Webb, *Retrofit for the Future: Reducing Energy Use in Existing Homes. A Guide to Making Retrofit Work,* Innovate UK (formerly Technology Strategy Board), April 2014

[3] M. Baeli., *Residential Retrofit: 20 Case Studies,* RIBA Publishing, 2013

[4] R.A. Sharpe, C.R. Thornton, V. Nikolaou & N.J. Osborne, 'Higher Energy Efficient Homes are Associated With Increased Risk of Doctor Diagnosed Asthma in a UK Subpopulation', University of Exeter Medical School, *Environment International,* 75, 2015, pp 234–44

[5] J. Lewis & L. Smith, *Breaking Barriers: An Industry Review of the Barriers to Whole House Energy Efficiency Retrofit and the Creation of an Industry Action Plan. Summary Report,* National Energy Foundation (NEF) & Energy Efficiency Partnership for Buildings (EEPB), March 2014

[6] Note: Ecology Building Society in the UK offers 'Renovation Mortgages' with reduced interest rates for energy-efficient homes

[7] S.J. Bright, D. Weatherall & R. Willis (University of Oxford), *Exploring the Complexities of Energy Retrofit in Mixed Tenure Social Housing: A Case Study from England, UK,* Springer, 2018

[8] N. May & C. Rye, *Responsible Retrofit of Traditional Buildings,* STBA, September 2012

[9] C. Bottrill, *Homes in Historic Conservation Areas in Great Britain: Calculating the Proportion of Residential Dwellings in Conservation Areas,* Environmental Change Institute, 2005

[10] C. Sanford, Listing Factsheet, Historic England, April 2018

[11] A. Carvajal, G. Unkaya, C. Botten & A. Dasgupta, *Minimum Energy Efficiency Standards and Heritage Properties,* Better Buildings Partnership, May 2018

[12] Dr E. Milsom, *Solid Wall Heat Losses and the Potential for Energy Saving: Consequences for Consideration to Maximise SWI Benefits: A Route-Map for Change,* Building Research Establishment, Watford, 2 March 2016

[13] Building Research Establishment

[14] https://wufi.de/en/

[15] K. Ueno, Masonry Wall Interior Insulation Retrofit Embedded Beam Simulations, Building Science Corporation, 2012

[16] N. May, STBA Internal Wall Insulation (IWI) Paper, 3 August 2012

[17] ECD Architects

[18] Ibid

[19] https://www.q-bot.co/about.html

[20] Smartwin: https://www.passivhausfenster.com/en/homeowners/products/smartwin.html

[21] This author

[22] N. Grant and M. Siddall, *Designing for Summer Comfort in the UK,* Passivhaus Trust, 2016

[23] ECD Architects

[24] J. Hines, S. Godber, B. Butcher, M. Siddall, P. Jennings, N. Grant, A. Clarke, K. Mead & C. Parsons, *How to Build a Passivhaus,* Passivhaus Trust, 2015

CHAPTER FOUR

[1] Energy Companies Obligation Final Report, OFGEM, 30 September 2015

[2] Autumn Statement by the Chancellor of the Exchequer (2013) and subsequent reduction in installation target

[3] Estimates of Home Insulation Levels in Great Britain, DECC, April 2013

[4] 'Implementing Deep Energy Step-by-Step Retrofits: EuroPHit: Increasing the European Potential' Passivhaus Institute, 2015

[5] Tomas O'Leary, MosArt Ltd, Wicklow, 2014

[6] Ibid

[7] Mariana Moreira, MosArt Ltd, Wicklow, Ireland, 2018

[8] 'Implementing Deep Energy Step-by-Step Retrofits: EuroPHit: Increasing the European Potential' Passivhaus Institute, 2015

[9] 'Long Life, Loose Fit, Low Energy', Sir Alex Gordon (PPRIBA), 1972

[10] Berthold Kaufmann: 'Step by Step Retrofits with Passivhaus Components', Passivhaus Institute, 2016

[11] MosArt

[12] Ibid

[13] Ibid

[14] Ibid

[15] MosArt

[16] Ibid

[17] Dame Judith Hackitt, 'Building a Safer Future: – Independent Review of Building Regulations and Fire Safety: Final Report', Ministry of Housing, Communities & Local Government, May 2018

[18] ECD Architects (reproduced courtesy of Westminster City Council)

CHAPTER FIVE

[1] M. De Groote, M. Fabbri, J. Volt & O. Rapf, *Smart Buildings in a Decarbonised Energy System,* Building Performance Institute Europe (BPIE), Brussels, June 2016

[2] Updated Energy and Emissions Projections 2017, Department of Business Energy & Industrial Strategy, January 2018

[3] Ibid

[4] S. Cran-McGreehin, et al., 'Heating Buildings: Reducing Energy Demand and Greenhouse Gas Emissions', Energy Research Partnership, October 2016

[5] Author's italics

[6] A. Menezes, *The Performance Gap: Carbon Bites from the CIBSE Energy Performance Group,* February 2012

[7] Note: Under UK Building Regulations L1B & L2B consequential improvement is not currently enforced for domestic properties. For non-domestic properties consequential improvement is only required when the proposed works affect more than 25% of a building element.

[8] S. Foster, J. Love & I. Walker, *Research on District Heating and Local Approaches to Heat Decarbonisation: A Study for the Committee on Climate Change: Main Report,* Element Energy, 20 November 2015

[9] Dr D. MacKay, Sustainable Energy Without the Hot Air, UIT, 2009

[10] B. Watts, W. Howard, J. Climas & T. Bentham. A Case Against the Widespread Use of District Heating and CHP in the UK, Issue 3, Max Fordham LLP, August 2010

[11] P. Elwell, B. Fitzsimons & E. Bleach, *Low Carbon Heat Networks: How to Optimise an Existing System for Improving Performance,* CBxchange Research Project, 3 November 2016

[12] 'Turning up the Heat: Getting a Fair Deal for District Heating Users', *Which?,* March 2015

[13] P. Elwell, B. Fitzsimons & E. Bleach, *Low Carbon Heat Networks: How to Optimise an Existing System for Improving Performance,* CBxchange Research Project, 3 November 2016

[14] B. Dixon, 'Efficient Heat System Design in Large Passivhaus Multifamily Buildings: UK Experience', International Passivhaus Conference, 2018

[15] J. Barnes, et al., *The Capital Cost of Passivhaus,* Passivhaus Trust/AECOM, January 2015

[16] Ibid

[17] J. Barnes, et al., *The Capital Cost of Passivhaus,* Passivhaus Trust/AECOM, January 2015

[18] *Passive House Plus,* issue 3 (UK Edition)

[19] J. MacLean 'Methodology to Assess Cost Optimality for Retrofitting Existing Scottish Housing Stock to Meet EnerPHit Energy Efficiency Standards' (A thesis submitted in partial fulfilment for the requirement of degree in Master of Science in Renewable Energy Systems and the Environment), University of Strathclyde: Department of Mechanical and Aerospace Engineering, 2015

[20] 'Wilmcote House, Portsmouth: Whole Life Cost: – A Study to Calculate the Whole Life Cost Implications of Retrofitting a Social Housing Tower Block to the EnerPHit standard', ECD Architects/Keegans, April 2014; International Passivhaus Conference, 2016

[21] M. Economidou, *Europe's Buildings Under the Microscope: A Country-by-Country Review of the Energy Performance of Buildings,* Building Performance Institute Europe, October 2011

[22] Sir M. Marmot, *Fair Society, Healthy Lives: The Marmot Review: Strategic Review of Health Inequalities Post-2010,* 2010

[23] Dr V. Press, *Fuel Poverty + Health: A Guide for Primary Care Organisations, and Public Health and Primary Care Professionals,* National Heart Forum, 2003

[24] Dr Ian Wilkinson (Chief Clinical Officer NHS Oldham CCG), 'The Impacts of Poor Housing on Health: Lessons from Oldham', Presentation given at Sustainable Homes Conference (Leeds), March 2015

[25] R. A. Sharpe, C.R. Thornton, V. Nikolaou & N.J. Osborne, 'Higher Energy Efficient Homes are Associated with Increased Risk of Doctor Diagnosed Asthma in a UK Subpopulation' *Environment International,* 75, 2015, pp 234–44

[26] J. Stephen, 'Summer Thermal Comfort and Overheating Risk Mitigation Strategies in Social Housing' (Unpublished Doctoral Thesis, Sustainable Energy Research Group, University of Southampton)

[27] Dr M. Sorensen, *Exploring Road Traffic Noise Pollution and Associated Health Risk,* European Research Council

[28] https://www.nkarch.com/blog/got-a-noisy-site-passive-house-brings-peace-and-quiet

REFERENCES

[29] *Next Steps in Defining Overheating*, Zero Carbon Hub, March 2016

[30] J. Stephen, 'Summer Thermal Comfort and Overheating Risk Mitigation Strategies in Social Housing' (Unpublished Doctoral Thesis, Sustainable Energy Research Group, University of Southampton)

[31] Ibid

[32] E. Vogiatzi, S. Pelsmakers & H. Altamirano, 'The PassivHaus Standard: Minimising Overheating Risk in a Changing Climate', University of Sheffield, 2015, S. orcid.org/0000-0001-6933-2626

[33] K. de Selincourt. 'Disastrous Preston Retrofit Scheme Remains Unresolved', *Passive House Plus*, issue 24

[34] J.L. Atkinson, 'Evaluating Retrofitted External Wall Insulation', Cardiff Metropolitan University, January 2015

[35] 'Buyers in Despair at Badly Built New Homes', *The Times*, 19 April 2018

[36] Dame J. Hackitt, 'Building a Safer Future: Independent Review of Building Regulations and Fire Safety: Final Report', Ministry of Housing, Communities & Local Government, May 2018

[37] Dr Peter Bonfield, 'Every Home Counts', DBEIS & DCLG, December 2016

[38] Z. Bastian, D. Arnautu, Dr J. Schnieders, Dr B. Kaufmann, T. MikeSKA & S. Peper, *Building Certification Guide (2nd Edition)*, Passivhaus Institute, February 2018

[39] J. Thema & J. Rasch, *Calculating and Operationalising the Multiple Benefits of Energy Efficiency in Europe (COMBI): Final Quantification Report*, Wuppertal Institut, May 2018

[40] Ibid

[41] Ibid

CHAPTER SIX

[1] 'UK Housing Energy Factfile', DECC, 2013

[2] 'UK Greenhouse Gas Emissions: Final Figures', BEIS, 2016

[3] 'Heating Buildings: Reducing Energy Demand and Greenhouse Gas Emissions', Energy Research Partnership, October 2016

[4] 'UK Housing Energy Factfile', DECC, 2013

[5] 'English Housing Survey', 2008

[6] Ibid

[7] *Europe's Buildings Under the Microscope: A Country-by-Country Review of the Energy Performance of Buildings*, Building Performance Institute Europe, October 2011

[8] NAO 'Green Deal and Energy Company Obligation', 8 April 2016

[9] Dr Peter Bonfield, 'Every Home Counts', DBEIS & DCLG, December 2016

[10] ARUP 'Towards the Delivery of a National Residential Energy Efficiency Programme', May 2016

[11] 'English Housing Survey', 2015

[12] Ibid

[13] 'UK Housing Energy Factfile', DECC, 2013

[14] 'Energy & Emissions Projections', DECC, 2014

[15] 'English Housing Survey', 2012

[16] D. Teli, T. Dimitriou, P.A.B. James, A.S. Bahaj, L. Ellison & A. Waggott 'Fuel Poverty-Induced "Prebound effect" in Achieving the Anticipated Carbon Savings from Social Housing Retrofit', University of Southampton, UK/Chalmers University of Technology (Gothenburg), Sweden. 10.1177/0143624415621028/

[17] J. Stephen, 'Summer Thermal Comfort and Overheating Risk Mitigation Strategies in Social Housing' (Unpublished Doctoral Thesis, Sustainable Energy Research Group, University of Southampton)

[18] Ibid

[19] Resident consultation events held between 19 and 26 September 2013, Portsmouth City Council

[20] ECD Architects

[21] D. Teli, T. Dimitriou, P.A.B. James, A.S. Bahaj, L. Ellison & A. Waggott 'Fuel Poverty-Induced "Prebound effect" in Achieving the Anticipated Carbon Savings from Social Housing Retrofit', University of Southampton, UK/Chalmers University of Technology (Gothenburg), Sweden. 10.1177/0143624415621028

[22] ECD Architects

[23] Ibid

[24] ECD Architects

[25] Ibid

[26] Ibid

[27] Ibid

[28] Dún Laoghaire Rathdown Council

[29] Ibid

[30] Ibid

[31] Ibid

[32] MosArt

[33] Ibid

[34] Donal Murphy Photography

[35] Ibid

[36] *Passive House Plus*, issue 23, pp 28–37

[37] Dún Laoghaire Rathdown Council

[38] Passive House Plus, Issue 23, pp 28–37

[39] Ervins Krauklis (Architect)

[40] Ibid

[41] Ibid

[42] Ibid

[43] Ibid

[44] Ibid

[45] Riga Technical University

[46] Peter Pierce Photography

[47] Peter Pierce Photography

[48] Peter Pierce Photography

[49] Ibid

REFERENCES

50 Feilden+Mawson Architects
51 Ibid
52 Ibid
53 FeildenIbid
54 Ibid
55 Ibid
56 Leonard Design Associates, M&E Engineers
57 Feilden+Mawson Architects
58 Ibid
59 Ibid
60 Ibid

CHAPTER SEVEN

1 Prof. T. Dixon (University of Reading) 'Scaling Up Commercial Property Retrofitting: Challenges and Solutions', *Estates Gazette,* February 2014
2 *Europe's Buildings Under the Microscope: A Country-by-Country Review of the Energy Performance of Buildings,* Building Performance Institute Europe, October 2011
3 Building Energy Efficiency Survey, 2014–15: Overarching Report, Department for Business, Energy & Industrial Strategy, November 2016
4 Ibid
5 'Heating Buildings: Reducing Energy Demand and Greenhouse Gas Emissions', Energy Research Partnership, October 2016
6 'A Tale of Two Buildings: Are EPCs a True Indicator Of Energy Efficiency?', Jones Lang LaSalle/Better Buildings Partnership, 2012
7 Prof. T. Dixon (University of Reading) 'Scaling Up Commercial Property Retrofitting: Challenges and Solutions', *Estates Gazette,* February 2014
8 F. Fuerst, P. McAllister; A. Nanda & P. Wyatt, 'Is Energy Efficiency Priced in the Housing Market? Some Evidence from the United Kingdom', University of Cambridge, Dept of Land Economy, 2013

9 *Building Energy Efficiency Survey, 2014–15: Overarching Report,* Department for Business, Energy & Industrial Strategy, November 2016
10 Ibid
11 Rongen Architects
12 Ibid
13 Ibid
14 Ibid
15 Ibid
16 Ibid
17 This author
18 Rongen Architects
19 Ibid
20 This author
21 Passivhaus Institute, Innsbruck
22 Thomas Jantscher (photographer)
23 Passivhaus Institute, Innsbruck
24 ATP Architekten
25 Passivhaus Institute, Innsbruck
26 Ibid
27 Ibid
28 Ibid
29 Passivhaus Institute, Innsbruck
30 Ibid
31 Thomas Jantscher (photographer)
32 This author
33 Ibid
34 S. Oehler, 'Emissionsfreie Gebaude', Springer Vieweg, 2017
35 Ibid
36 Ibid
37 Dirk Altenkirche (photographer)
38 S. Oehler, 'Emissionsfreie Gebaude', Springer Vieweg, 2017
39 Ibid
40 This author
41 S. Oehler, 'Emissionsfreie Gebaude', Springer Vieweg, 2017
42 Ibid
43 Ibid
44 Ibid

45 Draft Building Energy Law (GEG): German Government, 2017
46 S. Oehler, 'The Contents of a Future German Building Energy Law in Just Three Pages', DGNB, April 2018

CHAPTER EIGHT

1 International Passivhaus Database: https://passivhausprojekte.de
2 International Passivhaus Database: http://www.passivhausplaner.eu
3 *Building Certification Guide (2nd Edition)*, Passivhaus Institute, February 2018
4 ECD Architects
5 ECD Architects
6 Ibid
7 ECD Architects
8 Ibid
9 Ibid
10 Ibid
11 ECD Architects
12 Ibid
13 ECD Architects
14 Ibid
15 Ibid
16 Manufacturer's data sheet: Zehnder
17 ECD Architects
18 Ibid
19 Ibid
20 Ibid
21 ECD Architects
22 Ibid
23 S. Lewis, *PHPP Illustrated: A Designer's Companion, (2nd Edition)*, RIBA Publishing, 2017

POSTSCRIPT

1 The Economist, 'Efforts to Make Buildings Greener Are Not Working', 5 January 2019, https://www.economist.com/international/2019/01/05/efforts-to-make-buildings-greener-are-not-working

INDEX

Page numbers in *italic* indicate figures and in **bold** indicate tables.

ActiveHouse 22
Agar Grove, Camden, London 67
air pollution 11, 70
air quality, indoor 11, 18, 31, 70
airtightness 18, **19**, 20, **21**, 24, 31
    optimising 42, 155–6, *155*, *156*
Arbed programme, Wales 73
Association for Environment Conscious Building (AECB) 20, **21**

barriers to retrofit 8–10, 32–4, 124–5
BIM (Building Information Modelling) 6, 60–1, *61*, 73
Bonfield review 4, 10, 73
BREEAM 11, 22, 74
building envelope 8–9, 18, 20, 31
    cavity wall insulation 47, 48, *81*, *83*
    challenges of heritage buildings 34–5, *35*, *36*
    external wall insulation 8–9, 31, 38–9
    ground floors 26, 40, *157*, *158–9*, 159
    internal wall insulation 8–9, 20, 31, 37–8, *38*, *39*
    optimising thermal envelope 37–42, *38*, *39*, *40*, 156–60, *156*, *157*, *158–9*, *160*, *161*
    remaining potential to insulate 80, *81*, *82*, *83*
    roofs 40, *40*, 159–60, *160*, *161*
    solar gain and shading 18, 41–2, 162–3, *163*
    thermal bridges 18, **21**, 24, 26, 37–9, 55, *55*, 159–60, *160*, *161*
    see also windows
building form 31, 43, *43*
Building Information Modelling (BIM) 6, 60–1, *61*, 73
Building Performance Institute Europe (BPIE) 64, 70
building regulations 5, 6, 8, **21**, 23, 66, 68, *68*, 71, 73, 154, 162
Building Research Establishment Domestic Energy Model (BREDEM) 23
building services 31
building users 3, 16–17, 26, 32, 33

capital costs 68–70, *68*, *69*
carbon, embodied 37
carbon emissions 2, 3, 5, 6–7, 7, 71–3
    commercial sector 122
    residential sector 80, *80*, *81*
Carbon Emissions Reduction Obligation (CERO) 47, *47*
Carbon Emissions Reduction Target (CERT) 47
Carbon Saving Community Obligation (CSCO) 47, *47*

Carbonlite programme 20
case studies
    Ērgli Vocational School, Latvia 100–3, *100–3*
    Evangelical Church, Heinsberg, Germany 126, 128–35, *129–35*
    2 Gloucester Place Mews, London 114–19, *114–19*
    Rochestown, Phase 2, Dún Laoghaire, Ireland 94–9, *94–9*
    Sparkasse Bank, Gross Umstadt, Germany *41*, 126, 144–51, *144–51*
    Stella Maris House, Wicklow Town, Ireland *50*, 53–8, *53–9*
    University of Innsbruck, Tirol, Austria 126, 136–43, *136–43*
    105 Willow Street, Brooklyn, New York 104–13, *104–13*
    Wilmcote House, Portsmouth 69–70, *69*, *71*, *72*, 73, 86–92, *86–93*
cavity wall insulation 47, 48, *81*, *83*
certification 18–20, **19**, 74, 163
challenges 30–43
    barriers to retrofit 8–10, 32–4, 124–5
    funding 8, 32, 46–9, *47*, *48*
    heritage buildings 34–5, *35*, *36*
    success factors 30–2
    see also practical installation issues
CHP (combined heat and power) 66
climate change 2, 71–3
    see also carbon emissions
Climate Change Act 2008 3, 4, 33
Code for Sustainable Homes 5, 20
COMBI project 76, *76–7*
comfort cooling 71–3
comfort standard 11, 70–3, *71*, *72*
comfort, thermal 10–11, 16–17, 70–3, *71*, *72*
commercial sector
    achieving EnerPHit 122–7, *122*, *123*, *124*, *125*, *126*
    Evangelical Church, Heinsberg, Germany 126, 128–35, *129–35*
    simplified building energy model (SBEM) 23
    Sparkasse Bank, Gross Umstadt, Germany *41*, 126, 144–51, *144–51*
    University of Innsbruck, Tirol, Austria 126, 136–43, *136–43*
Community Energy Saving Programme (CESP) 47
condensation 18, 70
    and internal wall insulation 9, 37, 38, *38*, *39*
    interstitial 35, 37
consumer demand 33
contractors' prelims *69*, 70
costs
    capital costs of EnerPHit 68–70, *68*, *69*
    in step-by-step retrofit 52–3, *52*

damp-proof course (DPC) 39, 55, *55*
decarbonisation of grid 64, *65*
deep retrofit 7, 30
    barriers 8–10, 32–4, 124–5
    Energiesprong 23, 32, 67, 75
    funding 48–9, *48*, 74–5
    success factors 30–2
    see also case studies; EnerPHit; practical installation issues
designPH plug-in 17, 74, 165–7, *166*
Display Energy Certificates (DECs) 124
district heating systems 66–8, *67*
double glazing *9*, 10
draughts 11, 18

economic barriers 32, 125
Edward Woods Estate, London 168, 169
EHC (Every Home Counts) Quality Mark 4–5
embodied carbon 37
Energiesprong 23, 32, 67, 75
Energy Company Obligation (ECO) 47, *47*, 48
energy-efficiency measures, market penetration of *9*, 10
Energy Performance Certificates (EPCs) 5–6, **21**, 24, **24**, 80, 124
Energy Performance of Buildings Directive (EPBD) 5, 20, 23–4
EnerPHit 2–3, 11
    approach 154
    capital costs 68–70, *68*, *69*
    certification 18–20, **19**, 74, 163
    comfort standard 11, 70–3, *71*, *72*
    delivering 163–7
    funding 74–5
    performance standards 19, **19**, 20, **21**, *21*
    principles of 18
    quality control 25, 73
    as target for retrofit 64–6, *65*, 73–4
    see also challenges; commercial sector; practical installation issues; residential sector
EnerPHit Plus 26
EnerPHit Premium 26
EnerPHit Retrofit Plan (ERP) 26, 49–60, *50*, 164
    aligning planned maintenance 51–2, 59–60
    case study *50*, 53–8, *53–9*
    costs 52–3, *52*
    pre-certification 51, *51*, 74
EPCs *see* Energy Performance Certificates (EPCs)
Ērgli Vocational School, Latvia 100–3, *100–3*
EU Energy Performance of Buildings Directive (EPBD) 5, 20, 23–4
EU Horizon 2020 programme 75
EuroPACE 75
Evangelical Church, Heinsberg, Germany 126, 128–35, *129–35*

180   EnerPHit: A Step-by-Step Guide to Low Energy Retrofit

INDEX

Every Home Counts (EHC) Quality Mark 4–5
'Every Home Counts' report 4, 10, 73
excess winter deaths (EWDs) 70
external wall insulation 8–9, 31, 38–9
external walls 8–9, 31
    cavity wall insulation 47, 48, *81*, *83*
    external wall insulation 8–9, 31, 38–9
    internal wall insulation 8–9, 20, 31, 37–8, *38*, *39*
    optimising thermal envelope 37–9, *38*, *39*, 156–9, *156*

financing *see* funding
form factor 18
fuel poverty 7, *7*, 10–11, 70, 84, *85*, 169
funding 8, 32, 46–9, *47*, *48*, 74–5

2 Gloucester Place Mews, London 114–19, *114–19*
Government Soft Landings (GSL) methodology 6
Greater London Authority (GLA) 66
Green Deal scheme 4, 32, 33, 47, 75
ground floors 26, 40, *157*, *158–9*, 159

'hard-to-treat' properties *see* solid-wall properties
health 10–11, 70–3, *71*, *72*
heat recovery *see* mechanical ventilation with heat recovery (MVHR)
heatwaves 71–3, *72*
heritage buildings 34–5, *35*, *36*
    see also listed buildings; solid-wall properties
Hochhaus, Freiburg, Germany 168, 169
Home Heating Cost Reduction Obligation (HHCRO) 47, *47*
Horizon 2020 programme 75
humidity 11, 18, **19**, 35

indoor air quality 11, 18, 31, 70
insulation
    cavity wall 47, 48, *81*, *83*
    external wall 8–9, 31, 38–9
    ground floor 26, 40, *157*, *158–9*, 159
    internal wall 8–9, 20, 31, 37–8, *38*, *39*
    loft 9, 10, 40, *40*, *81*
    material types 37
    remaining potential 80, *81*, *82*, *83*
internal heat gains 24, 25
internal wall insulation 8–9, 20, 31, 37–8, *38*, *39*
International Passivhaus Database 154

KfW bank, Germany 32, 75

leasehold contracts 8, 34
LEED 11, 22, 74

legal barriers 8, 10, 34
listed buildings
    2 Gloucester Place Mews, London 114–19, *114–19*
lock-in of modest gains 48–9, *48*, 66
loft insulation 9, 10, 40, *40*, *81*
London Plan 66, 68

Marmot review 70
mechanical ventilation with heat recovery (MVHR) 11, 16
    capital costs 69, *69*
    cooling effect 17
    indoor air quality 11, 18, 31, 70
    optimising 42, 160–2, *161*, *162*
Micro-CHP (combined heat and power) 66
micro-energy hubs 64
Microgeneration Certification Scheme (MCS) 5
Minergie-P 20
Minimum Energy Efficiency Standard (MEES) 6, 48, 124
modelling software 17–18
moisture 9, 11, 37, *38*
    see also condensation; humidity
mould growth 11, 35, *40*, 70
MVHR *see* mechanical ventilation with heat recovery (MVHR)

noise pollution 70–1
non-renewable primary energy (PE) demand **19**, **21**
non-residential buildings *see* commercial sector
nZEB (near-zero energy in buildings) standard 5, 6, 20, 26, 33, *69*, 70

occupant parameters 16–17
occupants 3, 16–17, 26, 32, 33
offsite manufacturing 23, 32
overheating 11, 18, **19**, **21**, 35, 42, 71–3, *72*

Paris Climate Agreement 2, 4
party walls 39
PAS 2030:2017 specification 4, 73
PAS 2035:2018 specification 5, 73
Passive House Planning Package (PHPP) 17–18, 23, 24–5, 74, 154, 163–7, *165*, *166*
Passivhaus 2, 5, 16
    capital costs 68–70, *68*, *69*
    comfort standard 11, 16–17
    performance gap 25
    performance standards 19, **19**, **20**, **21**, *21*
Passivhaus-certified components 19–20, 74
Passivhaus Institute (PHI) 2, 18, 19, 20, 26, 154
Passivhaus Plus 26
Passivhaus Premium 26

Passivhaus Trust 16
Passivlink 17, 74
PassREg project 26
performance gap 6, 25, 34
PHPP *see* Passive House Planning Package (PHPP)
pilot projects 30–1, 32, 34, 49, *49*
    see also case studies
planned maintenance 46, 51–2, 59–60
political barriers 33, 46–7, *47*
pollution
    air 11, 70
    noise 70–1
practical installation issues 8–9, 33–4, 36–43, 155–63
    airtightness 42, *43*, 155–6, *155*, *156*
    external walls 37–9, *38*, *39*, 156–9, *156*
    ground floors 26, 40, *157*, *158–9*, 159
    mechanical ventilation with heat recovery (MVHR) 42, 160–2, *161*, *162*
    roofs 40, *40*, 159–60, *160*, *161*
    skills and training 32–3
    solar gain 41–2, 162–3, *163*
    thermal bridging 37–9, 159–60, *160*, *161*, 162
    thermal envelope 37–42, *38*, *39*, *40*, 156–60, *156*, *157*, *158–9*, *160*, *161*
    windows and doors 41, 160
pre-certification 51, *51*, 74
primary energy renewable (PER) demand **19**, **21**
Public Works Loan Board (PWLB) 75

quality control 25, 73

radiant asymmetry 11
Reduced Data Standard Assessment Procedure (RdSAP) 6, 23, 24, 80
renewable energy 23, 25–6, 64, *65*, 66, 169
    primary energy renewable (PER) demand **19**, **21**
residential sector
    achieving EnerPHit 80–5, *81*, *82*, *83*, *84*, *85*
    Ērgli Vocational School, Latvia 100–3, *100–3*
    2 Gloucester Place Mews, London 114–19, *114–19*
    Rochestown, Phase 2, Dún Laoghaire, Ireland 94–9, *94–9*
    Stella Maris House, Wicklow Town, Ireland 50, 53–8, *53–9*
    105 Willow Street, Brooklyn, New York 104–13, *104–13*
    Wilmcote House, Portsmouth 69–70, *69*, *71*, *72*, 73, 86–92, *86–93*
residents *see* occupants
retrofit
    barriers to 8–10, 32–4, 124–5

Index **181**

INDEX

challenges of heritage buildings 34–5, *35*, *36*
defining 3–4
drivers to 6–7, *7*, 10–11
Energiesprong 23, 32, 67, 75
EnerPHit as target for 64–6, *65*, 73–4
funding 8, 32, 46–9, *47*, *48*, 74–5
importance of 64
lock-in of modest gains 48–9, *48*, 66
performance gap 6, 25, 34
planning 31
previous schemes 4–5
quality control 25, 73
standards 5–6, 22
success factors 30–2
see also case studies; EnerPHit; practical installation issues; step-by-step retrofit
retrofit coordinators 31, 33
Retrofit for the Future programme 30–1
Revit 17, 74, 167
RIBA Plan of Work 60, 154
Rochestown, Phase 2, Dún Laoghaire, Ireland 94–9, *94–9*
roofs
  loft insulation *9*, 10, 40, *40*, *81*
  optimising thermal envelope 40, *40*, 159–60, *160*, *161*

SAP (Standard Assessment Procedure) *9*, 10, 23, 24–5, **24**, 42, 71, 80, *83*
shading 18, 41–2, 162–3
simplified building energy model (SBEM) software 23
site operations 31–2
SKA 22
SketchUp 17, 74, 167
skills 32–3
solar gain 18, 41–2, 162–3, *163*
solid-wall properties 8–9, 31
  challenges 34–5, *35*, *36*
  external wall insulation 8–9, 31, 38–9
  funding 47, 48–9, *48*
  internal wall insulation 8–9, 20, 31, 37–8, *38*, *39*
  remaining potential to insulate 80, *81*, *82*, *83*
space cooling demand **19**, **21**
space cooling load **19**
space heating demand **19**, 20, **21**
space heating load **19**
Sparkasse Bank, Gross Umstadt, Germany *41*, 126, 144–51, *144–51*
specific heat demand 64–6, *65*
Standard Assessment Procedure (SAP) *9*, 10, 23, 24–5, **24**, 42, 71, 80, *83*
standards, performance
  commercial sector 124
  EnerPHit 19, **19**, 20, **21**, *21*

Minimum Energy Efficiency Standard (MEES) 6, 48, 124
newbuild 5, 20
nZEB (near-zero energy in buildings) 5, 6, 20, 26, 33, *69*, 70
Passivhaus 19, **19**, 20, **21**, *21*
retrofit 5–6, 22
ultra-low-energy 20–1, **21**
statutory compliance 23–5, **24**
Stella Maris House, Wicklow Town, Ireland *50*, 53–8, *53–9*
step-by-step retrofit 26, 49–61, 74
  aligning planned maintenance 51–2, 59–60
  BIM as tool for 60–1
  case study *50*, 53–8, *53–9*
  costs 52–3, *52*
  pre-certification for 51, *51*, 74
success factors 30–2
Sustainable Energy Association Ireland (SEAI) 58

thermal bridges 18, **21**, 24, 26, 37–9, 55, *55*, 159–60, *160*, *161*
thermal comfort 10–11, 16–17, 70–3, *71*, *72*
thermal envelope, optimising 37–42, *38*, *39*, *40*, 156–60, *156*, *157*, *158–9*, *160*, *161*
training, deep retrofit 32–3

ultra-low-energy standards 20–1, **21**
United Nations Framework Convention on Climate Change (UNFCCC) 2
University of Innsbruck, Tirol, Austria 126, 136–43, *136–43*
unregulated energy loads 24, 25–6

vacuum insulated panels (VIPs) 37
ventilation 4, 5, 11, 17, 18, 31, 40, 70
  see also mechanical ventilation with heat recovery (MVHR)

weather files 24
105 Willow Street, Brooklyn, New York 104–13, *104–13*
Wilmcote House, Portsmouth 69–70, *69*, *71*, *72*, 73, 86–92, *86–93*
windows
  double glazing *9*, 10
  opening 11, 17
  optimising thermal envelope 41, 160
  solar gain 18, 41–2, 162–3, *163*
World Health Organization (WHO) 70